T0314187

Brahmin Capitalism

Brahmin Capitalism

Frontiers of Wealth and Populism
in America's First Gilded Age

NOAM MAGGOR

Harvard University Press

Cambridge, Massachusetts
London, England
2017

Library of Congress Cataloging-in-Publication Data

Names: Maggor, Noam, 1977– author.
Title: Brahmin capitalism : frontiers of wealth and populism in
America's first Gilded Age / Noam Maggor.
Description: Cambridge, Massachusetts : Harvard University Press, 2017. |
Includes bibliographical references and index.
Identifiers: LCCN 2016017873 | ISBN 9780674971462 (alk. paper)
Subjects: LCSH: Capitalism—United States—History—19th century. | Capitalists and financiers—
Massachusetts—Boston—History. | Capitalists and financiers—United States—History. | West
(U.S.)—Economic conditions—19th century. | United States—Economic conditions—1865–1918.
Classification: LCC HB501 .M2435 2017 | DDC 330.973/08—dc23
LC record available at https://lccn.loc.gov/2016017873

For Rebekah

Contents

Preface

W hen Americans went to civil war in 1861, the United States was the
leading supplier of the era's most important agricultural commodity—
cotton. By the early twentieth century, that same country had emerged as
the foremost industrial nation in the world, surpassing the manufacturing
output of Germany, France, and the United Kingdom combined. This was
arguably nothing less than the greatest leap in industrial capacity in human
history to that point. It catapulted a new set of industries—iron and steel,
mining, chemicals, meatpacking, and, most importantly, railroads—to the
core of American capitalism, radically recasting social relations, labor regimes, political institutions, and ideological commitments.

How did this momentous transformation come about? How did a slave-
owning, cotton-exporting republic become a hegemonic industrial nation
in the span of less than four decades? This question is central to our appreciation of the full arc of American history in the nineteenth century. It
is likewise crucial for our understanding of the origins of modern capitalism in America in an epoch that witnessed the rise of the large business
corporation, the accelerated formation of American state institutions, an
explosive growth of urban centers, and the rapid settlement of the Great
West. And yet this question has been elided more often than it has been
directly engaged. Standard accounts routinely invoke the revolutionary
power of technologies such as the railroad and the telegraph. Histories of
business chronicle the seemingly self-propelled rise of large bureaucratic
firms. Textbooks list the many tons of steel that were forged, the gross
product that flowed out of factories, the growing density of cities, and the
millions of immigrants who poured into the country. These narratives
allow the sheer magnitude of the process to overwhelm contextual historical analysis. They cast this transition as nearly inexorable, recounting the
drama in broad brushstrokes rather than interrogating, unpacking, and
explaining it.

This book challenges the overdetermined quality of these sweeping narratives. It revisits some of the key underlying processes that reshaped the American economy during those formative decades, asking not how Americans adapted to industrial capitalism, as studies of the period have typically done, but how industrial capitalism emerged in the United States in the first place. All history is contemporary history, and this book is not exceptional in drawing inspiration from recent events, in this case the global economic transformation of our own time. One of the crucial insights that scholars have drawn from the geopolitics of the present day is that the nation-state cannot be assumed to be the obvious unit of analysis. Although the nation-state could be imagined as the container of economic activity for much of the twentieth century, this is clearly not the case in the current global system. Nor was it in the late nineteenth century, a fiercely vibrant era marked by far-flung capital flows, metropolitan dynamism, and the absorption of continental interiors into the world economy. The renewed awareness of the permeability and malleability of political boundaries has already altered our historical understanding of the United States in the nineteenth century. Historians of the early national period, for example, have situated the young republic within a longer history of interactions throughout the Atlantic Ocean. Historians of slavery have traced the aggressive territorial expansion of the "Cotton Kingdom" in North America. Historians of native Americans have embedded the trajectories of Indian polities in interimperial networks of exchange, diplomacy, and power. Similarly, the formation of a national economy that extended across the continent in the late nineteenth century—the product of an array of highly contentious economic and political projects—cannot be taken for granted but must itself become a topic for historical inquiry.

Therefore, instead of tracing national economic growth over time, this book explores the formation of the new geography of American capitalism in the latter decades of the nineteenth century—an uneven and contradictory process not captured by macroeconomic indicators or master narratives of "industrialization." It locates many of the important trajectories of the era on *sub*national scales of analysis—city, metropolis, territory, and region—which have often been concealed under the blanket cast by more conventional national optics. Most crucially, the book tracks the movement of investment capital from urban centers in the East and into the Great West in the aftermath of the Civil War. It examines how the moneyed elite of Boston—the folks known as the Boston Brahmins—mobilized their saved resources out of cotton manufacturing in New England toward faraway destinations such as Michigan, Kansas, Illinois, and, increasingly, Colorado, Dakota, Wyoming, and Oregon. The migration of wealth from Boston and other old cities in the East toward bold new investment frontiers in the West financed railroads, mines, farms, stockyards, and many other business ventures. This redeployment of capital greatly expanded the territorial reach of American agriculture and transformed budding western enterprises into gigantic industries. This movement reoriented American capitalism away from the cotton-based Atlantic economy of earlier decades toward the new industrial political economy organized around an interconnected domestic market.

New frontiers of wealth and investment also delineated new frontiers of social contestation. The incorporation of remote sites and territories into an integrated economic whole was far from seamless. Moving up and down between geographical scales of analysis, this book engages political controversies that accompanied the formation of a national market at every level. It reveals how grassroots political mobilizations, in the urban East and the rural West, pushed back in a variety of ways against the pull of concentrated capital. As urban dwellers debated municipal budgets, metropolitan jurisdiction, and the uses of public space, they more fundamentally struggled over how best to position their own metropolis in an emerging interconnected system of cities. As settlers of western territories argued over the regulation of railroads, protection of labor, and extraction of natural resources, they contested the terms, rules, and payoffs of their participation in national commerce. These populist movements were not monolithic in their agenda. Nor were they limited to a particular party, organization, or region. They nevertheless drew on a shared producerist ideology to challenge centralized financial power. Against the tenets of liberal political economy, they conceived of economic change, not as derived from immutable natural laws, but as politically defined, and thus also politically malleable. They embraced the democratic possibilities of an urban industrial society, founded on free and empowered labor. They supported, and in many cases successfully enacted, capacious and democratically controlled state action on multiple geographical scales that promoted more decentralized and egalitarian development paths.

The controversies that surrounded the emergence of a national industrial economy in the late nineteenth century show that economic transformations, even massive ones, are never simply inevitable outcomes of technological breakthroughs or products of spontaneous market transactions between individuals. Nor do they ensue seamlessly in linear and irreversible fashion according to an evolutionary logic. These shifts proceed, rather, through the deliberate mobilization of strategic actors and intense battles over politically enforced rules, regulations, and entitlements. The political and legal infrastructure that creates markets can be put together in many different ways, with vast implications for the shape of development, the allocation of resources, and distribution of wealth. Only a magnificent sleight of hand can obscure the struggles that mold this infrastructure and propose its formation is bound to converge toward some logical or necessary endpoint. While the balance of power between contending social groups and contending visions of progress is uneven, the outcomes— then and now—are never predetermined. Few living in the 1850s could have predicted what lay ahead. How Gilded Age Americans made their history is, therefore, the subject of this book.

Brahmin Capitalism

Introduction

When pioneering financial journalist Henry Varnum Poor launched the *Manual of the Railroads of the United States* in 1868, he included, alongside the dense volume's many tables, statistics, and maps, a celebratory chronicle of the entwined rise of Western civilization and its roads. The historical sketch began with the highways of the Roman Empire and ended with the railroads of the United States, drawing an evocative parallel between the two epic networks of transportation. Rome's highways, Poor explained, had always represented the empire's "most striking displays of . . . greatness." "Radiating from the Imperial City," these roads "conveyed the pulsations of its mighty heart to the remotest provinces," serving Rome not only "to make known its will, but to enforce its prompt execution." The highways of the empire were more than means to secure political control over an ever-widening realm. They became conduits of trade, as well as instruments of civilization. Indeed, without these "most perfect and most durable roads," Poor proposed, the empire could have "neither commerce nor wealth; neither intelligence nor social order."

Poor envisioned American railroads as accomplishing a similar set of aspirations in North America, facilitating the "consolidat[ion of the entire continent] into a great empire." Three years removed from a bloody civil war that had laid bare the nation's sectional fault lines, Poor proposed that railroads would rule out a similar kind of internal fracturing in the future. They would serve to "hold together the different portions of our vast and widely-separated domain." Even as American settlement spread rapidly across large territories in the Great West, iron rails would connect "the Eastern and Western States . . . geographically and commercially" into "one system." This imperial system would allow nothing less than the "complete utilization of the resources and wealth of a great continent," an endeavor of a scale "infinitely more grand than even Imperial Rome ever attempted."[1]

Poor presented his vision of a sprawling capitalist empire as almost pre-ordained, in keeping with the conventions of the boosterist genre that he and his fellow journalists had helped to perfect. Yet he knew full well that his manifesto was a premature celebration of an embryonic project. His notion of a fully integrated North American political economy—one interconnected market from sea to shining sea—was at that juncture an improbable and highly controversial vision, in line with the wildest aspirations of the gentlemanly element on Wall Street and in the other financial centers on the Atlantic coast. Faced with what seemed like overwhelming obstacles on a variety of fronts, it was not a necessary trajectory and, of course, far from an accomplished fact.

For starters, the railroads of the United States constituted a unified network only in the far-fetched conjectures of a relatively small group of promoters.[2] The much heralded first transcontinental track of the Union Pacific, which has since become an emblem of postbellum national unification, had not yet been finished, let alone proven technologically or financially viable. Its completion, commemorated at the iconic driving of the Golden Spike at Promontory Summit in Utah in 1869, more properly signaled the launch, not the culmination, of the effort to consolidate American dominion over the entire continent. Meanwhile, the skeletal foundations of railroad infrastructure, almost all of it east of the Mississippi and mostly north of the Mason-Dixon line were characterized by immense unevenness and fragmentation. The most prominent feature of the existing railroad network, the interregional trunk lines linking the Atlantic cities of New York, Philadelphia, and Baltimore to their trans-Appalachian hinterlands, were built with hefty public subsidies, not with national or continental considerations in mind, but in a competitive mode as a way to aggrandize a particular urban center over others.[3] Other parts of the railroad grid similarly bore the imprint of the local and regional priorities that had prompted their construction. Most railroads, like canals before them, were designed to connect midsize cities to their adjoining countryside, not to facilitate shipping over long distances or to power the growth of mega-metropolises. Within this disjointed patchwork of lines, divided among a large number of uncoordinated operators, long-haul freight traffic moved slowly and haltingly, routinely being broken up at various transfer points between different gauges of track, within cities that had several unconnected terminals, and at river crossings, which were as yet unbridged.[4] It took a great deal of optimism and rhetorical flair to imagine this tangle of lines adding up to a seamless national system of transportation.

Segmentation and uneven development were not confined to railroad construction alone. From a financial standpoint as well, the East and the West were sharply differentiated. Whereas the Northeast was saturated with banking institutions, investment houses, insurance companies, and savings banks—all in possession of enormous pools of capital in need of new investment outlets—other regions of the country remained capital poor and relatively cut off from the lifeblood of national commerce and large-scale industry. The National Banking Act, passed by Congress in 1863 to enable the U.S. government to finance the war effort, provided a federal basis for the banking system, but it did not diminish, and in some ways it further accentuated, the lopsided geography of the financial land-scape.[5] Urban centers in the West, in spite of their rapid growth, could not hope to match the far superior resources of older cities on the Atlantic coast. In 1868, New York and Boston, the two largest financial centers in the nation, had several dozen national banks in operation, with more than $157 million and $60 million of notes in circulation, respectively. Chicago and Cincinnati lagged far behind, with only thirteen and eight banks, respectively, with each city's national banks issuing less than $9 million of notes. The gap was even more insurmountable farther west, where large swaths of states and territories possessed virtually no banking resources. Colorado and Montana together had four national banks, with a grand total of $368,245 in circulation, providing barely enough liquidity for local transactions.[6] Left to their own devices, and given the uneasiness with which money flowed between the regions, the residents of these territories could hardly fund the most rudimentary infrastructure that was required to open up these regions for development.[7]

Most consequentially, the American state seemed ill suited to provide a stable and coherent institutional framework that could support the integration of a national market. The formation of markets is not often thought of as a political project. The idea that markets are spontaneous expressions of universal human proclivities, rather than historically specific and politically constituted institutional arrangements, is one of the pervasive fallacies of our own time. Nevertheless, all iterations of capitalism, as historian Richard White recently pointed out, are ever and always co-productions of state and market actors.[8] An integrated North American

economy could not cohere without the legal foundations, public resources, and coercive military and police powers that only governments
could muster. Its consolidation rested in indispensable ways on political
authorities that could adjudicate property rights, charter corporations,
compile volumes of reliable information, build and sustain infrastructure, and mediate between capital and labor, altogether establishing the
groundwork for market transactions.

In analyzing state and market relations in the United States during the
late nineteenth century, the conventional scholarly focus, almost by de-
fault, has been on the federal government, which in many ways projected
back in time Washington, D.C.'s supremacy in the twentieth century.[9]
This teleological emphasis has misread the locus of American state capacity over the course of the nineteenth century, misconstruing a balance
of power that in fact consistently favored local and state authorities over
the federal government. This emphasis has also privileged the nation-state
as the taken-for-granted framework of economic activity, presuming that
national borders provided a natural container that market actors were
bound to gradually and steadily pervade. In the nineteenth century, however, the multitude of state and city governments far outpaced the national
government in terms of public spending, legislative activity, and ongoing
promotion and regulation of economic change. Less encumbered by the
constricting mandate of the U.S. Constitution, they had broad authority to
shape market conditions. It is impossible to grasp the variegated density of
state involvement in American economic life, spanning a wide array of
policy areas—government finance, infrastructure, industrial relations,
natural resources, business regulation, public space, and others—without
accounting for the many pivotal legislative and legal efforts that took place
on the subnational level.[10]

In a political system overwhelmingly dominated by state and local governments, the Civil War was indeed the nineteenth century's most emphatic moment of federal hegemony. The war empowered the national
government to overturn the South's labor regime (eliminating the Union's
most obvious case of regional "peculiarity"), subsidize the construction of
transcontinental railroads, tether the nation's currency to the international
gold standard, and enact a high-tariff regime that protected American
manufacturers from international competition.[11] Most tragically, the federal government deployed its newfound powers out west, where military
forces violently crushed indigenous polities, thereby opening new territo-

4

ries for settlement.[12] The authority of central national authorities, however, remained limited, in ways not atypical for many states in the Western Hemisphere at the time.[13] The failures of postwar Reconstruction in the South were not regionally specific but rather were symptomatic of the generally embattled position of the federal government within the overall structure of the American state. Federal authorities fell far short of obliterating the bewildering institutional diversity that characterized American governance at the state and local levels that, if anything, greatly compounded over the following decades. Instead of converging toward a seamless whole on the national level, the drive of market integration accelerated a contradictory trajectory of political fragmentation. As metropolitan areas splintered into cities and suburban towns, and territories out west became new states, the number of semiautonomous political authorities rapidly multiplied.[14] To the dismay of business elites, who were developing a national purview and were growing increasingly frustrated with this unwieldy political apparatus, city and state governments remained far and away the principal sites where economic policy questions were settled. Each one of these governments, controlled by democratic majorities, continued to pursue its own priorities relatively independently of other communities.

For all of these reasons—the incredible fragmentation of existing infrastructure, regionally unbalanced financial system, and capacious government power on the state and local levels—the effort to extend market dominance to all corners of the continent remained an improbable undertaking. The vision that Henry Poor and other financial prophets charted so triumphantly was liable to rupture and implode. Over the last several decades of the century, it faced enormous entrepreneurial, political, and ideological challenges that were overcome strenuously and always incompletely.

Most historical accounts of the period, however, have not done enough to interrogate the pursuit of this grandiose project. Instead of treating this issue as a historical problem that required critical scrutiny and explanation, the standard works have narrated the emergence of the new interconnected political economy at the end of the nineteenth century as being nearly indistinguishable from the unfolding of modernity itself.[15] The notion that the United States possessed exceptional features, including, for example, uniquely stable political institutions and a population steeped in the tenets of Lockean liberalism and the Protestant work ethic, has allowed observers to perceive the American path to industrial modernity in almost evolutionary terms, as unusually simple.[16] What seemed dubious, crisis prone, and always bitterly contentious in other large economies in the Americas and elsewhere—Mexico, Argentina, Russia, India, and the Middle East, to name several examples—has been viewed in the case of the United States as necessary and unproblematic.[17]

With these presuppositions in mind, the canonical works about American industrialization in this period have been derived from an overdetermined and technologically driven template of "modernization." These works have cast American industrialization as a sweeping, almost automatic, process that was triumphantly carried forward by transportation and communication technologies—the railroad and telegraph above all. Taking for granted the national contours of the market and its eventual consolidation, they viewed the era's dramatic capitalist transformation in bureaucratic terms, as synonymous with the inexorable rise of the modern corporation.[18] This overpowering trajectory has often seemed remarkably unperturbed by the labor strife and social unrest that erupted in this period. The dominant historical actors in these forceful narratives have been either a colorful cast of rapacious "robber barons," crony capitalists whose financial shenanigans threatened to sabotage an otherwise necessary historical transition,[19] or an emerging class of salaried technocrats and professionals, who tackled the logistical challenges of market integration but never pondered its political and social dimensions.[20] Either way, the final outcome was never really in question. These paradigms tended to cast political challenges to this capitalist transformation as either dangerously reactionary, even proto-fascist, or as hopelessly utopian and therefore hardly pregnant with viable alternatives.[21] They have severely understated the lasting imprint of these challenges on the modern political economy.[22]

This book pursues a different mode of investigation into the emergence of modern capitalism in the United States, attending to two intimately linked aspects of this monumental transition. First, it examines how business elites mobilized to reinvent the American economy in the decades after the Civil War, reorienting it away from cotton and toward the project of continental industrialization. Then, it looks at their entwined efforts to recast political institutions to better facilitate the formation of a seamless national market.[23] It focuses in particular on a cast of gentlemanly bankers from the Northeast, particularly Boston. After the collapse of slavery, these powerful men gradually extricated themselves from the cotton-based economy of earlier decades, in which their class had been deeply embedded as textile manufacturers. They moved their attention, and their immense financial resources, toward mines, stockyards, railroads, real estate, and a host of other business ventures in the Great West. This unprecedented wave of capital migration from the East transformed the West's fledgling industries. The region's economic development, which had been fragmented, fragile, tentative, and gradual, became rapid, centralized, robust, and systematic. Large western territories—abundant with minerals, fertile land, dense forests, and other natural resources—were pulled firmly into the economic orbit of the United States. The integration of this North American market drove the emergence of enormous urban centers and the rise of large-scale manufacturing. It transformed the United States from its former position in the world economy as an exporter of agricultural commodities into the leading industrial nation in the world.[24]

The new geography of capital that these affluent Bostonians (and their counterparts in New York and Philadelphia) so strenuously worked to create hinged in crucial ways on amenable state institutions. But as these scions of wealth stepped beyond the private sphere of the market, where their authority was rarely questioned, into a democratic public arena—both out west and much closer to home, in their own metropolis—they faced a rude awakening. Government institutions, under the control of workers, farmers, miners, mechanics, and small businessmen, did not yield easily to, let alone prioritize, the imperatives of the emerging interconnected system. Largely autonomous, and responsive to popular pressures, these governments pushed back against the hegemony of financial power. Suffused by populist commitments, they pursued a more democratic, state-driven, and decentralized path toward economic modernity. Numerous corners of the political system thus became the sites of acrimonious battles over the very terms of market integration. The evolving relationships between economic centralization and decentralization, state and market institutions, capital and labor, urban and rural, core and periphery, were debated not as technocratic problems to be addressed by experts but as political questions to be determined by enfranchised majorities. Rather than being isolated episodes, these confrontations revealed competing efforts to define the economic trajectory of the United States as a whole, making the period one of the most explosively contentious in American history.[25]

Boston's illustrious business elites, the book's chief protagonists, seemed unlikely to embrace Poor's grand vision of an empire in the American west.

7

Over the course of the nineteenth century, they cultivated the identity of exceptionally prudent and deeply rooted businessmen, not the type to get caught up in risky experiments across the continent. As one of their chroniclers put it, they came to stand for "a conservative pattern of financial behavior quite in contrast with that of America generally."[26] In other words, they were assumed to be (and are still commonly thought of) as the antitheses of aggressive and overreaching American capitalists. This reputation, however, is much belied by the historical record that reveals them to have been dynamic risk-takers who never lost their business instincts and entrepreneurial drive. In the first half of the nineteenth century, it was a leading group of New England merchants—Francis Cabot Lowell, Patrick Tracy Jackson, Nathan Appleton, Abbott Lawrence, and Amos Lawrence—who inaugurated the industrial revolution in the United States. Leveraging their mercantile fortunes, easy access to southern cotton, and the availability of female labor in the countryside, they made Waltham, Lowell, and several other New England rural locales into bustling centers of textile manufacturing. Their reputation as conservative and prudent men notwithstanding, they positioned themselves in the vanguard of global capitalism, making New England, alongside Lancashire, Normandy, Flanders, Saxony, and Catalonia, into one of the most heavily industrialized regions in the world.[27]

By midcentury, after several decades of rapid growth, cotton manufacturing entered a period of declining profitability and one of crisis, which reached a climax in a series of bankruptcies in 1857. This was a profoundly disorienting juncture for the Brahmins, who had staked their fortunes on cotton manufacturing and expected it to propel them in perpetuity. With their primary industry no longer able to absorb large-scale investment and produce steady dividends, members of the same elite families again showed an astonishing ability to adapt. In what was yet another watershed moment, they dramatically redeployed their saved resources into bold new ventures and reinvented themselves as financiers. The old generation of textile magnates passed away or retired from public life, having lost their credibility in their desperate efforts to appease their cotton suppliers in the South and save the Union. The war dealt a death blow to this older coalition of what Senator Charles Sumner derisively called "the lords of the loom and the lords of the lash." But an ambitious new generation, a new vanguard group from within the old elite—including such figures as Henry Lee Higginson, Alexander Agassiz, Charles F. Adams Jr., and Thomas Jefferson Coolidge—

came to take their place. In the aftermath of the war, this younger generation, who had genuine antislavery credentials and had joined the military effort, began long careers in business. They successfully mobilized the financial resources of the city's affluent families toward brave new horizons.

These powerful men did not sit back and wait for ambitious westerners to take the lead, nor did they expect to realize their designs from the comfort of their private chambers in eastern financial districts. They did not resemble the declining, detached, and effeminate elite depicted in the literary works of Edith Wharton and William Dean Howells. Charged with managing the accumulated savings of dozens of wealthy Bostonian families, they came down from the "commanding heights of the economy" and scoured the treacherous terrains of the broad continent in search of lucrative investments, especially ones that could soak up large amounts of capital. They crossed the continent numerous times, observed development, gathered information, and built networks of business connections. Rather than withdraw into their private parlors, country estates, and social clubs, they moved through the untamed wilderness in trains, steamboats, coaches, and on foot. They embraced continental integration as a heroic undertaking and infused it with an exhilarating sense of grandiosity. Only gradually, as a result of their incessant work, did western properties that would normally have been considered highly speculative become mainstays in the portfolios of moneyed eastern families.

The progenies of old moneyed families thus showed an extraordinary capacity to reinvent the economy and reinvent themselves, time and time again, as befitting members of a commercially oriented bourgeois class. This ability has often been overlooked by observers of the United States, who, guided by the works of Benjamin Franklin and Alexis de Tocqueville, associated American capitalism with the unleashing of pent-up entrepreneurial energy from the grass roots.[28] These canonical texts allowed commentators to ignore some of America's most powerful economic actors and prematurely announce the death of "seasoned wealth" in American life.[29] As a result of this well-entrenched interpretive orientation, scholars have rarely examined the archives of elite Bostonians, the quintessential old-money capitalists on the American scene after the Civil War, for their involvement in business. Unlike their counterparts in the South, who often stood in the center of controversy and debate, the trajectory of northern capitalists has often appeared unremarkable. The complicated links between their business practices, politics, and ideology have withstood relatively little scrutiny.[30] Stock narratives about the period have mostly overlooked the involvement of these capitalists in the economic life of the United States, dwelling instead on their much loftier engagements as social reformers, diplomats, philanthropists, and sophisticated literary figures. These narratives have often emphasized the Bostonians' alienation from the modern industrial society that, ironically, they were instrumental in creating and over which they presided.[31]

Indeed, the relentless business drive and instincts of the Boston Brahmins remained very much intact, allowing them to take key roles in the great capitalist drama of the late nineteenth century. Their age-old fortunes, instead of eroding over time, moved into cutting-edge investments and continued to earn remunerative returns. As economist Thomas Piketty recently observed in relation to the top wealth owners in all developed economies over the course of the nineteenth century, their share in the overall economy did not wither but rather continued to expand.[32] The returns on their various properties handsomely sustained a class of wealthy Bostonians, and their social and cultural institutions, into the twentieth century. This persistent ability to accumulate had profound implications far beyond Boston's fashionable residential neighborhoods or even the city's financial district. The control over this massive movement of capital allowed the business leadership of this class to reinvent major industries, establish new urban centers and recast old ones, revolutionize the ecologies of entire regions, and set whole populations in motion. In extending their reach into the deep interior of North America, these men were not unique. They acted very much like capitalists elsewhere around the world during those decades, who similarly mobilized to intensify their domination of continental hinterlands and pull vast territories in India, Egypt, Asia, Africa, and Latin America into the world economy.[33] In more than one way, therefore, the Brahmins reveal the formation of modern capitalism in the United States to have been far less unique than previously assumed. They broaden the analytical framework beyond the familiar idiom about a distinctly American "Gilded Age," situating it instead in a much longer history of capitalism—a history of constant invention and reinvention—and in a broad comparative perspective, as part and parcel of a much larger global transformation.[34]

The corollary trajectory of the American state over the same decades further complicates the story, making the history of capitalism into much more than the history of capital and capitalists. Expanding beyond a narrow focus on market transactions between consenting individuals, it places much greater emphasis on the role of collective mobilization, rival ideological commitments, and political contestation over the very rules that governed markets. It considers a much wider cast of characters and engages other types of historical sources, complementing the papers and memoirs of affluent Bostonians with government records that documented fierce battles over public policy. These documents reveal that modern capitalism did not emerge in accordance with a set of universal laws or the dictates of new technologies, or directly out of the elegant blueprints of the rich and powerful. Rather, it was the contingent historical outcome of messy and drawn-out confrontations between social groups with competing visions of political economy. At stake in these confrontations was not merely the distribution of the material rewards—although that was certainly a chief concern—but also the very foundations of the capitalist marketplace itself. On the table as open-ended questions in these debates were some of the most fundamental underpinnings of the capitalist economy, including the rights and privileges associated with private property, the full meaning of "free labor" in the aftermath of Emancipation, the separation between private and public, and, crucially, the power of democratic political processes to dictate policy and ultimately mold economic change.

The federal structure of the American state meant that battles over policy were fought not in a single unitary site such as Congress but in the many sites within the political system. Given that a central government capable of superseding the thicket of local arrangements was not remotely on the horizon, the integration of a national market hinged on capitalists' ability to recast political institutions on the subnational level, rendering these institutions congruent with a new, interconnected economic order. Much of the tendency for development in the United States to splinter was directly linked to the decentralized structure of the political system, which allowed each state and city government to pursue its own economic policies independently of a single centralized design. National elites, the Boston Brahmins being one very telling case in point, therefore mobilized to reorient city and state governments toward greater emphasis on their position in a broader capitalist geography. They worked to make subnational governments into compatible nodes in a larger integrated whole. This agenda proved highly controversial and faced powerful opposition in a democratic political system where Americans of different walks of life had a voice and exercised considerable power. Large areas of American politics that historians have often written off as immaterial or irredeemably corrupt—the domain of ethnic jealousies, naked opportunism, and party bosses—were in fact crucial in molding the economic trajectory of the United States. They became the sites of deeply ideological and surprisingly principled contests over industrial modernity.

This book examines these fateful contests in two crucial locales, metropolitan politics in the urban East and territorial politics in the Great West. It identifies populist politics—broad grassroots efforts to politicize and shape market integration—as a key feature of state formation in this period in both of these locales. Disciplinary divides between "urban" and "western" histories have customarily treated these sites as separate, but as national elites readily recognized, they were two frontiers, each with their own unique features, in a broader struggle over the creation of a national political economy.[35] The relationships between financiers and political constituencies in the East and in the West were, of course, very different. Westerners' entanglements with eastern bankers were primarily financial. These westerners resided in communities whose development rested on eastern financial resources. Eastern urbanites' link to bankers was primarily political. These easterners lived in political communities that counted among their members the nation's most important financiers and that were home to some of the most powerful banking institutions in the United States. Despite these differences, urban and western variants of American populism nevertheless overlapped in meaningful ways. Drawing on a shared ideological producerist legacy, both opposed the unchecked power of centralized financial authority. They identified the relationship between political and economic democracy as necessary and insisted on the inherently political nature of economic policy. They converged around creative efforts to use a democratic state to shape industrial development, promote a more equal distribution of wealth, and secure a just reward for labor. Populists in both the East and the West did not oppose commerce or look back wistfully to a preindustrial past. They were passionately modern and remained optimistic about the democratic potential of industrialization. Their goal was not to abolish market exchange but rather to embed it in a democratic political framework.[36]

The transformation of a city like Boston from the hub of an industrial region into a large financial center with a continental reach triggered an array of political clashes. In the 1870s and 1880s, the republican language of "productive labor" that had mobilized the urban population against slaveholders and their northern partners rendered financiers politically and culturally suspect. It gave policymakers in city government a public mandate to pursue a democratic vision of urban-industrial progress. These urban leaders, many of whom were neighborhood businessmen, shopkeepers, and tradesmen, prioritized metropolitan industry and housing, not interregional financial networks or banking institutions. They radically expanded the territorial political jurisdiction of the city and used robust public investment in infrastructure and services—roads, water, sewers, parks, schools, libraries, and a slew of other initiatives—to promote dynamic and broad-based metropolitan development. These efforts produced meaningful benefits for wide segments of the population. They swelled the diverse industrial base of the city, for the first time making Boston, rather than its rural industrial satellites, into the largest center of manufacturing in the commonwealth. They also greatly enlarged the city's housing stock, creating a large population of working-class homeowners.

These policies, however, not only caused a sharp increase in taxation on property but also produced a gritty metropolitan landscape and a populist mode of governance that became anathemas to elite sensibilities. They made the city less desirable for the affluent residents whose savings sustained the financial sector. Those who sought to nurture Boston's emergence as a financial hub thus worked to stem any further additions to the city's territory and to cement a new political divide between city and suburb. They attempted to impose strict limits on public spending and to exempt financial assets from the city's list of taxable properties. This elite program aimed to reallocate resources from the rapidly growing neighborhoods on the metropolitan periphery to the financial district and the posh areas of downtown, which elites identified as the wellsprings of urban eminence and prosperity. Fully integral to this agenda were attempts to redefine urban culture around a new set of dichotomies. Urban workers and mechanics at the time championed the integration of physical and intellectual labor. They believed that free labor amalgamated manual dexterity and mental development. Elites dismissed these deeply entrenched ideas, introducing new conceptual divides between useful and beautiful, practical and aesthetic, production and consumption, highbrow and lowbrow. They challenged a proto-modernist industrial ethos that celebrated the cacophony of urban life and spurned the separation of form and function, art and craft, and, by implication, social stratification. They instead proposed a more hierarchical emphasis on connoisseurship and taste.

They founded or reconfigured an array of civic institutions and venues, such as the Boston Symphony, Museum of Fine Arts, Massachusetts Institute of Technology, and Boston Common, that fortified these new values in the public imagination and imprinted them on the urban landscape.

Analogous political and ideological battles raged in the Great West, the destination of ever-growing Bostonian investments. As eastern money poured into places such as Colorado, Montana, Idaho, Wyoming, Washington, and the Dakotas, it made the western territories of the United States into a crucial new arena of political conflict. Faced with unprecedented corporate power backed by eastern finance, settlers in these territories began to forge a robust regulatory framework. They envisioned a capacious democratic state that would empower them in their relations with what they considered to be "foreign" interests. They advocated for government regulation of railroad shipping rates and a legal framework that would secure for settlers broad access to land and water. They sought state protection of workers' safety, prohibition of child labor, and the right to organize collectively. Determined to avoid narrow regional specialization on the extraction of raw materials, they aimed to structure the relationship with distant capitalists in ways that would harness eastern money in the service of more balanced and sustainable development. Eastern investors, in Boston and elsewhere, were deeply concerned about this agenda, which they viewed as misguided and ultimately counterproductive. They and their compradors in the region mobilized to retract these legislative initiatives and subsume western political institutions under a set of general, legible, and predictable principles that would stabilize the property rights of investors. They worked to secure the primacy of finance capital over a democratic state and of the integrated national market over relative regional autonomy.

Brahmin Capitalism is thus an urban history with a continental scope, and a continental history with a strong urban focus. Only by considering the East and the West together does it become possible to make sense of the leverage elites gained in politics, despite being a tiny minority in a democratic system. Their clout rested on their ability to mobilize on both ends of the new capitalist geography. They placated constituencies in the urban East with the allure of gaining a share in the "wages of empire" in the Great West even as they trumped western constituencies with arguments about severe penalties to communities that proved hostile to eastern investors. Elites thus had the upper hand not because approaches that were more democratic were at odds with the immanent logic of modernity but owing to their ability ultimately to muster their own structural advantages, forge resilient networks over long distances, and organize effectively around key issues.

The national market that emerged in the late 1890s, most dramatically in a triumphant wave of corporate consolidations known as the "great merger movement," launched the economy of the United States into the twentieth century. Whereas the decades that followed the Civil War were economically challenging for the nation's business elites, the turn of the century signaled a change for the better. The overall economic landscape had shifted markedly in their favor. The underpinnings of the new corporate economy nevertheless remained creaky. The American state bore the deep-seated marks of several decades of inconclusively re-solved conflicts that left intact much of the authority of subnational po-litical institutions. The turn to federal authorities to supplant local and regional ones continued to be an embattled process. Corporate hege-mony extended far and wide, but its reach was generally shallow. It was largely limited to core economic sectors, leaving sizable portions of the economy to emerge via the proliferation of proprietary and regionally ori-ented industries. The language and ideological imagination of the popu-lists was never extinguished from the political system, even as it lost some of its power and political coherence. The critique of financial elites who produced little, consumed a disproportionate amount, and held unwar-ranted power remained viable, as was the populist tendency to understand economic policy in political terms. In all, the formative period of the late nineteenth century left a thorny legacy of deep structural wrinkles in the blanket of the corporate liberal modernity, wrinkles that continued to per-vade the American political economy deep into the twentieth century.

CHAPTER ONE

Anatomy of a Crisis

I n September 1865, Henry Lee Higginson marched through Georgia in search of the future of American capitalism. Honorably discharged from service in the Union Army the previous year, the young patrician Bostonian joined forces with two fellow veterans in an effort to demonstrate the viability of cotton cultivation based on free labor. It was an experiment in social reform and political economy that also promised considerable material rewards. "Making money there," Higginson was judiciously advised upon commencing the enterprise, boiled down to the "simple question of being able to make the darkies work."[1] The stakes were high. If slavery was indeed inferior to free agricultural methods, and if the emancipated slaves could be effectively mobilized with monetary incentives instead of physical coercion, capitalism in the United States could be reconstructed along radically new lines. The market doctrine of the young New Englanders would be vindicated, as would their moral sentiments. A great supply of cotton would flood the marketplace and put the postbellum United States on a prosperous economic trajectory.

The three partners took the necessary precautions to set themselves on the path to success. One of the partners, Channing Clapp, was dispatched to Boston to secure financial backing from acquaintances and family. "He will call on you for $9500," Higginson alerted his father. The other partner, Charles F. Morse, traveled to the Sea Islands of South Carolina, where New Englanders had conducted a similar experiment on a much larger scale during the war. He consulted with Edward Atkinson, a vocal champion of cotton production with the use of free labor, who shared his experience and even provided the young entrepreneurs with seeds of a vigorous Egyptian variety of cotton.[2] Higginson drafted a business plan, figuring that with generous use of manure (much neglected under slavery in his view) they could yield in the first season a minimum of 32,000 pounds of cotton. This would allow each partner to reap almost $6,000, a nice sum, which was bound to increase in the coming years. With this plan in hand, the three Yankees headed down to Savannah and acquired "Cottonham," a plantation deep in the woods of Bryan County. The estate included 5,000 acres of land and a roomy "big" house surrounded by beautiful oak trees, as well as several barns, a cotton gin, and a grist mill. There were also workers' quarters, where about sixty former slaves resided.

Despite the optimism that surrounded the project, the enterprise floundered from the get-go. Among the complications the Bostonians were not prepared for, having had no prior exposure to rural life, were a variety of pests and less than ideal weather conditions, especially intense summer heat and untimely rainfall. Their relations with their workers, however, remained the crux of the challenge. Higginson devised an elaborate contractual scheme that paid workers a basic rate per acre tended, with the rest earned by the pound for picking, sorting, and moting. Families could earn extra wages for more work around the plantation and also raise their own crops and keep pigs and chickens on small plots that were allocated to them. To ease the freedmen's transition to the new incentives, the Bostonians did their best to introduce new attitudes about the ennobling qualities of work. Higginson scrubbed, whitewashed, and hammered alongside his workers as they fixed up the big house. His partners joined the laborers in the field, drove mules, cleaned horses, ploughed, chopped, and hoed. They tried to give manual labor "a new aspect" in the minds of their employees and inspire "life into their movements." Higginson expected that the plan would support the freedmen handsomely and allow the more industrious of them to save enough to purchase their own land within a few years.[3]

The former slaves were not similarly sanguine about their prospects under the new leadership. They utterly refused to work under their previous master, but the new bosses from Boston, despite their good intentions, appeared only marginally better. Before the arrival of the three, the freedmen thought it would only be fair that they become the rightful owners of the land that they had worked for generations. They "have been indulging in a belief or hope that the lands were to be divided," Higginson noted. They never really surrendered the expectation, which he dismissed as "chimerical," to gain "a horse and forty acres from the United States." Furthermore, they thought the wages the Bostonians proposed to pay were grossly inadequate, and so the planting season that began after Christmas was punctuated by work stoppages and strikes. To win over their workers, the employers tried the "carrot," offering for sale a stock of calicoes and flannel fabrics, shoes, and other goods that the impoverished freedmen were "much pleased to see." "They see the work brings wages and the wages bring food and clothing," Higginson cheerfully observed, hoping to soon have "a good, reliable set of hands."[4] Too often, however, he turned to the dull "stick" of market forces. As free laborers on the land, the former slaves had to choose between, as Higginson starkly put it, "work or starvation." If they did not earn wages, they would be allowed no credit at the store and would face eviction from the plantation. Higginson was clear that if they refused to work, "we shall put other laborers, black or white, into their houses."[5] This ethic was foreign to the freedmen, who expected to live on the premises and receive whatever provisions were available. When they were denied what they wanted, they simply helped themselves, greatly infuriating their employers.[6]

The first season fell far short of Higginson's projections, owing to a thin crop and the worldwide decline in the price of cotton. The second season, like the first, began with a cycle of labor negotiations. The initial buoyancy and the notions of paternalism wore off, to be replaced with frustration and even outright anger. Higginson's wife, Ida, the daughter of famous Harvard naturalist and polygenesist Louis Agassiz, joined the group in Georgia to model bourgeois domesticity. She articulated the sense that "these darkies have been very well paid, kindly treated, taught, helped by us, but they feel no gratitude for all this." Earlier assumptions about the power of market incentives drastically softened. They were replaced with a growing conviction that the former slaves could not be counted on to work without constant "supervision, and spurring on and urging and system to guide them." "How much more hopeful they appear at a distance than near to," Mrs. Higginson confessed.[7] The season ended with greater losses than in the first, reinforcing the realization among the Bostonians that they would not be able to produce cotton profitably under those circumstances. By the end of May 1867, the Higginsons had packed their bags and headed back to Boston, where Henry launched a decades-long career with his father and uncle's powerful private banking house of Lee, Higginson, and Company.

For Higginson and his associates, "Cottonham" signaled the unlikely coda of the cotton economy's heroic age in the United States and the launch of a new industrial order. The fraught labor of southern Reconstruction resumed,

1.1. Major Henry Lee Higginson, soon to become Boston's most important investment banker, posing in his Union Army uniform, 1863.

Credit: Bliss Perry, *The Life and Letters of Henry Lee Higginson* (Boston: Atlantic Monthly Press, 1921).

of course, but, with the New Englanders' retreat (initially economic, then gradually political), the drama of American capitalism shifted decisively to other landscapes. The efforts to resuscitate cotton cultivation in the aftermath of Emancipation thus marked a key moment in a long historical arc whose constituent parts have conventionally been kept conceptually discrete, segmented along regional and temporal lines: the careers of Bostonians like Higginson—and the long trajectory of American capitalism more generally—cut through these divides. Rooted in an old American city with a long and ever-changing engagement in business, they highlight a dynamic history of cross-regional connections, continuities, and discontinuities. They bridge deeply entrenched compartments that separate antebellum and postbellum economic change; North, South, and West; and national, regional, and metropolitan scales of development. They reveal the understudied mechanisms and historical actors that propelled the cotton economy of earlier decades to give birth to a new regime of capital accumulation—new industries, new labor systems, new geography—in the war's aftermath.[8]

The chronology of industrial capitalism over the course of the nineteenth century was not simple or linear, nor was it free of crises and false starts. For half a century before the Civil War, Boston's business leaders had staked their fortunes on the spinning and weaving of cotton in water-powered mills near the streams and rivers of northern New England. Cotton manufacturing generated robust profits that were continually reinvested in the industry. Millions of dollars poured into the waterworks that powered the mills, the massive land improvements at the new factory towns, and the construction of mill buildings, machine shops, and workers' housing. Large financial resources funded railroads, warehouses, and maritime facilities that connected the sites of production to supply and distribution chains at home and worldwide. Over time, the streams and waterfalls of the New England countryside, the region's arteries of transportation, the commercial docks and wharfs in Boston Harbor, the lives of thousands of mill workers, and, crucially, the financial institutions that held the savings of the city's affluent families all pulsated according to the ebbs and flows of textile production. Cotton manufacturing dominated the economy of Massachusetts and its adjoining states. It also defined the interregional connections that made industrialization possible, especially the powerful bonds between New England and the agricultural economy of the South, where the raw cotton was grown, picked, ginned, and baled by slave labor.[9]

Cotton-based industrialization in those days was much more than an economic system. It was deeply embedded in New England's political institutions, social arrangements, and civic institutions. Government action, class formation (at the top and bottom of society), and the intellectual and cultural life of the region were intimately bound up with the development of this particular industry. Its broad foundation—extending beyond the realm of business—made the cotton complex remarkably resilient. Over time, the profitability of textile mills eroded, and the industry endured a severe crisis. The viability of cotton manufacturing as an engine of growth became doubtful. The self-reinforcing dynamics of the system nevertheless predisposed elite Bostonians to pursue recovery and even further expansion. These elites warded off political challenges and dug in their heels in the face of social unrest. As evinced by Higginson's escapades in Georgia, many of them continued to look for ways to reignite the cotton economy, even after the Civil War destroyed the unfree labor system that made raw cotton cultivation possible on a mass scale.

Standing among the ruins of the "Cotton Kingdom" as the nation began the difficult work of Reconstruction, Higginson and other elite Bostonians were soon disabused of the hope of inaugurating a new age in cotton agriculture. The enthusiasm around "cheap cotton with free labor," which was intended to give the antebellum cotton economy a second lease on life, quickly faded. With their flagship industry in crisis, unable to profitably absorb additional heavy investment, the urgency to forge new circuits of accumulation inspired the emergence of a whole new business orientation. The Bostonians thus made a fateful departure and set off on a new trajectory. They began to reenvision American capitalist development, not in modifying and salvaging the arrangements of earlier decades but in a far more ambitious program of continental industrialization. In a bold pivot that many at the time considered implausible, especially for an established elite with a reputation for being feeble and conservative, they dramatically broadened their business horizons. They retreated from cotton and moved into a host of groundbreaking ventures in the Great American West— mining, stockyards, and railroads.

The implications of this momentous turn to the Great West could not have been more profound. The shift reinvented Boston, previously the hub of a manufacturing region, as a major financial center of national significance. It opened new avenues for profitable investment after a decade of stagnation, unlocking grand vistas of enterprise for a young generation of affluent Bostonians, who readily embraced the challenge. It revitalized the urban elite's financial prospects and introduced a new sense of purpose into the old community. The city's business district on State Street soon bustled with an extraordinary volume of activity. Urban politics became the site of conflict over the city's new position within the emerging national economy. Just as significantly, large infusions of investment from places like Boston began to reshape the West. The unprecedented wave of eastern capital penetrated deeply into the interior of the continent, greatly intensifying the West's enmeshments in circuits of commodity exchange. It allowed financiers to transform what had been ad hoc, fragmented, and often flimsy industries into systematic, robust, and highly capitalized endeavors that were governed in centralized fashion from the business districts of eastern cities. The hugely profitable new industrial sectors moved into the core of American capitalism. In a manner that was politically controversial and socially explosive, they made the West and its seemingly endless supply of natural resources, valuable minerals, and agricultural commodities into an integral part of the U.S. economy.

The abandonment of textiles and turn to the west was almost unthinkable for Bostonian businessmen only decades earlier as they moved headlong into cotton manufacturing. "It is true that a good deal of capital is going into this business," merchant-turned-industrialist Nathan Appleton assured a skeptical acquaintance in 1821, "but so wide is the field before us that I think it will not soon be overdone."[10] This confidence characterized the founders of the textile industry, whose rosy beginnings have consistently overshadowed its longer and much grimier lifespan. A tight cohort of New England merchants, led by Francis Cabot Lowell and Patrick Tracy Jackson, first launched the Boston Manufacturing Company on the banks of the Charles River in Waltham, Massachusetts, in 1813. They secured a corporate charter and capitalized their venture at about ten times that of the smaller cotton mills that preceded it in Rhode Island. They created the first fully integrated factory in the United States, combining the spinning and weaving portions of the process. The mills turned raw cotton into finished cloth and churned out hefty profits.

In 1822, the astounding success in Waltham inspired the founders to launch Lowell, a more ambitious undertaking to be erected near a thirty-foot waterfall on the Merrimack River. Before long, the immense infrastructure at the site powered nineteen large-scale textile mills. The once rural locale became the second-largest city in Massachusetts and, by 1840, among the largest twenty cities in the United States. The workforce was to be made up of "sober" and "industrious" young women, who were recruited from the New England countryside to operate the mills and live in supervised boarding houses for several years before marriage. Free from a permanent class of wage earners and nestled in the salubrious rural surroundings, the venture was advertised as a uniquely American model of industrialization, fully compatible with republican institutions.[11]

Over the next two decades, Lowell's promoters reinvested their earnings back into the industry and financed a proliferation of cotton mills throughout the region, in Manchester, Saco, Dover, and Chicopee.[12] They forged an interlocking system of related enterprises in banking, transportation, distribution, and machinery, all under the control of a cohesive milieu of owners. In time, regional railroads such as the "Boston and Lowell" and "Boston and Worcester" brought many millions of pounds of raw cotton to the mills and carried the finished cloth to Boston Harbor. Machine shops assembled the devices that made mass production of yarn and fabrics possible. Commercial banks and financial firms provided liquid capital to an industry that kept large resources in fixed assets. A set of selling agents distributed ever-growing quantities of cloth to places far and wide throughout the United States and abroad.[13]

This industrial system reached its apex in the 1840s. In the course of a single generation, a core group of about eighty Bostonians, who owned more than thirty of the largest textile corporations, each of which employed hundreds of workers at dozens of mill buildings, cemented their economic, social, and political power.[14] Older mercantile families such as the Jacksons and Lowells reestablished themselves financially and socially. Newcomers such as Abbott Lawrence and Nathan Appleton, who had migrated to Boston from the countryside as young men, became towering figures in the community and in the nation at large. A class of Bostonians who owned the lucrative shares clustered in elegant homes in a residential enclave on Beacon Hill. They contributed funds and sat on the boards of prominent civic institutions such as Massachusetts General Hospital, the Boston Athenaeum, the Lowell Institute, and, most importantly, Harvard College. They nurtured a long list of prominent writers, legal theorists, theologians, and intellectuals, who set the tone for the period as a whole. These luminaries—men such as Joseph Story, Henry Wadsworth Longfellow, Oliver Wendell Holmes, and many lesser figures, long forgotten—earned the urban hub of the industrial revolution in the United States the improbable label of "Athens of America." Finally, with the Whig Party as their political vehicle, and its eloquent leaders, Edward Everett and Daniel Webster, as close associates, the cotton magnates enjoyed decisive influence in government affairs on both the state and federal levels.[15] At that point, this thickly knit operation appeared to be foolproof. Young Amos A. Lawrence, who was reared to one day preside over this large-scale complex, brimmed with confidence upon his graduation from Harvard in 1835. He reasoned that if he would merely have "mercantile tact enough to carry on the immense though safe machine which my father and uncle have put in operation, it will turn out gold to me as fast as I could wish."[16] He fully expected this intricate arrangement to continue to pay steady dividends in perpetuity.

A stable accumulation strategy, however, proved to be an elusive goal. With profits flowing in from existing properties, Bostonian investors found it increasingly challenging to find new outlets for their ever-growing pools of capital. Water power at Lowell and elsewhere had reached their outer limits, precluding slow, linear expansion, and so, in the generally prosperous 1840s, plans were already afoot for a new phase of development in two promising locales, which were christened "Lawrence" and "Holyoke." Capitalized at unprecedented amounts, the two projects signaled efforts to replicate earlier accomplishments on an even grander scale. Promoters poured enormous resources into the initial phase, including huge dams and canals, the most advanced machine shops, and grand city layouts with allowance for churches, schools, parks, and workers' boarding houses. Altogether, the founders furnished the two sites with sufficient water power for 1.5 million spindles, which alone would have gradually increased the number of spindles in New England by about 50 percent. They anticipated each town to match the population of Lowell, which was around 33,000, within five years. Mill construction that could bring these industrial sites to complete utilization would have absorbed anywhere between $30 million and $40 million in additional investment.[17]

Lawrence and Holyoke were not haphazard enterprises. They commenced, as William Appleton, who was one of the investors, explained, "by men of capital & intelligence . . . on a large scale."[18] The incorporators of the new towns were not rapacious upstarts but Boston's best and brightest, "men of forecast, scientific attainments, and practical knowledge of heavy manufacturing and engineering operations," as another memorialist put

24

it. Their actions were guided by the best available business projections, and they thus "harbored no fear of failure."[19] Thoughtful action, and the leadership of Boston's most experienced men of business, provided no immunity from disaster. As early as 1850, Appleton diagnosed a persistent problem of "over production" in the industry. Lawrence and Holyoke greatly exacerbated this problem as their mills began to dump additional product into already glutted markets. Appleton accurately estimated that despite being located in "a magnificent place for a Manufacturing City," Lawrence would not yield income for "years." He doubted whether the machine shop, which was expected to provide spinning and weaving machinery to a booming city, was "worth anything."[20] For a time, the project's backers sustained confidence among investors, buoying the shares of the parent firm, the Essex Company, despite large operating losses.[21] Soon enough, however, the venture's financial hardships could no longer be ignored, and the stocks began to drop. The Hadley Falls Company, the company behind Holyoke, fared even worse. The availability of water power far exceeded demand. Costly machinery ran at less than full capacity. The proprietors could not attract new textile mills to the site and instead leased space at lower rates to smaller enterprises—a flour mill, a wire plant, and a paper factory.[22]

The financial panic of 1857 pushed the languishing Lawrence and Holyoke into insolvency and wiped away an estimated $10 million of investment.[23] As large-scale, fully planned, Boston-controlled mill towns, they were the last of their kind. As bankruptcies extended from the most recent entrants to the industry as a whole, the deep-seated nature of the crisis became all the more clear. Manufacturing stocks, to the extent that they were traded, were priced at 40 percent to 60 percent less than their par value. Five large companies declared bankruptcy, as did two of the industry's largest distributors. Several others were widely assumed to be worthless. In all, the industry lost an estimated third of its former valuation.[24] As Amos A. Lawrence observed, "our manufacturing interest is for the present completely broken down and discredited." He noted in particular the disorienting effects of the panic on what was a tight community of investors, who viewed themselves as prudent and gentlemanly. "Most kinds of property have no value, nor is there confidence between men of the ability to perform contract," he explained. "Many who relied on it extensively have been beggared: among them are some of my dearest friends."[25] William Appleton, in what were by his own admission "the most

25

trying" days of his long career, spent long days in desperate efforts to inject liquidity into his failing properties.[26] He observed that "many of our acquaintances and some of our neighbours who thought themselves rich find they have no property."[27]

The downturn forced a painful disillusionment among elite Bostonians. The Board of Trade of Boston reported at length on the crisis and decried its "deadening effect on the capital of our State, where a large amount of this property is held." The unambiguous diagnosis was "excess of investment in mills and machinery."[28] The Board lamented the "vast projects" that were pushed forward despite the rapid increase in the manufacturing capacity of existing mill towns. Overproduction kept down the price of goods "to the starving point" and propped up the price of raw cotton, the supply of which proved relatively inelastic.[29] "A glance at the prices of the corporate stocks in New England at this time, and at the list of dividends for the past ten years, show what a beggarly business we have been doing."[30] Dividends of cotton manufacturing corporations indeed consistently declined from an annual average of 11.4 percent up to 1836 and 9.7 percent from 1836 to 1846 to an average of 5.8 percent from 1847 to 1859, with several companies unable to make regular dividend payments.[31] A reckoning of a worldwide glut, driven by the rapid growth of manufacturing in the United Kingdom as well as on the Continent in Germany, Austria, France, and Switzerland, offered little room for optimism. This sober assessment made it clear that this was not a temporary setback but rather a lasting structural challenge. The Board read the writing on the wall and cautioned against any further expansion. It advised that the "present generation of manufacturers will regard more the importance of keeping alive and of strengthening what is already created, than of forming new schemes."[32] The recommendations officially announced that the strategy that had for quite a while carried the region's economic development had lost its viability as a vehicle for further growth.

This intractable impasse was very bad news indeed. For almost half a century, elite Bostonians assumed that cotton mills would be able to absorb older profits from commercial endeavors and pay regular dividends, which would in turn be redirected back into more textile manufacturing capacity.[33] The political economy of the entire region rested on this presupposition. Maritime trade, which had been the main focus of business for affluent New Englanders in earlier centuries, resumed, but even Bostonians with deep-seated roots in long-distance commerce slowly moved their holdings to manufacturing stocks and the regional railroads. Veteran traders such as Henry Lee and Harrison Gray Otis, who were at one point vocal critics of the tariff protections that nurtured local industry at the expense of cheap imports, fully embraced this form of investment. By 1847, Lee owned stock in twenty-two manufacturing companies; two regional railroads; one cotton machine shop; and three water power companies, at Lowell, Lawrence, and Saco.[34] William Sturgis, who had accumulated his fortune in the East India trade, similarly became a prominent investor in the textile industry. Sturgis held stock and served as a director in at least six textile companies and four regional railroads.[35] Sturgis's good friend John Perkins Cushing, upon his return from three decades as a merchant in the port of Canton, similarly withdrew his capital from trade and moved it into New England's industrial economy. By 1851, his property included $428,494 in nineteen manufacturing corporations and $128,794 in railroads, adding up to 35 percent of his very large holdings.[36] The movement of these men into manufacturing signaled that the "lustrous and fragrant products of Coast and Islands" had been emphatically replaced by the much more "prosaic fruit of New England looms."[37]

The area's financial institutions followed a similar strategy. The largest depository of accumulated maritime fortunes in Boston, the Massachusetts Hospital Life Insurance Company, formed in 1823, initially invested its reserves in land mortgages. After the limited market in Boston was exhausted, the company's actuary, in search of alternative investment outlets, extended lending into the New England countryside, offering credit to farmers in the commonwealth's western districts. These loans, however, became administratively cumbersome and politically controversial. After 1838, the company therefore scaled back these loans, allowing funds to flow into less unwieldy loans to manufacturing and regional railroad corporations. In what was a mutually beneficial arrangement, the company was relieved of the bureaucratic burden of dealing with a mass of unknown borrowers. It instead found a ready and ever-expanding outlet for its funds among a group of insiders within the city's business community, who borrowed large lump sums. The company, in turn, became the textile industry's single largest source of credit. Unlike commercial banks, which lent moderate amounts for periods that lasted at most several months, Massachusetts Hospital Life provided large-scale loans that often extended uninterrupted over several years.[38] Overall, between 1845 and 1855, direct loans to manufacturing companies and loans to individuals in the industry, which were secured by manufacturing stock, increased from $300,000 to nearly $4,000,000. This was about half the total resources of Massachusetts Hospital Life at that point. Almost $600,000 more was invested in Massachusetts railroads.[39]

By the late 1850s, the steady movement of Bostonian capital into cotton manufacturing led to an overwhelming concentration of resources in the industry. It was at that point the largest industry in the United States, with more capital invested and the largest annual value produced. The six New England states dominated this sector, with roughly 3.8 million of the 5.2 million spindles nationally and 93,000 of 126,000 looms. By 1860, even after its valuation declined by about a third during the crisis, almost $70 million was invested in cotton manufacturing in New England alone. The industry employed more than any other industry in the region, approximately 80,000 workers, the majority of them women.[40] For the upper echelons of the business community of Boston, diversification of investment mostly meant dividing ownership between a large number of mills at several sites in the region, each producing a different type of fabric in mass quantities. With the exception of the area's railroad network, itself an integral part of the textile complex, the move into cotton manufacturing occasioned little carryover of large-scale capital into other industries. As mentioned, this was evident in the portfolios of Boston's leading businessmen, such as Lee, Sturgis, and Cushing. Upon Nathan Appleton's death in 1861, his estate included shares in twenty-five cotton mills and water-power firms, which he had systematically acquired since 1813. Estimated to be worth $827,700, they represented 54 percent of his invested property, dwarfing his investments in railroads (20 percent), financial institutions (10 percent), real estate (13 percent), and utilities (3 percent).[41] Amos A. Lawrence's portfolio was even more heavily concentrated in textiles. In 1857, it included seventeen mill companies, which added up to 67 percent of his investments. The rest was lent out to individuals (21 percent) or held in real estate (21 percent).[42] These affluent Bostonians took on a tremendous stake in cotton manufacturing, with hardly any entanglements in other types of industrial ventures.

Over time, the ownership of cotton mills spread beyond these prominent figures. One of the most important features of the corporate form was its ability to facilitate the seamless transfer of ownership without disrupting day-to-day business operations. This transfer, however, did not diffuse to a mass market of anonymous investors, nor did it absorb capital from outside the region. The affluent owners of the shares rarely traded them in the open market, and their high par amount put them beyond the reach of other classes of savers. Two decades after its inception, the Merrimack Company of Lowell, which had drawn its initial investment from a dozen men, had about four hundred shareholders. As stocks moved beyond the original incorporators, large holdings were distributed among a sizable but ultimately confined group of merchants, manufacturers, lawyers, physicians, and their female heirs.[43] As late as 1859, three-quarters of all the shares in the eleven largest mills were held by about 750 shareholders, almost all of them New Englanders.[44] Much of the diffusion took place between family members. A few decades after the incorporation of these companies, the lists of stockholders showed large numbers of shares in the possession of clusters of close relatives. At Merrimack, forty-three of the one hundred names on the books in 1846 belonged to nine well-known families connected with the original incorporators, including ten Appletons, seven Lees, seven Lowells, and six Abbotts.[45] These families continued to dominate annual shareholder meetings via proxy votes, and they populated key positions at their companies with their close friends or kin.[46] Regardless of their professional occupations and the particular makeup of their portfolios, members of these expanding family clusters had a joint stake in the textile industry as a whole.

The same type of concentration permeated the region's major charitable and educational institutions that fed off of the gifts and bequests of wealthy Bostonians.[47] Privately endowed funds became the financial basis of what emerged as major bastions of elite power. Membership in the Boston Athenaeum, for example, overlapped with that of the directors of New England's largest cotton mills. The major stockholders were all members and prominent benefactors of the exclusive club, making it the best-funded private library in America.[48] Harvard College had been initially established as a state school that was controlled and funded by the Massachusetts legislature. The school's relationship with the commonwealth loosened in the first half of the nineteenth century as more and more of its resources came from private donors. The influx of contributions from wealthy Bostonians gave business interests decisive influence within the college's governing bodies. This money sponsored professorships, professional faculties in law and divinity, libraries, chapels, and research facilities, establishing the new orientation of the school as a private institution and a key site of elite socialization.[49] The sizable permanent endowments—$152,000 in the case of the

Athenaeum, $200,000 in the case of Massachusetts General Hospital, and more than $640,000 in the case of Harvard (as of 1840 and rapidly increasing)—were managed like private estates to yield steady but safe returns.[50] These institutions thrived as centers of learning, charity, and refinement, even as they became progressively more reliant on the industrial economy of the region.

All of this meant that by 1857, when the Board of Trade announced that cotton manufacturing had reached the point of saturation, Boston had developed an entire class of men and women whose livelihood and social standing depended heavily on income from this industry. The accumulation and preservation of wealth, which had been risky and erratic on the high seas, had been effectively systematized and regularized.[51] The steady stream of revenue supported elite Bostonians and the civic organizations that bound them together, gave them a shared set of values, and enabled them to socialize newcomers into the group. This financial and organizational foundation allowed the growth of a community of bourgeois wealth owners unmatched in its internal cohesiveness at that point anywhere in the United States.[52]

The unresolved problem in the basis of the entire apparatus was that the core of the "Waltham-Lowell system"—the use of the highly capitalized industrial corporations to yield steady returns—had yet to be replicated in other manufacturing activities.[53] Whether owing to the staggering growth of cotton manufacturing, which occupied the city's chief businessmen and their resources for several decades, or a more general difficulty in deploying technology to achieve similar economies of scale in the production of other goods, no obvious alternative presented itself. In the existing constellation, a new reality of diminishing profits spelled steady economic decline, with far-reaching implications for the city's elites, its institutions, and the region's population as a whole.

To make things worse, an industry-wide malaise that had been brewing for over a decade exploded in the 1850s into a much broader social and political crisis. By then, cotton manufacturing had clearly moved beyond the initial takeoff phase. Narrow profit margins prompted managers to intensify the production process and push workers to labor harder in deteriorating working conditions. The number of spindles per worker more than doubled. Weavers tended a multiplying number of looms. Wages stagnated. Workers experienced erratic bouts of unemployment.[54] "Labor," critics pointed out, "has been pressed from low, even lower, and down to the least per diem that will support life." With work stoppages designed to curtail overproduction becoming a pervasive practice, the workers "have been turned out without provision for the present or their future return," even as dividends and executives' salaries often resumed."[55] The makeup of the workforce also changed drastically. Native-born women, the temporary labor force of the early years, slowly vacated the mills. Mill owners replaced them with a more vulnerable population of immigrants—males, females, and children. In one typical mill, the percentage of foreign-born workers increased from 3.7 percent in 1836 to 38.6 percent in 1850 and 61.8 percent in 1860.[56] Housing deteriorated as well, as managers reversed their earlier commitment to maintain decent living conditions. The proportion of employees who resided in company-owned boarding houses dropped, and more of them lived in crowded tenements.[57] Mill sites shed their pastoral aura and became crowded and grimy cities, the home of a permanent class of wage earners. They were no longer plausible as an exceptional model of industrialization, free from the ills of European proletarianization.

These deteriorating conditions undermined the rhetoric of high-minded paternalism that had formerly rallied voters to support the Whig Party, the industrialists' political vehicle. For decades, Massachusetts Whigs had touted a vision of modernizing society, led by a virtuous elite and organized to pursue the harmonious interdependence of all groups in society. In the context of the crisis, critics such as Charles Sumner, Henry Wilson, and, most scathingly, Theodore Parker turned the tables on this vision. They laid bare a more dour reality of deep-seated social antagonism and class conflict. They warned against growing disparities between a privileged "class of men" and the "mighty multitude . . . poor, ill-born, ill-bred, ill-bodied, and ill-minded." They mocked the aristocratic pretensions of Harvard College, the elite's most cherished institution but also increasingly a symbol of class rule and reactionary politics.[58] Unflinching, they assailed the moneyed elite and their political minions for prioritizing financial gain over and above all and manipulating public institutions to their advantage.[59] They lambasted "the controlling classes" and "the power of consolidated riches" and warned against "the peril which accumulated property may bring upon the liberties of an industrial commonwealth."[60]

Looming large over this crisis was the controversy over slavery. It became the industrialists' biggest political liability, one that they were unable to suppress despite incessant efforts. As the masses in Massachusetts embraced the politics of antislavery, the powerful connections between the industrialists and their cotton suppliers in the South undermined the man-ufacturers' moral authority. They became known pejoratively as "Cotton Whigs" and the willing accomplices of the "Slave Power." The rift was aggravated when the Fugitive Slave Act, which sanctioned the return of escaped slaves to their masters, triggered a succession of violent confronta-tions in the streets of Boston. Exposing their allegiance to the South, the manufacturers stood firmly with their partners in the Cotton Kingdom and pressured officials in Massachusetts to uphold "law and order." The controversy further defined antislavery as a class issue as much as a sec-tional question.[61] It is with the conjoined concerns about slavery and elite power that Sumner famously condemned the "unholy union" between "the cotton-planters and flesh-mongers of Louisiana and Mississippi and the cotton-spinners and traffickers of New England—between the lords of the lash and the lords of the loom."[62] These types of attacks mobilized a sequence of oppositional political movements—the Free Soil, Know Nothing, and finally the Republican Party—that dealt the Whig Party a series of electoral defeats. The platforms and constituencies of these move-ments varied, but they shared an uncompromising opposition to slavery and a bitter hostility toward the textile magnates, who came to epitomize the evils of the social order.[63] In time, these movements removed compro-mises from the political agenda and led the way to civil war.

Beset by economic, social, political, and ideological challenges, the high bourgeoisie of Boston were indeed assailed on all sides during the 1850s. The industrial system that they had painstakingly put together was in shambles, unable to yield profits and expand any further. American in-dustrialization, long thought to be benign, in contrast to its European equivalents, proved unexceptional and devastating in its effects for a large, impoverished population of working families. With every passing election, their political organ disintegrated. Its celebration of cross-class harmony and good leadership rang hollow. It was no longer able to command the support of the region's voters. Finally, these elites' standing as stewards of the public good and as the most revered individuals in the community collapsed. As willing apologists and direct beneficiaries of the South's slave system, they were unable to reclaim the high moral ground.

Many of the early architects of New England industrialization either passed away or retired during those years of crisis, so the onus of setting political and economic strategy was thrust on a new generation. This younger generation, born to wealth and comfort, hardly inspired confidence among observers at the time. Dr. Oliver Wendell Holmes, a physician and a professor at Harvard Medical School, spoke as an insider when he observed the new generation's lack of heroism, the lack of "thorough manhood" and "high-caste gallantry." In what was widely read humorous fiction that nonetheless betrayed a sense of anxiety, he parodied these sons of a "decayed gentry," who were too busy "driving their chariots, eating their venison over silver chafing-dishes, drinking Madeira wine chilled in embossed coolers, wearing their hair in powder, and casing their legs in long boots with silken tassels." He noted that any such class of people, whose status was based on commercial profits, not aristocratic privilege, would be bound to decay over time. This destiny was in the natural order of things "unless some special means are taken to arrest the process of disintegration in the third generation . . . which is so rarely done, at least successfully."[64]

Members of the younger generation were indeed not known at the time for their capacity to take decisive action. In what was yet another, more existential dimension of the crisis, many of them spent the 1850s demoralized, melancholically in search of meaningful avenues for action. Nevertheless, when faced with these pessimistic predictions and the impending decline of their class, they more than embraced the challenge. They responded to the crisis in one of two ways. They could either fight tooth and nail to sustain the existing arrangement in the face of economic decline and political controversy or, alternatively, they could join the antislavery cause, resuscitate the elite's moral legitimacy, and work to define a new economic order. Both routes proved decisive for the future trajectory of the city and of American capitalism more generally.

The conservative response came from those most deeply entrenched in cotton manufacturing, who tried desperately to preserve the status quo and avert sectional conflict. They hoped that a new compromise with the South would not only facilitate the expansion of cotton agriculture within the framework of the nation-state but also include new tariff protections, which would allow cotton manufacturing to recover from its depressed state.[65] Amos A. Lawrence, the industry's heir apparent—son of Amos, nephew of Abbott, and son-in-law of William Appleton—led the charge. Lawrence entered the industry during its heyday. He served his apprenticeship at his father and uncle's firm before starting business on his own as a commission merchant.[66] In 1843, he formed "Mason & Lawrence," a selling agency that secured an exclusive contract to distribute the fabrics of the

Salmon Falls Cocheco Companies, in which the family held a large stake. As was the custom, he served terms as treasurer and president of these companies. He sat on their boards of directors, as well as those of several others, including a commercial bank, an insurance company, and later Hospital Life, from which he was also a large borrower. These connections positioned Lawrence at the strategic center of the cotton manufacturing industry.[67]

Lawrence's links in the South were established early in his career. His first destination as a young businessman was the city of Lowell, where he studied the operation of several of the mills. Soon after, however, he was sent to the South, with letters of introduction from his uncle, who was a well-known figure in the region. Lawrence's task was to drum up a clientele for New England textiles among wholesalers and, just as importantly, forge relationships with the local elite, with whom he collaborated in the decades to come.[68] This journey, and several similar expeditions that followed, gave Lawrence opportunities to observe the rapidly expanding southern frontier from up close. Moving through Louisville, Nashville, and Montgomery in late 1836, he learned about the speculative fever in land, noted the sites of Indian attacks, saw "cotton piled everywhere" in places which were not long settled, and observed "wagons full of Negro children & women" moving across state lines.[69] The realities of slavery and the slave trade drew little comment from him. He was primarily concerned with the general ruggedness and lack of "cultivation" in this frontier region. By contrast, he admired the cosmopolitan "Parisian-like levity" of New Orleans, noting the magnificence of the St. Charles Hotel, which captured "the grand scale on which operations are carried on in this growing city." He found his hosts—the cotton planters and merchants of the city—to be congenial gentlemen, who were full of "good will" and "high opinions" of New Englanders.[70] These were men he was comfortable doing business with.

Lawrence's position as a cotton manufacturer, and his intimate relations with the planter class, made him acutely sensitive to any threat to interregional cooperation. He was keenly aware that the industry rested on a cheap and reliable supply of raw cotton. Viewing himself as a clear-eyed realist not prone to the "fanaticism" of either side in the slavery controversy, he sought to anticipate and disarm any policy that threatened to bring the conflict to a head. His moderate position seemed feasible at first. He endorsed the compromise of 1850 and backed the New England Emigrant Aid Society, which sought to use peaceful and legal means to keep slavery out of Kansas. The violence that erupted around the Fugitive Slave Act in Boston and the violent struggle over Kansas, however, made a middle course less and less tenable. When a group of free blacks rescued a captured slave named Shadrach Minkins from the Court House in 1851, Lawrence was aghast and demanded forceful action against the abolitionists from the U.S. marshal in charge.[71] As proslavery settlers gained the upper hand in Kansas, Lawrence cautioned against resistance to government authorities and instead sought to appease southerners with a proposal to ban slavery in the state in return for new slave states elsewhere.[72] The commitment to the preservation of the Union above all else predisposed him to be sympathetic to southern attitudes and intolerant of antislavery forces. John Brown, he concluded, was "an unpatriotic and deluded man," Sumner "monomaniac on the subject of slavery," and John Andrew, the governor of Massachusetts, "anti-slavery in the extreme . . . [an] advocate [of] a 'higher law' than the Constitution."[73] Lawrence confided to his diary that he just could not understand "what good can result from liberating six millions of negroes, and making them politically equal to the whites. . . . What can result from that except the degradation of the Southern states and the expulsion of their best population."[74]

Lawrence spent the two years before the war in unrelenting attempts to regain control over public sentiment. He supported and ran for office as a candidate for the American Party in 1858 and the Constitutional Union Party in 1859, a cross-sectional initiative that promised to stand by the U.S. Constitution and allow "cooler heads" to prevail against fanaticism of any sort. Lawrence reversed his earlier inhibitions about westward expansion and embraced the party's compromise position on slavery, which allowed slavery to expand to the Pacific south of the Missouri line. He pressed the party to promote the protection of industry—"the great manufacturing and producing interests of the country"—thereby breathing new life into the older coalition that had sustained the cotton economy.[75] These efforts made little headway in the North, where they were ridiculed as irrelevant, but also in the South, where global demand for cotton raised its price and nurtured the popularity of free-trade ideas, making a protected American market less and less compelling.[76] Even after Abraham Lincoln's election, Lawrence organized the "Boston Union Saving Committee" with fellow ex-Whigs, violently cracking down on "treasonous" abolitionist meetings and "unconstitutional" personal liberty bills, and finally traveling to Washington to plead for a compromise with the South.[77] These efforts, and the personal connections that coordinated them, continued until the very last moment, when the first shots of the war were fired.

Young elite Bostonians with fewer direct entanglements in the cotton industry pursued a very different course of action. High society in Boston had long been hostile to antislavery and to any heady notions that might prove disruptive to the existing arrangements. As the 1850s drew to a close, however, many members of the younger generation reversed course. In what was a stunning change of heart, they sensed the collapse of the cross-regional détente and became more receptive to radical ideas that pointed the way toward violent confrontation. This turn was most clearly felt at Harvard, the cherished civic institution of the cotton magnates. In previous years, the college had been a hotbed of conservative sentiment. Students greeted antislavery speakers such as Charles Sumner, Horace Mann, and Ralph Waldo Emerson with heckles, hisses, and hoots.[78] The "men who reigned supreme in College circles," as they were commonly referred to, made their sentiments known when they alienated Sumner, an eminent and prolific legal scholar, and instead offered a university professorship to arch conservative Edward G. Loring, the U.S. commissioner of the Circuit Court, the man in charge of the rendition of fugitive slaves. As of 1852, the students overwhelmingly approved.[79]

But the atmosphere changed drastically as the decade progressed. When Loring became embroiled in public skirmishes over the fate of escaped slave Anthony Burns in the spring of 1854, Harvard grew increasingly polarized. It was now Loring's turn to be received for his lectures with "a storm of hisses, and other marks of disapprobation."[80] By 1860, even as the leadership of the school remained averse to abolitionism, the student body had been thoroughly radicalized.[81] However nurtured by cotton they had been in their earlier years, the relationship of younger Bostonians to the cotton industry was revealed to be ultimately malleable. It could not outlast a prolonged economic decline and political controversy. These younger Bostonians were unwilling to allow cotton manufacturing to dictate their own decline or render them captive to the designs of southern cotton planters. As sectional tensions mounted, they threw themselves wholeheartedly into the war effort and enlisted in the Union Army in disproportionately large numbers.[82]

The prominent leaders of the new political and economic orientation that emerged after the Civil War tended to come from elite families that had few direct connections to cotton manufacturing. Henry Lee Higginson, of "Cottonham" glory, who was destined to become the city's most prominent investment banker in the postwar industrial order, was born in 1834 to a long line of well-connected New England merchants and grew up among his extended kin on Beacon Hill. Although his father's brokerage firm occupied a central position on State Street and traded in cotton shares, among other assets, the Higginsons remained a degree or two removed from the core of the textile industry. Retaining their primary identity as merchants, they did not serve as treasurers or sit on the boards of cotton companies. This made them more receptive to antislavery ideas than many of their acquaintances. "Very many of the people whom we naturally saw, old and young, in Boston, were interested in cotton manufactures and had many friends in the South," Higginson explained many years later. They thus "did not share the strong feeling that we held about slavery."[83]

With no clear business prospects at the time, the young Higginson seemed, in the words of his biographer, "uncertain of himself, unconscious of his deepest motives, unaware as yet of his true aim."[84] He dropped out of Harvard because of an illness and entered a two-year apprenticeship with India Wharf merchants Samuel and Edward Austin, whose modest trade reached as far as Calcutta, Manila, Java, and Australia.[85] Higginson acquired valuable accounting skills and honed his commercial instincts, but ultimately he was not particularly enamored with this old line of business, which, with the closing of the age of sail and the rise of steam transportation, was then on its last legs. He instead spent the 1850s traveling in Europe, spending most of his time in Vienna. He attempted to study music but more often indulged his sociable personality at the opera and the theater, frequently with visitors from Boston. He corresponded with his father, who begged him to abandon his life of leisure, to choose a vocation and "pursue it with zeal and perseverance," but he could not settle on any respectable occupation.[86] For the time being, he continued to live on "legacies" inherited from his uncle and grandfather, although his expenses more than offset the profit from the property. He remained largely aloof from politics, even as sectional conflict escalated. Only the actual breakout of the war finally inspired him to action, and he was soon, at twenty-six, together with many of his former Harvard classmates, swept up in the enthusiasm of the moment. He served for four long years in the second Massachusetts regiment and later the first Massachusetts cavalry, seeing battle at Bull Run and Aldie, where he suffered several injuries.

Charles F. Adams Jr., one of Higginson's schoolmates and friends growing up, emerged as another prominent leader in Boston's new business orientation. Descended from an eminent political family strongly associated with opposition to slavery, the Adamses kept away from cotton-related investments. The family fortune was derived via the marriage of Charles F. Adams Sr. to Abigail Brown Brooks, the youngest of four daughters of Peter Chardon Brooks, a merchant and a pioneer in the field of marine insurance. Brooks's fortune could not fail to have been derived, in some measure, from the commerce in slaves and slave-produced commodities.[87] The portion that passed on to the Adams family, however, was held almost entirely in real estate in downtown Boston and in their hometown of Quincy, with only negligible amounts in cotton manufacturing stock.[88] The conservatism of the portfolio generated sufficient revenue to handsomely support the elder Adams, who carried on the family's tradition as a congressman and diplomat, and furnished an annuity of several thousand dollars for the younger generation, but not enough to keep the younger Adams from desperately searching for new sources of income that would place him in better financial standing.

Given his renowned ancestry, Adams was haunted from his youth by the specter of generational decline, which he felt driven to dispel, but, like Higginson, he identified no clear career path. Upon graduation, he trained as a lawyer, apprenticed in a reputable office in downtown Boston, and passed the bar. He became involved in managing the family's properties. He collected rents and quarreled with contractors. These commitments hardly matched his outsized ambition.[89] For the time being, Adams channeled his engagement with world events into journalism. He weighed in on the urgent question of the day in the pages of the *Atlantic Monthly*, arguing that the reign of King Cotton hung "upon a thread." The merchants of Liverpool and industrialists of Manchester, he argued, would soon take decisive action to undercut the dominance of the American South over the cultivation of raw cotton. They would not allow the southern agricultural tail to wag the industrial dog for much longer and find alternative sources of cotton elsewhere around the world, in "the jungles of India, the well-nigh impenetrable wilderness of Africa, the table-lands of South America, or the islands of the Pacific." He pointed out that "hundreds of miles of railroad in India" were already opening "vast regions" to cotton cultivation, threatening to deal "a death blow" to the southern monopoly over the precious commodity.[90] Adams presciently sensed that the rising price of raw cotton would lead not merely to sectional tensions within the United States, but more generally to a profound change in the organization of the world economy. Unlike Lawrence, whose embeddedness in the existing system rendered him opposed to any disturbances, Adams was more attuned to the dynamic nature of political economy. He counted himself among the optimists in Boston who believed that industrial capitalism would survive the end of slavery.

The Civil War began soon after the article was published, and Adams enthusiastically joined the military effort, becoming an active participant rather than an observer. The war offered not only an escape from the mundane pursuits of his postgraduate career, allowing him to break out from the confines of his social milieu, wear leather boots, and spend months in field conditions in the manly camaraderie of military life. It also gave Adams, and many of his friends, an opportunity to take part in a transformative historical event and begin to restore the Bostonian elite's eroded moral standing in the public sphere.[91]

Thomas Jefferson Coolidge more opportunistically straddled the line between conservatives like Lawrence on one end and forward-looking men like Higginson and Adams on the other. Like other members of his class, Coolidge was born in Beacon Hill and was descended from an old New England family. On his mother's side, he was also the great-grandson of the third president of the United States, Thomas Jefferson. In the 1830s, Coolidge's father relocated to Canton to become a partner in the trading house of Russell and Company, leaving his four sons to grow up in boarding schools in Geneva and then Dresden. When Thomas returned to Boston in 1847 to attend Harvard after ten years in Europe, he spoke English poorly and felt generally out of place among Boston society. He served an apprenticeship to a merchant and started to trade on his own account, only to almost lose everything during the panic of 1857. He and his partner were saved from ruin, he wrote, only because of their "connections with wealthy men who helped our credit." After his near failure, his father-in-law, William Appleton, pressed on him a position as a mill treasurer of the Boott Cotton Mills, a position that brought him a steady monthly salary. For a time, his political affinities lay firmly in the antiabolitionist camp with the other cotton industrialists. Coolidge was identified among the elite "broadcloth" mob, who violently disrupted an antislavery meeting in the runup to the war. Ultimately, Coolidge's commitment to cotton proved tenuous. He was not bred into the industry and entered it in an era of decline. This pragmatic relationship allowed him to extract himself from cotton manufacturing and reposition himself after the war as one of Boston's leading financial men.[92] Against expectations, a young cohort from within the established elite—Higginson, Adams, Coolidge, and many others—reversed Boston's declining fortunes in the aftermath of the Civil War. They found creative ways to deploy the savings of the community to yield high and steady returns.[93] New profitable investments in far-flung western sites did not simply present themselves to these men, nor were they necessary or seamless outgrowths of earlier patterns of development. As textile manufacturers, in fact, elite Bostonians had been deeply ambivalent about westward expansion, which tended to drain labor to the frontier, increase wages, and dilute New England's political power.[94] Groping for success (but hardly immune to failure), the Bostonians fundamentally rethought their place in a national economy. They traveled staggering distances and went to great strenuous lengths to forge these new vehicles of accumulation. Driven by the disintegration of the cotton economy and the prospects of their decline as a hegemonic class, they acted with a marked sense of urgency. They leveraged their entrepreneurial instinct and values, stretched their organizational skills to the utmost limit, drew on the latest scientific and technical expertise, and where necessary took aggressive and even violent measures in mobilizing labor. Their access to the large financial resources back east gave them the confidence and ability to lead and play a pivotal role in shaping the American political economy of the following decades.

With the war and two seasons of cotton planting behind him, Higginson found surprising business success far away from Beacon Hill on the remote Keweenaw Peninsula of Michigan, where he and his partners reinvented copper mining as a capital-intensive industry. By the mid-1860s, copper mining on the shores of Lake Superior had been under way for nearly two decades. The discovery of copper in the area in 1842 prompted the federal government to seize the land from the Chippewa Indians and open it to hundreds of prospectors, who descended on the swampy, densely wooded region, extracting any easily detachable copper from the surface and the ridges. This initial speculative boom fizzled and gave way to industrial-scale operations. Joint-stock companies looked for rich veins that yielded large copper masses. Cornish immigrants, versed in English mining methods, arduously removed these masses from the ground bit by bit with drills, sledges, and gunpowder. The copper rocks were rolled along in wheelbarrows to mine shafts, where they were hoisted up to the surface in iron buckets by men and horsepower. To isolate the copper, the miners experimented with water-powered stamps that hammered the rock, allowing them to pick out the metal by hand from the processed sand.[95]

These methods allowed the settlers on the peninsula to produce about fourteen million pounds of copper annually. The copper mining industry, however, was far from sound. Only six of ninety-four mining companies became profitable. Between 1845 and 1865, investors sank a total of $13.1 million into mining companies and reaped only $5.6 million in dividends.[96] The high cost of extracting and transporting the copper meant that only very rich deposits proved viable. Those "bonanza finds" captured the imagination and fueled speculation but were ultimately rare. By the end of the 1850s, the three largest, high-yield mines on the peninsula showed signs of depletion.[97] New copper deposits in the area existed in low-content bedrock. Whereas the conventional wisdom had been that to be mined profitably a vein had to contain at least 40 percent copper, these conglomerate belts contained only 2 to 4 percent. Copper in this form was finely and unevenly disseminated in lodes that stretched deep into the ground. There had been at that point no previous experience of remunerative mining under these conditions.[98]

The investors from Boston, with a new magnitude of financial resources itching for profitable fields of action, exerted tremendous efforts to overcome this impasse. They stepped in in the summer of 1866 to acquire the low-grade Calumet mine, an undeveloped mineral body in the Portage Lake district. Having soon after extricated himself from his involvements in Georgia, Higginson placed the resources of Lee, Higginson, and Company and its network of wealthy Bostonians solidly behind the enterprise. His two brothers-in-law, Quincy A. Shaw and Alexander Agassiz, not only gained control of the venture but moved to recast the entire operation. Agassiz was the man on the ground. Alexander was the son of Louis Agassiz, the brother of Ida Higginson, and a renowned naturalist in his own right. He had earned a degree in civil engineering and was therefore sent to Michigan in March 1867 to take charge of the properties. He stayed at the desolate site for twenty arduous months and worked to put the operation on an entirely new footing.[99]

The only way to extract copper from low-density rock at profitable rates was to run a continuous operation on a very large scale, thus lowering the cost per unit. This had never previously been accomplished in copper mining. Armed with unprecedented financial backing from Boston, Agassiz rammed through the various bottlenecks in the mining process. The supply of water for a stamping station was a big concern. Agassiz deemed the supply from the nearby stream to be insufficient and led the construction of a five-mile railroad (capitalized at several million dollars, controlled by the Higginsons, and headed by Agassiz) through dense forest, which connected the mines to a stamping station by the lake. Another subsidiary company dredged a two-mile channel, making the mine docks, warehouses, and smelting works at Portage Lake accessible to large steamers from Lake Superior.[100] Since mines produce rocks of varying densities and hardnesses, Agassiz and his staff experimented for several months before the stamping mill was able to produce uniform raff for the automatic washers that separated the copper from the small pebbles. It was not until September that Agassiz announced that the stamps operated uninterruptedly, "hammering away day and night and not stop[ping] again." The two heavy stamp heads hammered the rock ninety times per minute and worked through 800 tons of rock each day.[101]

With a much enhanced capacity to process rock in the facilities above ground, the new management transformed work within the mines themselves. Agassiz insisted that the mine would be redesigned to allow a greater volume of operations. Teams of miners underground began to use high explosives and air drills, tramming rock from drifts to main shafts, where it was dumped into heavy, high-capacity skips, each carrying several tons. An engine with 1,000 horsepower capacity (at that point, most likely the largest dynamo in the United States, if not the world) hoisted the skips to the surface. The skips then moved on elevated tracks to a rock house several hundred feet away, where the hard extract was crushed to pieces with a six-ton steam hammer and corrugated iron-jaw rock breakers. Next, at the stamp mill, the copper was jigged free from the sand and gravel and was finally moved into smelting works that purified it and cast it into ingots, bars, bolts, and cakes.[102]

In the damp and sulfurous bowels of the mine, almost a mile below ground, a thousand of the company's employees worked ten-hour shifts "with great regularity" year-round. Five hundred more manned surface operations. The community around the mines grew to about five thousand people by 1875, the majority of whom were foreign born: Cornish, Irish, Italian, Austrian, and Finish. Higginson and his partners pursued

1.2. Miners being lowered into the Boston-owned Calumet and Hecla Mine Shaft No. 2, Calumet, Michigan, 1906.

Credit: Library of Congress Prints and Photographs Division, Washington, DC. Detroit Publishing Company Photograph Collection. LC-DIG-det-4a13086.

paternalist policies toward the workers, contributing to an employees' aid fund, building a hospital and a school, and supporting the churches of the various denominations. They did not, however, allow the workers to challenge their control over the community or engage in collective action.[103] The first major strike occurred in 1872, primarily around wage reductions and the demand for a shorter workday. The local sheriff and eighteen deputies confronted six hundred workers armed with clubs, rocks, and other makeshift weapons and were rebuffed. Management then called in four companies of the United States First Infantry from Detroit. The troops jailed the leaders of the strike and allowed ownership to reestablish control of the property.[104] Agassiz instructed the superintendent to hold firm against workers' wage demands: "We cannot be dictated to by anyone. . . . Wages will be raised whenever we see fit and at no other time." The company sustained a vigilant stance against any presence of the "Knights of Labor" or other attempts at unionization. He attributed labor unrest to "the lack of force exhibited in the handling of discontented employees."[105]

Overall, the new operation as conceived and carried out by the Bostonians proved an immense business triumph. Working the deepest mine shafts in the world and some of the lowest grade ores in the United States, it produced large amounts of copper, with output increasing from 16 million pounds of copper in 1871 to over 50 million pounds in 1885, which represented almost 90 percent of all new copper extracted in the United States during those years.[106] By then, the renamed Calumet & Hecla Mining Company was no longer a single profitable mine but a vast operation, with over a dozen large-scale and deep shafts, in control of the richest copper reserves in the United States. Shipped out continuously on railroads that extended via the Boston-owned Marquette, Houghton, and Ontonagon Railroad, the so-called copper road, it repositioned the United States, previously a net importer of copper from suppliers in the United Kingdom and Chile, as the world's largest copper producer, most of which was consumed by a growing domestic market. Between 1869 and 1884, the company paid out over $25 million in dividends. This was about 80 percent of all dividends paid by the American copper industry during this time span.[107] Its valuation rose from $4.9 million in 1870 to $10.6 million in 1874 and $23 million in 1880. By the end of the century it hovered around $57 million and continued to grow very fast.[108] The Higginsons, who had invested in the mines "to the extent of their ability," were among the main beneficiaries of the venture. "Our office was a sort of headquarters for the property, and our friends bought a great many shares," Higginson later explained. The dividends secured Higginson's financial future and established Lee, Higginson, and Company as one of two leading investment banks in Boston and in the nation at large.

Charles F. Adams Jr. was partially involved in the windfall at Calumet and Hecla and worked tirelessly in the 1870s to replicate this financial accomplishment in another industry. Where else could the investment of large financial resources recast an industry and yield steady profits? His efforts bore fruit in the budding city of Kansas City and its adjoining region, which were utterly transformed by the influx of capital from Boston. Kansas City was not the most populous city among several vying for supremacy in the region. Its small size, however, became an advantage as it allowed members of the local Board of Trade to avoid internal schisms and lobby for the support of eastern financial interests. The Bostonian investors, convinced that the board indeed had a firm grip on affairs in their city, acquired the Hannibal and St. Joseph Railroad in 1869. They then flexed their political connections in Washington, DC, to make Kansas City the site of the first railroad bridge across the Missouri River. The bridge gave their new hub in the area a direct connection to Chicago and a distinct advantage over its competitors.[109] Still, it was not at all clear at that point that development in this frontier region would become sustainable from a financial standpoint.

Adams began to visit the area frequently in the early 1870s, inspecting properties, studying conditions, and forging connections with prominent businessmen. Kansas City was one destination among many, including St. Joseph, Council Bluffs, Ft. Scott, and Baxter Springs, all of which were in the running for regional preeminence.[110] In 1876, Adams engineered the reorganization of the Kansas City Stock Yards Company, of which he became president. Adams acquired the underfunded stockyards from local interests and financed, to use industry terms, the "combination of conveniences" that made Kansas City the choice site for the "reception, care, sale, and delivery" of livestock from the Southwest. Access to Boston's financial resources allowed the yards to grow exponentially. The company purchased forty-two additional acres of easily accessible land, built pens and loading docks, installed scales and sheds, and constructed a three-story exchange building, complete with company offices, two banks, rental space for several dozen commission merchants, a restaurant, a billiard hall, and

1.3. Kansas City Stock Yards, Kansas City, 1887, a new magnitude of industrial enterprise made possible by large-scale financing from Boston.

a barber shop.[111] The dispersed and fluctuating cattle trade, conducted in an impromptu fashion by different railroad carriers in a scattering of midsized cities, became a gushing flow through a state-of-the-art facility. This commerce catapulted Kansas City's growth, making it a gigantic hub for the livestock trade, second only to Chicago (in whose Union Stockyards Bostonians were also heavily invested).

To oversee day-to-day operations, Adams recruited none other than Henry Lee Higginson's former partner Charles Morse, who came from a modest upbringing but had been closely associated with the Bostonians since their days at "Cottonham." Adams had initially called on Morse to oversee the Bostonians' mining properties in Michigan. "We [Higginson, Shaw, Agassiz, and Adams] want someone up there, who is more akin to us than those head workmen & mining captains promoted, however good and able they may be," Adams wrote to Morse in 1872, emphasizing (in what was a most effective form of flattery) Morse's dissociation from the ranks of labor, not his superior managerial skills. Morse could not stomach the conditions in the mining region and instead chose to pursue a career in railroading. He spent several years in the employ of the Burlington and Missouri River Railroad in Iowa and Nebraska, and the Atchison, Topeka, and Santa Fe Railroad, both of which were Boston owned and controlled.[112] He distinguished himself in this last role by faithfully upholding a strict line against unions. When members of the Brotherhood of Locomotive Engineers—"strikers and hoodlums," as he referred to them—occupied the railroad yards in 1878, Morse called up two companies of the state militia to restore "normal conditions," then summarily discharged the two-thirds of his workforce who were union members.[113]

The Bostonians rewarded Morse's loyalty with a position as general manager in the Kansas City cattle yards. Working diligently to cement Kansas City's supremacy, Morse became involved in all aspects of the business. He launched and became president of the Livestock Exchange, which standardized and regulated trade. He headed the Stock Yards Bank, which financed the commerce in livestock. He then launched the Kansas City Fat Stock Show Association, which disseminated breeding and fattening techniques and established the city as a center of livestock know-how.[114] With Adams and Morse at the helm, the yards became a big success. Cattle, hogs, and sheep moved through the facilities in ever-increasing numbers, reaching the millions within a few years.[115] The annual value of stock handled at the yards increased rapidly from about $6.5 million in 1875 to $40 million by 1885. By 1890, it had surpassed $75 million.[116] Beyond profitable revenues from renting yardage, selling feed, and charging fees from commission merchants, the yards generated a steady stream of traffic for railroads. By 1880, the Boston-owned Atchison, Topeka, and Santa Fe Railroad became the undisputed leading carrier of cattle, hogs, and sheep into the city. In 1890, it alone brought to Kansas City over 660,000 head of cattle and 460,000 hogs from all corners of the Southwest and West. The trade "made the road a paying concern," an industry chronicler accurately concluded. It fueled the railroad's rapid expansion into one of the great railroads in the United States.[117]

The backing of eastern bankers allowed Kansas City's credit networks to reach deep into Kansas, Iowa, Nebraska, Colorado, Texas, and even California, financing the raising of a steady stream of animals.[118] Heavy traffic in livestock fueled agricultural development in Kansas and the adjoining states, as range-bred cattle were fattened on locally grown corn closer to the point of slaughter. After 1875, corn overtook wheat as the leading crop in Kansas, increasing from 16 million bushels in 1870 to 110 million bushels in 1880, with corn production occupying 40 percent of the state's agricultural lands.[119] The number of farms in Kansas more than tripled, from 6,000 to 21,500, the expansion being financed through heavy mortgage borrowing from the East.[120] Next came meatpacking. Fostered by the large supply of livestock that passed through the city, as well as by financial incentives—land, facilities, rail connections, and cash—from the stock exchange, the industry boomed in the 1880s. The numbers were again staggering and climbed quickly—581,000 cattle, 199,000 sheep, and 2,348,000 hogs by 1890.[121] Unlike Chicago, which developed a diverse urban economy, Kansas City remained almost entirely dedicated to the livestock trade and the meatpacking industry. Meatpacking employed more than 4,600 employees, more than 70 percent of the city's industrial workforce, in six large facilities, which were capitalized at $9 million. The value of the product, almost $40 million by 1890 and $73 million by century's end, accounted for 90 percent of the city's industrial output.[122] The growth of the city's leading industry created a rapid increase in population, from less than 10,000 at the end of the war to more than 160,000 by the end of the century, opening up a range of opportunities in urban development that the Bostonians capitalized on. As Adams's main representative in Missouri, Morse coordinated the acquisition and development of streetcar properties that became the Metropolitan Street Railway Company (of which he likewise became president). He disclosed that he also oversaw "numerous . . . land transactions."[123] Many years later, after retiring to Boston in his old age, he explained that "these Boston people seemed to depend on my helping them out," which he was indeed in an excellent position to do.[124]

New ventures such as the Hecla and Calumet Mining Company and the Kansas City Stockyard Company demonstrated to eastern investors that western development could be viable and remunerative. Organized around heavily capitalized facilities that extracted and processed commodities from the natural bounty of the West, they radiated out from their manufacturing core to a broad range of other sectors, generating freight traffic for railroads, building up demand for livestock and agricultural output, and boosting the value of urban real estate in new urban centers. These industries heralded a pivot of Bostonian capital away from cotton manufacturing and toward finance.

Thomas Jefferson Coolidge's contribution to this reorientation was two-fold. Like other Bostonians, Coolidge continued his association with cotton manufacturing in the coming years, serving as treasurer and director of cotton mill corporations. His involvement, however, facilitated the beginning of the withdrawal of funds from the industry. As the incoming treasurer of the Boott Cotton Mills after 1857, for example, Coolidge introduced a particularly vigilant approach to spending on equipment and repairs. Machinery at the Boott, in operation for more than twenty years at the time, was deficient and outmoded. Many of the looms were unable to produce cloth of marketable width. Waterwheels did not produce enough power to carry out operations at full capacity at a sufficient rate of speed. Quite clearly, Coolidge reported upon entering the position, "the Mills are old, have been run very hard . . . the goods produced cost high, the waste is too large, the yarn uneven, the cloth not what it should be." He concluded that only with "very great expense" could these difficulties be adequately addressed.[125] Coolidge's policy as treasurer, however, in consultation with the directors of the company, was set against any heavy spending on repairs or improvements. Earnings poured not into further investment in infrastructure, which was kept to a minimum, but into the "Quick Capital" account from which owners drew their dividends.[126] Coolidge's approach as treasurer was to squeeze labor to the utmost, run the machinery at a bare minimum, and pay steady dividends to the owners, who were able to invest their profits elsewhere. Hardly unique to the Boott, this industrial program was most emblematically exposed when the five-story Pemberton Mills at Lawrence collapsed in January 1860, trapping hundreds of men, women, and children in the rubble, killing 88 and seriously injuring 116 others. The disaster, the worst in Massachusetts history, was linked to faulty iron columns that management knew about but, in an attempt to be financially prudent, failed to replace.

The long-term trajectory of Coolidge's own investment portfolio reflected the new priorities. It recorded the dramatic movement of Bostonian financial resources into new fields. In 1868, Coolidge's holdings, passed down in part from his father-in-law, William Appleton, were heavily concentrated

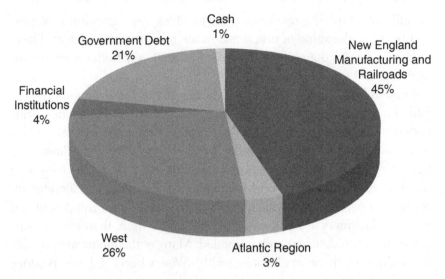

1.4. From New England textiles to national industrialization: The investment portfolio of Thomas Jefferson Coolidge in January 1868. Compiled from the Coolidge Family Business Records, Baker Library Historical Collection, Harvard University.

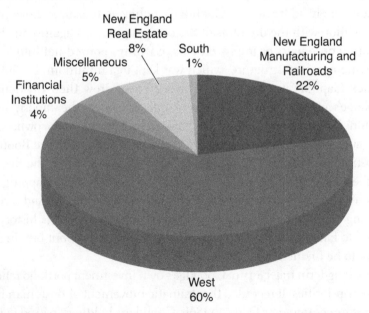

1.5. From New England textiles to national industrialization: The investment portfolio of Thomas Jefferson Coolidge in January 1883. Compiled from the Coolidge Family Business Records, Baker Library Historical Collection, Harvard University.

in cotton manufacturing and New England railroads. Almost half of his portfolio, over $160,000, was invested in these nearby properties. A much smaller but still sizable amount, at 26 percent, or over $84,000, was invested in western ventures, primarily the Kansas City–based Hannibal and St. Joseph Railroad. The rest of Coolidge's portfolio was held in government securities, valued at almost $84,000, primarily the U.S. bonds that helped finance the war effort (see figure 1.4). Over the next fifteen years, this allocation drastically shifted in ways that were typical for the investment community in Boston as a whole. Cotton manufacturing and New England railroads remained important but were dwarfed by new holdings out west. By 1883, despite Coolidge's continued association with the textile industry, his New England investments had shrunk in relative terms to about 20 percent of his portfolio. Investments elsewhere on the continent expanded to occupy more than 60 percent of his holdings, adding up to almost $1.9 million at that point. This part of the portfolio included extensive holdings in Kansas City and Chicago stockyards, four mining companies (including the Calumet and Hecla), and sixteen western railroads, including the Atchison, Topeka, and Santa Fe, of which Coolidge later served as president for a year (see figure 1.5). Coolidge's western holdings continued to proliferate and dominated the portfolio, even as cotton manufacturing stocks steadily declined and were then entirely phased out.[127]

The profound changes in investment strategy that Coolidge documented in his business ledger in his office on State Street in Boston reverberated throughout the continent. They did not merely chart changes in his individual portfolio or even a new regime of accumulation. These notations signaled an entirely new direction for American capitalism as a whole, away from its origins in the cotton economy and toward continental industrialization. Over time, these new directions repositioned affluent Bostonians vis-à-vis the national economy that their financial resources helped develop. This shift also redefined their relationship to their own city, which was fast becoming one of the major financial centers in North America. But as Coolidge added up his expanding list of assets and the large revenue they generated for him, he recorded more than the accumulation of dollars and cents. The changing portfolio betrayed a much grander sense of triumph. It affirmed the continued vitality of yet another generation of elite Bostonians who confronted the breakdown in their flagship industry, weathered a political storm, and lived to see another day. Unlike other elites who were bound to a particular economy and place, and as a result withered, the Bostonians were able to sustain their dominance and cohesion over time. They leveraged the advantages their forbears accrued in the past to move forward and shape the future, recovering their sense of confidence and gaining a whole new magnitude of wealth and power.

CHAPTER TWO

Cultivating the Laissez-Faire Metropolis

The success of the new industries out west in the aftermath of the Civil War infused upper-class Boston with an exhilarating sense of endless possibilities. The dour prospects of the 1850s had been averted, and the city was set on an exciting new trajectory. Whereas elite investments previously focused on the securities of New England mills and railroads, they now increasingly turned to large-scale undertakings in remote places throughout the continent. The shift in orientation and volume of activity was striking. As one Bostonian recalled: "One had not to look back far to see one or two brokers running about State Street and trying to get someone to buy or to sell a few shares of a cotton mill or one of the little New England railroads, and thus doing all the brokerage business that was offered." After the war, this situation quickly changed. Within a few years, a "lavish outpouring of bonds and stock" combined to make a stock exchange that would have dazed the old-time broker.[1] The business district on State Street became the home of a proliferating number of financial firms, about two hundred in number by 1868, including eighteen private banks, seventy-seven brokerage firms, and forty-three national banks.[2] On the Boston Stock Exchange and the investment portfolios of affluent Bostonians, regional securities such as the Merrimack Manufacturing Company, the Connecticut Railroad, and the Vermont Central Railroad started to give way to the distant Atchison, Topeka, and Santa Fe Railroad, the St. Louis and San Francisco Railroad, the Chicago, Burlington, and Quincy Railroad, and the Calumet and Hecla Copper Mining Company.[3] Boston's cotton-based economy of the antebellum years was morphing into a powerhouse of finance.

As it shed its former regional emphasis, State Street became one of the preeminent centers of banking and finance in North America. As of 1880, for example, the nine New England railroads that radiated from Boston, built mostly before the war, were capitalized at a total of $120 million and had roughly 1,700 miles of track. By then, among many other properties, Bostonians owned and managed three large-scale railroad systems out West that were capitalized at over $340 million. Together these railroads had more than 10,000 miles of track and were quickly growing.[4] The ventures launched by the upper echelons of the business community were gaining an entirely new scale and geographical outlook. For members of this elite cohort, the city's importance as a place of manufacturing and movement of physical goods had clearly diminished. It instead became a strategic site where they amassed and mobilized financial resources, gathered and shared information, forged their identity and cohesion as a class, and made strategic business decisions with repercussions in places far and wide.

Moneyed Bostonians were not alone in this movement toward investment in the West. The reorientation encompassed other urban elites in the United States who similarly moved their accumulated savings away from the cotton economy of the antebellum decades and toward new geographies and industrial sectors. The descendants of New York's mercantile families, long beholden to the cotton trade, turned to the financing of industrial development. After the Civil War and the end of slavery, as historian James Livingston has argued, these former "handmaidens of international commerce" remade themselves into the close allies of "domestic industries."[5] These scions of wealth did not take a backseat to newcomers but instead involved themselves directly in the running of the national industrial economy. By one assessment, 60 percent of the leadership of New York's national corporations, investment banks, and railroads in 1890 were descended from the old mercantile elite.[6] Philadelphia's mercantile elite, which had depended heavily on southern trade and harbored significant pro-confederate sentiment, emerged in those years as another financial center that funded large-scale industry, with prominent figures such as Jay Cooke, E. W. Clark, and A. J. Drexel at the helm. The Stock Exchange loosened Philadelphia's commercial connections to the South and directed savings into the extraction and processing of oil, coal, and steel in western Pennsylvania and the Midwest.[7] Altogether the mobilization of capital from older northeastern cities drove the creation of a continental industrial economy.[8]

The transformation of cities like New York, Philadelphia, and Boston into major banking centers in the aftermath of the Civil War, however, did not take place in the private realm of business, on the stock exchange and in ventures halfway across the continent. It proceeded, more soberly and much closer to home, within urban government, where the economic futures of these cities became entangled in hotly contested political questions. For Boston's leading men of business, who looked for profitable ways to deploy their large pools of capital, the turn away from the manufacturing economy of the region seemed straightforward enough. With nearby textile industries in crisis, they sought new avenues for lucrative investment and found them elsewhere. They saw the growth of Boston as a financial hub as the key to bright economic prospects. For most other Bostonians, this shift represented a highly controversial proposition. They were skeptical that Boston's ever-growing banking resources, invested elsewhere, would trickle down and benefit broad segments of the population. Urban leaders in the democratically elected city government, where the business elite had no presence and exercised little direct influence, came primarily from the upper strata of the working class or the lower middle class: neighborhood businessmen, skilled workers, mechanics, and tradesmen. Vindicated by the Civil War and the republican language of producerism, these middling men forged a powerful political challenge to the elite's policy designs. They were keen not on turning away from manufacturing but rather on democratizing their "industrial commonwealth." These populist urbanites aspired to make Boston the site of a vibrant and diverse manufacturing economy whose rewards, including access to home ownership, would be widely distributed. Soon enough, the two programs collided in a series of political contests that pitted against one another not merely competing legislative agendas but rival visions of the modern city and its position within the political economy of the United States.

None other than Chares Francis Adams Jr. jump-started the debate in 1868 in a two-part article entitled "Boston" that appeared in the highbrow *North American Review*. For Adams, the rise of manufacturing over the previous several decades had signaled a wrong turn in the history of the region. With the cotton economy clearly in decline, he minced no words in disparaging the achievements of the leading businessmen of the preceding generation, who turned the city, historically a prominent Atlantic port of global commerce, into the hub of an industrial region. Boston had once been a "city of great foreign trade and enterprise," he rhapsodized, a routine destination for ships from "China, from Calcutta, from the African coast and the Mediterranean, from Russia, South America, and the Pacific coast." "Stately ships, rich in the association of distant lands," he continued, populated Boston Harbor, "bringing teas and spices from the East and wines and silks from Europe." Whereas most observers at the time would have considered industrialization a remarkable breakthrough, Adams argued that the hegemony of manufacturing had in fact made Boston more "provincial." "The merchant and the manufacturer . . . no longer [able] to move forward with equal steps," he argued, the city had become "in comparison with great, commercial, cosmopolitan New York, what Manchester was to London."[9]

The main obstacle to the restoration of Boston to its former eminence was not business initiative or access to financial resources, of which there was no shortage, but effective political institutions. To recapture its "cosmopolitan" glory among American cities, Adams argued, the city had to seize the business of the West and better nurture "fresh channels through which the wealth of the newly-developed West could be poured into her lap." Boston's popularly controlled government, however, seemed to him ill equipped to facilitate the necessary economic reorientation. The "ebbs and floods of a democratic form of government" undermined the ability of the local state to devise broad-minded policy and make the city a favorable place for business. Adams associated good policy not with government inaction or retreat—far from it—but with government deference to what he perceived to be the scientific principles and forces that controlled economic change. Boston had forgotten, he charged, "that she lives in a material age, an age of *laissez faire* and political economy." Its disregard for "certain great laws and forces of modern development" had "jeopard[iz]ed the material growth, independence, and influence of the community." It was only through "the ascertainment of these laws and in the cultivation of these forces" that governments could reverse course and bring about real recovery. Adams identified the recasting of political institutions toward a single-minded focus on the "ascertainment" and "cultivation" of those transcendent powers—and doing so in the midst of democratic politics where all was "flounder and spasm"—as the era's most pressing political economic challenge.[10]

The relationship between democratic government and "cosmopolitan" economic development was not just a problem of political theory, contemplated by Adams and his polite readers, but an urgent question that played out in very concrete battles over policy. The most consequential of these policy debates were the confrontation over the redrawing of the political boundaries within the metropolis and its close corollary, the confrontation over government finance. Both of these supposedly local contests were most fundamentally struggles over the relationship between the city and much broader economic transformations throughout North America. As Bostonians debated these policy issues, they struggled between the competing imperatives of their city as a junction in a wide-ranging web of investment and capital flows on the one hand and its internal dynamics as an industrial metropolis in its own right on the other. Each perspective prescribed radically different priorities for city government. Should the municipality expand its territory and subsidize the development of new industrial and residential districts for working families on the urban periphery, at the cost of heavy fiscal obligations, or should it retain its narrow boundaries, allowing the edges of the metropolis to be governed by independent rural towns, ideal for the homes of the city's most powerful business elites? Should revenues be raised from taxes on financial forms of property, which may consequently lead its owners to flee to other cities, or should finance capital be left unencumbered, protecting investors and shifting the tax load to less geographically agile homeowners and tenants? The full immersion of Boston within the political economy of the United States was not in doubt, of course. At stake, rather, was the particular institutional framework that would define the relationship between the city and the emerging national market, with far-reaching political, economic, and social consequences.

The links between the political structure of American cities and the formation of the national market have gone relatively unnoticed in the scholarship about metropolitan development in the United States. Cities typically appear in this literature as discrete containers of social and political processes. They are analyzed as microcosms or as stand-ins for the nation as a whole, not as interconnected sites in a larger political economy. This scholarly approach has produced wonderfully textured, fine-grained local research but generally pushed broader, supra-local geographical trajectories such as the cross-regional flows of capital, goods, and people into an unexamined historical backdrop.[11] As a result, some of the most contentious debates that raged in American cities in the late nineteenth century have been overshadowed or explained narrowly in terms of political culture.[12] To a surprising extent, however, the connections between urban policy and national economic change were clear to contemporary Bostonians. They passionately debated the economic implications of urban policy and understood full well that urban dynamics were shaped by, and in turn shaped, industrial development on the national and continental scales.

The debate over the decentralization of political jurisdiction within the metropolis was a poignant case in point, bringing the politics of urbanization to the fore and demonstrating the dynamically entwined character of urban and national processes. Ironically, even as elite Bostonians obliterated economic boundaries, forging capital networks that reached deeply into the interior of the continent, they simultaneously mobilized to cement borders and divides within their own city. They opposed popular attempts to unify the metropolis under a central government authority, insisting instead that the metropolitan area of Boston be governed by a large number of independent, fiscally disempowered towns. The fragmentation of the metropolitan area sheltered the rich from high city taxes and preserved the rural lands around the city for their picturesque homes and estates. They thus had a narrow self-interested reason to oppose greater metropolitan integration. Even more significantly, however, a decentralized political structure was a safeguard against what the financial elite perceived to be misguided municipal activism that sought to reshape the city's social and economic geography. Political disunity greatly attenuated the capacity of the urban state to meddle in economic issues, allowing development to be governed instead, as proponents of decentralization explained, by the "natural law of demand and supply."[13] In the decades after the war, the workings of this economic "law" mostly meant the unfettered movement of investment to other regions of the continent in search of high returns and the transformation of Boston into a preeminent center of banking and finance.

The fragmentation of the metropolitan area faced a powerful and remarkably successful grassroots challenge. Precisely as business elites began to look for new channels of investment far beyond New England, a broad coalition of middling Bostonians mobilized to energize metropolitan growth by merging their city with the adjoining rural municipalities, massively expanding the territory under Boston's jurisdiction. They encouraged city government to raise taxes on large landholdings and extend urban infrastructure—water, sewers, roads, schools, firehouses, police stations, branch libraries, and public parks—beyond the existing boundaries of the municipality. Anticipating the ideas of radical political economist Henry George about the relationship between taxes and the distribution of land, the plan aimed to stimulate the rapid subdivision of large estates in outer districts of the city and open new land for residential and industrial development.[14] The goal was to relieve population density in the inner city, provide "citizens of every occupation" with adequate housing, and spread the commercial and industrial center of the city beyond the inner city to more peripheral districts.[15]

The vision behind what became known as the "annexation movement" turned the fiscal logic of political fragmentation on its head. If fragmentation weakened the political institutions of the city, kept taxes low, and held public resources from redistribution across urban space, the annexation of adjoining municipalities into Boston accomplished the reverse. It greatly enhanced the ability of city government to shape economic conditions in the region and facilitate the flow of resources from the urban center to an emerging metropolitan periphery. Advocates were unabashed about the increase in municipal taxes and public spending they expected to go along with this plan. "With an extension of territory, and an increase of population," one of the early advocates of this agenda explained, "there will also come a spirit of liberality and a greater degree of public spirit than can exist within narrower confines." A centralized municipality would be more capacious than a multiplicity of independent towns and have the ability to operate "promptly and simultaneously throughout large districts, wherever the occasion calls for action." As supporters of the plan well understood, the distribution of resources across space was inextricably linked to distribution between social classes. They deliberately aspired to affect "an equal distribution of benefits to every part and portion of the whole community."[16]

This government-driven approach to metropolitan development first appeared in the 1850s and made powerful headway in the aftermath of the Civil War, winning broad popular support because of its strong association with the politics of "free labor."[17] In the context of rapid population growth and a housing shortage, this vision of robust urban development, driven by public investment in infrastructure and funded through an increase in property taxes, gained a near consensus within city government. To the great consternation of Boston's top business leaders, the city's board of aldermen issued an open call for surrounding cities and towns to pursue "mutually desirable" unions with Boston.[18] Two municipalities that adjoined Boston to the south—the city of Roxbury and town of Dorchester— were successfully absorbed into the metropolis in 1868 and 1870, respectively, more than tripling the jurisdiction of the city from 3,270 acres to almost 10,000 acres. A city commission appointed to study the issue in 1873 contemplated the incorporation of up to fifteen additional towns, which would have again doubled the area of Boston to about 20,000 acres as an initial phase, with even more land to be added at a later point.[19] Undeterred by the high fiscal costs, elected representatives envisioned a wide array of improvements that would foster urban settlement in the annexed lands, including "reclaiming and tilling marsh lands; constructing systems of sewerage; laying out main thoroughfares; locating engine-houses, police-stations, and school-houses," and, most importantly, providing "a certain and unlimited supply of water."[20] In what greatly alarmed wealthy taxpayers, they promised their constituencies in the city that the new wards would be gradually brought up to "the same footing with the other parts of the city."[21]

Government spending on urban infrastructure in those years indeed flowed disproportionately to the annexed districts of Roxbury and Dorchester, transforming their rural territories into city neighborhoods. Overall, between 1867 and 1874, the two annexed wards were the beneficiaries of over 60 percent of new water lines (see figure 2.1) and more than 50 percent of its new sewer lines (see figure 2.2), even though the two districts combined for only about 20 percent of the city's population (in 1870). These two districts were also the sites of massive road construction as, in the words of the mayor, "thoroughfares for travel and transportation have been made more ample, and extended; old avenues have been improved, and all made free from tolls; new avenues have been built, and business conveniences established," altogether facilitating easy communication between the inner city and the outside neighborhoods. To the elite's fascination with continental economic interconnectedness, this populist campaign responded with an ever tighter and equalizing integration of the different parts within the metropolis.

The extension of urban improvements to areas of low population density during those years, in anticipation of development, promoted a more unified metropolitan space. The process delineated the territory of urban Boston as distinct from those of the surrounding rural towns, for whom city conveniences remained prohibitively expensive. After being confined to the inner city when public water was first introduced in the 1840s, running water now became standard throughout Boston, bringing the system to a whole new scale.[22] Sewers, paved streets, and gas streetlights also represented distinctly urban infrastructure. By 1873, Boston boasted 55 miles of paved streets and 122 miles of sewer lines. The much more territorially

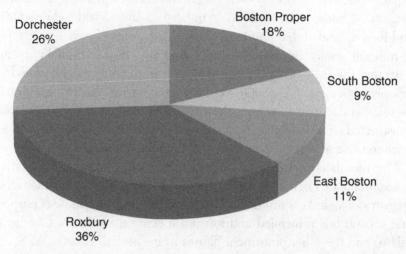

2.1. The distribution of miles of water pipes constructed between 1867 and 1874 among city neighborhoods. Compiled from the annual reports of the Cochituate Water Board, 1867–1874. Boston City Documents.

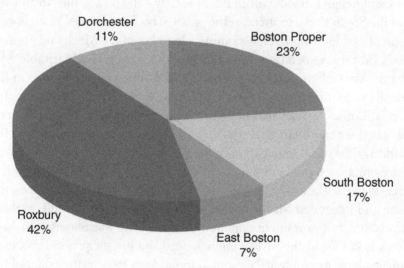

2.2. The distribution of miles of sewer lines constructed between 1867 and 1874 among city neighborhoods. Compiled from the annual reports of the Superintendent of Sewers, 1867–1874. Boston City Documents.

expansive towns around Boston (West Roxbury, Somerville, Brookline, Brighton, Charlestown, Medford, Winthrop, Everett, Malden, Watertown, and Revere) had at that point a total of only 7 miles of paved streets and 17 miles of sewers. Beyond water and other amenities, the public institutions that the Boston city government built in the new neighborhoods—schools, police and fire stations, and branch libraries—further established these areas not as retreats from the city, but as vital parts of it. They were constructed on a large scale, with the assumption that they would soon accommodate a growing concentration of the population.[23]

The members of the board of aldermen who promoted annexation rested their case not merely on practical administrative considerations, but on firm ideological commitments. They acted with a strong sense of purpose that was no less principled and forward looking than that of Charles F. Adams and the other prominent figures in his milieu. Charles W. Slack, the chairman of the board and a member of the special commission on the annexation of Roxbury, had a long-standing association with the radical labor interests in the city.[24] The son of one of the leaders of the early labor movement in Massachusetts, Slack was born in 1825 and raised in different neighborhoods within the inner city—the center, the North End, and the South End. He attended the public schools and served an eight-year apprenticeship as a printer, becoming a member of the Mechanic Apprentice's Library Association and later the Massachusetts Charitable Mechanic Association. Slack began his political life as an abolitionist in the late 1840s, joining the followers of Theodore Parker, the cotton magnates' fiercest critic.[25] Slack's first impact in public service came when he collaborated with William Cooper Nell and other black abolitionists in the battle against racial segregation in the public schools of Boston. As a state representative in the House in 1855, Slack chaired the Committee on Education that successfully reversed the state supreme court's decision on the issue and integrated Massachusetts public schools.[26] For his role in these efforts and as a prominent opponent of slavery, he was honored on New Year's Day 1863 as the first to publicly read the Emancipation Proclamation at a large assembly at Tremont Temple. After 1864, as the editor of the Republican organ the *Commonwealth*, he advocated for radical reconstruction and universal enfranchisement.[27]

Aldermen like Slack highlight the links between mobilization for the Civil War and the egalitarian, desegregationist vision embodied in the annexation campaign. In their view, the defeat of the "Slave Power" paved the way for urban policy that would champion the interests of workers. "Our Southern brethren," Slack wrote in his paper at the end of the Civil War, "in the days when we complacently licked their boots and politely asked them to observe how humble we were, were accustomed to designate the industrious masses of the North as 'greasy mechanics.'" The outcome of the war, however, represented "the triumphs of skill and labor," giving these workers their day in the sun as unsung heroes. "With one hand, it is not hyperbole to say, they directed the operations of the greatest of armies, and with the other fostered all the amenities of peace."[28] Annexation was intended to benefit precisely these "industrious masses." "We are crowded for accommodations to young mechanics," he explained. "We want room to enlarge and push the activity and skill of our people." Annexation would relieve these working people of the "high rents and difficulties of obtaining shops and houses," providing them with greatly expanded "opportunities for business and comfort." Slack's rhetorical coupling of "business" with residential "comfort," mechanical "shops" with "houses," militated against elite ideals that prescribed strict separation of "home" from "work." The seamless pairing of the two spheres in his rhetoric was not coincidental. The population Slack had in mind aspired not to a detached home in a rural setting away from the bustle of the city but rather to a convenient place of residence and an opportunity to practice their trade in an urban setting. "These persons do not wish to lose the advantages of residence in Boston," Slack noted. They would always prefer "good schools, well-kept streets, abundant water, creditable government, social and intellectual advantages of a compact city . . . over the casual advantages of any neighboring town." The high public costs of providing these amenities and supporting the well-being of this population, he explained, would be "a mere song compared with the advantages."[29]

For annexationists like Slack, growing social polarization between rich and poor was not an unfortunate if necessary part of city life but rather a dangerous anomaly that had to be addressed by political action. Against the notion that economic change was best governed by private market forces, they introduced an overtly political approach to public policy. Their petitions repeatedly emphasized that the "importance of retaining the industrial classes of our community within the city limits [could not] be overestimated." They explained that working Bostonians were not drawn to the countryside for aesthetic reasons but rather were pushed out by the conditions of the dense and costly housing in the inner city. These families nevertheless remained thoroughly urban in their sensibilities. They "will always remain in the city if they can live as cheaply and comfortably as elsewhere, not only because the interests of their labor are here, but because of its better facilities of education, recreation, libraries, and other advantages which the metropolis affords."[30] The new wards on the periphery offered lower population density and improved sanitary conditions over the inner city but were still intended to become urban neighborhoods. Public improvements, not the salubrious effects of natural surroundings, were the main appeal. Petitioners repeatedly praised the advantages of "drainage, of Cochituate water, of the Public Library, of the schools." These could only be provided by the resources of a large city. "A town," they explained, "will not build drains and sewers, any more than it will build streets and sidewalks." Educational facilities were also important since schools outside of the city did not "compare with the schools of Boston. . . . [We] do not know of a city or town in the Commonwealth where they do."[31]

Business elites in Boston saw the annexation program as a wrongheaded, ineffective, and wasteful plan that meddled with private market forces and could potentially derail Boston's future as a financial center. They mobilized in every imaginable way to obstruct the realization of this ambitious metropolitan vision. They used a three-pronged strategy that challenged annexation in politics, in law, and, finally, in historical memory, thus leveraging their own authority in the field of political economy, their legal training and expertise, and their sway over historical knowledge.

First, with the backing of the best authorities on issues of political economy, elites dismissed both the viability and desirability of the plan. Edward Avery, a Harvard-trained lawyer, who spoke for the opposition to Roxbury's annexation at a public hearing in the statehouse, argued that the overall prosperity of a city rested not on robust development within the metropolitan area but on its advantageous commercial and financial relations with other cities and regions. "Within the experience of those who have made this matter a study," he explained, "we are told that it is the facilities of trade, and not the aggregation of population, that go to make up a commercial mart."[32] In this expert view, some regional trade would inevitably center in Boston because of the combined market of the surrounding region. Commerce within this regional market, however, was "not a trade which gives extensive commercial advantages or position to any town or city." The far more desirable economic relations—"trade that comes from abroad"—rested entirely on "the aggregation of capital and enterprise" and the ability to forge "inter-communication" with remote places. Annexation could do little to enhance these long-distance business connections. It would therefore merely bestow undue government favors on a narrowly self-interested array of neighborhood factions—builders, carpenters, mechanics, and shopkeepers—whose profits, in this view, contributed nothing to the overall well-being of the city. If annexationists thought of an expanded metropolis in positive terms as nurturing local industry, having a multiplier effect on the creation of jobs in manufacturing, retail, and construction, Avery and his colleagues saw this mostly as a form of "pork barrel" corruption. They pointed to the example of the neighborhood of East Boston, a thriving Boston neighborhood where, due to the bountiful public spending, "the contractors, architects, mechanics had for a long time a feast of fat things."[33]

In place of an expansive metropolis, opponents of annexation envisioned a territorially small and bureaucratically lean municipality. Unencumbered by heavy fiscal obligations and high taxes, this municipality would much better empower the city's elite businessmen to boldly traverse the continent. Benjamin W. Harris, another Harvard graduate who represented the opposition to the annexation of Dorchester in 1869, elaborated this idea. He argued that Boston's metropolitan growth should be governed by the "natural" laws of political economy: "it need not be stimulated, it ought not to be stimulated, by any act of legislation."[34] The city's economic future, in his view, did not rest on its urban manufacturing base or its working population but on its merchants, bankers, and financial institutions, all of whom would be adversely affected by annexation: "It is State Street, with its hundreds of millions in values, in banking, and capital and exchange; its trusts and banks of discount and deposit. It is the railroads that . . . bring their freights from the North and West, from the lakes and the mines, and from the wells down below them both. . . . It is these that bring their tributes to enhance the commercial importance of the city of Boston. . . . It is these, more than extended areas and far reaching lines of boundary, that conduce to the prosperity and importance of our New England city." The annexation of additional territory would in fact have an adverse effect on Boston's future prosperity.

Like Avery, Harris ridiculed the notion that urban policy should facilitate residential and industrial development. He interpreted the annexationists' expansive metropolitan program as a decidedly parochial proposition. It made no sense to him that "the wealth which has built up Lowell and

Lawrence, the wealth which opens the mines of Pennsylvania and the mines of Colorado, should be employed here, in building up Washington Village and Dorchester!"[35] It was instead undeniably "better for the honor and fame of Boston and Massachusetts," he argued, "that Boston should send her capital forth to civilize, enlighten, and educate the world than that she should sit supreme upon a few hills, and reign over a single port." Since "the commerce of Boston is dependent for its prosperity upon the business of the broad continent," he concluded, there was no reason to think "annexation will have the slightest influence."[36]

As Charles F. Adams Jr. predicted, the political system, driven by enthusiasm for annexation among broad segments of the population, pushed back against Harris's positions, despite his scientifically authorized convictions. Politically weak in a democratic system, the opponents of the annexation scheme turned to the legal sphere and took their case to the Supreme Court of the Commonwealth. In 1873, led by William Minot, a downtown lawyer with a large estate in the rural town of West Roxbury, fifty of the town's largest taxpayers pleaded with the court to annul the impending unification of Boston with the surrounding towns. The petitioners cited, alongside various technical irregularities in the annexation process, the impairment of property rights—"controversies respecting property"—that made the act unconstitutional. Given that Massachusetts towns had an inviolable "proprietary and private" character, they reasoned, the parties to the annexation question were not "the political corporations"—cities, towns, and counties—but the private citizens and inhabitants, the corporations being mere "trustee[s] for their private interests and estates." These private interests were protected by the state's Bill of Rights and could not be constitutionally impaired. Beyond the residents and inhabitants of the towns, the petitioners added, annexation infringed on the rights of the various towns' creditors, who lent money to a particular municipality expecting "all the property in the town, and the estate of each inhabitant as [their] security therefor." In merging the town with Boston, this property would become "equally available for the city of Boston creditors" and thus rendered less secure.[37]

Unfortunately for Minot and his neighbors in West Roxbury, their effort to recast Massachusetts towns as private entities that were constitutionally protected from external government intrusion had no standing under the law of the commonwealth, where an expansive notion of public welfare sanctioned broad authority to the legislature. The court therefore unequivocally affirmed the legislature's power to "alter the boundaries of the counties, towns and cities" for purposes of "public expediency." It emphasized the political nature of the towns, which was irreducible to the individual property owners. The towns' existence was derived not from a compact among the individual inhabitants but in a corporate capacity from the sovereignty of the legislature. They did not exercise their power "under a grant, or by virtue of any contract express or implied." Rather, they were "political organizations, created for political purposes, and as mere instrumentalities by which the Legislature administers certain laws within particular limits."[38] In short, the creation and removal of political boundaries was an entirely pragmatic affair at the legislature's full discretion. Following a similar logic, the court disagreed that annexation impaired the property rights of municipal bondholders. The bonds were secured, it clarified, not by the private estates of the inhabitants but by the public property of the towns. Following annexation, this property would simply become "vested in the city of Boston," which would be fully liable for . . . all the debts, obligations, duties, [and] responsibilities." There was therefore little justification to allow the bondholders to thwart the legislature from pursuing what was in the public's best interest.

The court's decision struck a blow not only to the privatist conception of the towns as an aggregation of taxpayers but also to their sanctification as organic or "original" communities. The Tocquevillian trope about the sacred status of small towns in the history of New England, which was often cited by the anti-annexationists, obscured the remarkable malleability of political boundaries over the long history of the region since the beginnings of European settlement. The towns of the commonwealth were neither primordial nor invariably small. As political territorial units, they were in fact the outcome of a slow and deliberate process of partitioning (and unification) of the twelve original town charters that together occupied the entire eastern part of the colony. The process of partitioning accelerated in the middle of the nineteenth century as the region industrialized. Rural districts, the home of commercial farms and the estates of the well-to-do, sought separation from their urbanizing and increasingly fiscally burdensome neighbors, leading Somerville to break from Charlestown, Revere from Chelsea, Melrose from Malden, West Roxbury from Roxbury, and Swampscott and Nahant from the shoe manufacturing center of Lynn, all between 1842 and 1852.[39] This complex and uneven history did not prevent opponents of annexation from casting their position as a defense of the ostensibly inviolable independence of Massachusetts towns, which was bolstered by a proliferation of local town histories and the infusion of art and culture with a new antiquarian spirit.[40] "Save us simply those rights which are in harmony with the old and well-settled policy of this Commonwealth," Harris tapped into this discourse as part of his argument against the annexation of Dorchester. "Leave us in the enjoyment of that individuality and identity which belong to us."[41]

The inauguration of new town hall meetings in West Roxbury and Brookline in 1868 and 1873, respectively, was emblematic of the reification of the long-standing autonomy of the two towns. Determined to commemorate their independent political status and signal their determination to preserve it, the dedication ceremonies dwelled in painstaking detail on every minor dispute between the towns and their adjoining municipality since the seventeenth century. In Brookline, local orator and retired politician Robert C. Winthrop warned his audience that incorporation into Boston would "relapse [the town back] into the condition from which your fathers in 1705, and thirty years before, struggled so hard to release themselves." In West Roxbury, whose status as a destination for commuters from Boston led to its separation from Roxbury hardly two decades earlier, Arthur W. Austin told his listeners of the town's age-old grievances and longings for "self-government." "Judging from the records," he argued, it appeared that West Roxbury was for many years ruled by the lower part of the town (now Roxbury) that "always having numerical superiority refused what it pleased and considered what it granted as a boon and not as a right."[42] Annexation into Boston, these speakers suggested, would place Brookline and Roxbury under foreign and arbitrary rule.

These dubious invocations of history carried enormous cultural weight, especially as they were repeated ad nauseam. But they did not go unchallenged by ordinary observers, who were thoroughly familiar with the history of the region. William W. Wheildon, a Charlestown printer and amateur historian, for example, accurately pointed out that as far back as the colony's origin, "municipalities or townships were made as large as anybody wanted them, and ten times larger than was requisite. Nobody cared to make them small." He saw through the attempt to invent a tradition of small towns. "To advance the doctrine [of the sacredness of small towns] now, and claim for it the prestige of antiquity," he argued, "is peculiarly refreshing in our age and country. We esteem it simply ridiculous and essentially octogenarian." Others similarly pointed out that the celebration of the traditional independence of New England towns allowed affluent citizens "to escape their just share of the expense of support of the poor and of education and to form . . . small town[s] exclusively of men of wealth and to which others of like character would resort to escape equal taxation elsewhere."[43]

The debate over annexation thus produced an inverted alignment by which Boston's most prominent business visionaries, who were powerful agents of continental industrialization, stood firmly for "tradition" and localism in their urban political outlook. This was especially blatant in the case of Brookline, an adjoining town that became home to many of the most affluent residents of the Boston area, including members of the prominent Bowditch, Winthrop, Sargent, Dwight, Lee, Amory, Gardner, and Lawrence families. Brookline resident Henry V. Poor, for example, had been the founding editor of leading financial publications such as *American Railroad Journal* and *Poor's Manual of the Railroads of the United States*. He used these organs to celebrate financial interconnectedness as a defining feature of civilization and mocked opponents of North American economic consolidation as the equivalents of tribal "predatory chieftains" who represented "the inveterate foes to whatever was fitted to promote the progress and welfare of mankind."[44] On the metropolitan level, however, Poor was a staunch localist. He not only fiercely objected to Brookline's incorporation into Boston but also proposed to reverse annexation where it had already been consummated. Since annexation, he argued, Boston was "steadily going from bad to worse. The only remedy [was] . . . to decentralize the administration . . . to break up [the various] portions of the city into local organizations, charged with the conduct of their own affairs."[45]

Poor was not an exception. Edward Atkinson, another Brookline resident and one of the age's most prolific liberal writers, traveled the continent preaching the gospel of free trade. In Brookline, he devoted his scientific knowledge to locating a source of water for the town that would help Brookline stay independent from Boston's water system and thereby maintain its municipal autonomy.[46] Most outspoken of all was Alfred D. Chandler, a downtown lawyer and expert in private corporate law, trust estates, and landed interests, who was also Brookline's chairman of the board of selectmen. Even as he served as treasurer and counsel to private railroad corporations, and thus certainly understood the economies of scale and scope, Chandler remained vigilant against metropolitan growth, which he associated with inefficiency and corruption. "What we must guard against in this country," he explained, "are our overgrown cities, badly managed and tending *from their very size* toward corruption. Better an aggregate of small cities, or communities under town governments, wisely administered, than a metropolis great in population, but badly or unwisely governed."[47] For Poor, Atkinson, and Chandler, the cry of town autonomy and metropolitan fragmentation represented not a rebellion against economic integration but one of the interconnected political economy's key features. Political decentralization made economic consolidation possible.[48]

The struggle against annexation thus crystallized the financial elite's conception of the laissez-faire metropolis that, rather than mere government absence or inaction, entailed a much more elaborate configuration of intertwined dualities: home and work, public and private, tradition and progress, sacred and profane, local and national, and, metaphorically, the "natural" law of the marketplace and the pristine beauty of "nature" in the rural countryside. From this perspective, the capitalist transformation that swept through North America, gradually merging all communities and regions into an integrated whole, was counterbalanced by an emphatic celebration of tradition and localism at home. The thorough conversion of downtown Boston into a financial district was coupled with the elevation of suburban towns into privatist residential havens, exclusively devoted to domesticity and thus free from political and commercial encroachments. The natural forces of supply and demand, which operated just like "grass grows, or water runs," as Harris very aptly put it, would in this way be combined with the natural beauty of preserved countryside around Boston, which was "a park more beautiful than [the man-made] Central Park, ten thousand times over." Unadulterated by dense settlement and urban improvements, this land that "surround[ed] and embrace[d] the city of Boston"—but of course kept strictly separated from it—would remain a sparsely settled, pastoral domain "covered all over with the evidences of art and taste,—fine streets, fine avenues, beautiful residences, grand gardens; variety, beauty, everywhere."[49] In this harmonious vision, centralization and fragmentation, modernity and tradition, commercial and pastoral, continental and local could all be peacefully reconciled.

The battles over the political structure of the metropolis did not reach a clear resolution. In the late 1860s and early 1870s, Boston's boundaries expanded to include the large, sparsely settled territories of adjoining towns.

Following Roxbury and Dorchester, the city incorporated the municipalities of West Roxbury, Brighton, and Charlestown in 1873. The town of Brookline rejected annexation into Boston in 1873 (and did so again in 1875, 1879, and 1880). It retained its status as an independent municipality. Development in annexed and unannexed territories took very different forms.

The pattern of development in territories that became parts of Boston proceeded in line with annexationists' best hopes and in clear defiance of elite prescriptions. Under Boston's jurisdiction, the ownership of large parcels of land on the metropolitan fringe, taxed at higher rates at full valuation, became prohibitive. Publically funded urban amenities made dense settlement viable. As expected, these policies led to the rapid subdivision of large estates on the city's periphery. The process drastically expanded available housing for working families.[50] The annexed districts became the fastest growing neighborhoods in the city, housing an increasing percentage of the population of Boston. These new neighborhoods were where most urban growth took place in the closing decades of the century. While the population of Boston proper increased by only 20 percent between 1860 and 1890, the combined population in the annexed territories of Roxbury, Dorchester, West Roxbury, and Brighton more than tripled, jumping from roughly 44,591 residents to over 145,000 (compared to approximately 160,000 in the inner city).[51] As the outer neighborhoods expanded, their demographics radically changed. The population shifted from the former dominance of elite families, commercial farmers, and their associated domestic laborers and agricultural workers to a heterogeneous urban population, especially small manufacturers, shopkeepers, tradesmen, low-level white collar workers, and industrial laborers. In contrast to areas of the inner city, which tended to be socially polarized between rich and poor, the new neighborhoods were occupied by the households of a wide range of occupations such as carpenters, printers, machinists, blacksmiths, clerks, bakers, dealers, grocers, and teamsters, as well as large numbers of common laborers and domestic workers.[52]

The landscape of the districts that became part of Boston had several distinctive characteristics. Unlike in inner city neighborhoods, where a small number of elite families had gained a near monopoly on land, the new outer neighborhoods fostered relatively high rates of property ownership. Land in these areas was not leased on a long-term basis, as had been the practice downtown, but rather sold "free and clear." As a result, if the typical percentage of property owners in working-class districts within the inner city hovered between 3 and 7 percent of adult males, the number reached much higher proportions in the outer wards, climbing to anywhere between 17 and 26 percent by the early 1890s, which by nineteenth-century standards was exceedingly high.[53] Many thousands of working families became property owners. The majority who continued to rent made payments to a relatively large group of landlords, who tended to live in the vicinity and typically were not themselves major property owners.[54] The neighborhoods, furthermore, did not become exclusively residential. They developed as mixed-use areas where residences coexisted in close proximity to commercial and industrial corridors that were nurtured by and nurtured urban growth. On main thoroughfares and near transportation hubs, housing was interspersed with retail establishments, including butchers, bakeries, grocery stores, apothecaries, dry goods shops, florists, clothiers, stationery, and hardware. Nascent manufacturing corridors similarly expanded, becoming sites for a large variety of industries including, among many others, foundries, machine shops, lumber and brick yards, breweries, tanneries, print shops, shoe factories, furniture, musical instruments, fans and ventilation equipment, and chemical works.[55] With different social classes and land uses in close proximity, these urban districts were defined by what historian Sam Bass Warner astutely labeled a diverse "weave of small patterns."[56]

One of the ubiquitous industries in the new neighborhoods was construction, which received an immense boost following annexation. Earlier in the century, a significant portion of Boston's residential property was developed by large private syndicates that funded the preliminary land improvements, sanitation, and infrastructure in preparation for house construction. After annexation, the city government assumed fiscal and administrative responsibility for this groundwork, taking on the de facto role of large-scale land developer.[57] In this environment, the extension of urban amenities was driven by petitions and political leverage of the population within city government, not by easy access to private credit. Private land companies with deep financial pockets lost their competitive advantage in these areas. The city's public umbrella, responsive to grassroots pressures, created a business environment that appeared too unpredictable and chaotic to major developers. In contrast, this politically driven regulatory setting proved uniquely hospitable for several thousands of petit builders and contractors, who thrived in the annexed wards.[58]

2.3. Residential construction in the annexed districts (89 Mozart Street, Roxbury, Massachusetts). Note the proximity to multiple family homes, the unpaved street, and the construction materials in the background, all making this residence less than properly bourgeois. The railroad tracks, manufacturing workshops, and commercial establishments nearby also do not conform to elite-prescribed notions of privacy and domesticity. The visual association of the home with a male breadwinner, in this case immigrant builder Jacob Luippold, also contrasts with bourgeois associations of the domestic sphere as feminine.

Credit: Jacob Luippold Architectural Collection, Historic New England, Library and Archive. GUSN: 181071, Ref. Code: AR016.

The scant resources of these builders meant subdivisions tended to be irregular and small, often creating only a few lots of varying sizes at a time. Acting independently on a very moderate scale over decades, they constructed a blend of wooden houses—single-, double-, and three-family homes in close proximity to one another.[59]

The patterns that predominated in the annexed lands contrasted sharply with development in the independent Brookline that came to embody the suburban ideal. Under a town form of government that was controlled by wealthy residents, Brookline assessed undeveloped land at low valuations and kept property taxes purposefully low, creating little encouragement to subdivide the land.[60] This policy, combined with the town's notoriously tightfisted policies concerning the extension of urban infrastructure, led to a slow and sparse settlement pattern. Residential development proceeded along an exclusive character on sizable lots, with detached homes arranged on curvilinear streets that were designed to evoke natural beauty. Restrictive covenants prescribed generous setbacks from the street, minimum cost of construction, and sole use of land for dwelling houses "exclusive of all yards, shops, or other conveniences for manufacturing or mechanical purposes."[61] These nonresidential uses, along with the poor immigrant population that was associated with them, were segregated to "the Marsh," a lowland area by the railroad tracks that was deemed unfit for respectable residences.[62] As profits poured in from investments in the remote corners of the continent, elite residents of Brookline remained little concerned about spurring industrial activity nearby. They were instead able to revere the pastoral beauty of their town and mock the crass developmental aspirations of neighboring communities.

The uneven results of the annexation battles left the metropolitan area in a severe fiscal bind going forward. On the one hand, Boston brought large territories under its jurisdiction, territories that required urban infrastructure on an equitable scale with the other neighborhoods. Over the following decades, these territories provided homes and employment to a growing urban population, but they also strained municipal budgets that were vital for their growth. At the same time, more ambitious annexation proposals that aimed at towns like Brookline were effectively blocked, solidifying the fragmented government structure of the metropolis. Politically autonomous, the wealthy towns around Boston provided tax shelters for many of the city's largest property owners. The migration into these towns constrained Boston's tax base precisely at the moment when its financial needs began to grow exponentially. This fiscal contradiction, which was produced politically, was the foundation on which the modern metropolis emerged.

The fiscal contradiction plaguing the metropolis of Boston became more and more pressing in the 1870s and 1880s, shifting the conversation to a vigorous debate on the related issue of property taxes and public finance.

The debate revolved around a similar social and political axis. Again, a broad populist coalition pushed to make city government an engine of metropolitan development and wide distribution of property, triggering a powerful reform effort by elite business interests. The contests over control of the public treasury clearly played an important role in defining relationships between urban social groups. On the terrain of municipal budgets, private wealth did not translate seamlessly into political influence, and elites watched helplessly as popular constituencies impelled city governments to spend, borrow, and tax on ever-increasing scales. Just as significantly, as all observers recognized, public finance had far-reaching implications for the course of industrial development. Municipal taxes and spending had profound effects on metropolitan economies, potentially attracting (or deterring) commerce and investment, fostering manufacturing and industry, configuring a city's housing stock, shaping powerful civic and cultural institutions, and supporting some economic sectors at the expense of others. As cities became essential sites in a larger economic system, the repercussions of public finance in each city extended beyond a particular locale in a way that proved decisive for the development of intercity and interregional economic activity. Yet again, what at times seemed like local questions carried implications for the formation of an interconnected urban network that provided the backbone for the North American political economy as a whole.[63]

Especially in the aftermath of annexation, Boston epitomized the process of urban state formation more than any other American city. Labeled (somewhat hysterically) by contemporaries as the "heaviest taxed city in civilization," Boston municipal budgets were more lavish than those of all other cities in the United States. Its per capita taxes in the late 1860s were, by some measures, 40 percent higher than those in Chicago and Philadelphia and 17 percent higher than that of New York, which was itself considered heavily "burdened."[64] Overall, between 1860 and 1873, the annual budget of Boston City Government leaped from $3.5 to $17.8 million, which in real terms amounted to an increase of 325 percent, with most of the rise occurring after 1865. Despite the territorial expansion of the city and a population that more than doubled in this time span, annual expenditure per capita climbed from $20 to over $50, hitting an all-time high of approximately $64 in 1873 (see figure 2.4).[65] The debate surrounding municipal finances took place in the context of this massive rise in spending. Broad ranging in style and substance, the debate touched on

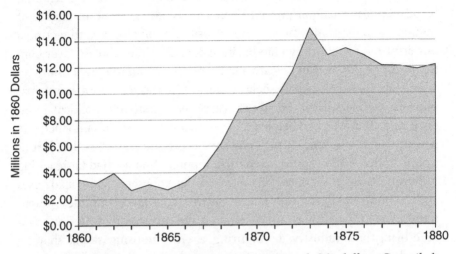

2.4. Boston municipal spending, 1860–1880, in adjusted 1860 dollars. Compiled from Charles Phillips Huse, *The Financial History of Boston* (Cambridge: Harvard University Press, 1916).

some of the fundamental questions of modern political economy, such as the limits of state sovereignty in a liberal society, the role of democratic politics in shaping economic policy, the nature of private property, and the proper relationship between the state and the economy, as well as between the state and civil society.[66]

The main source of revenue in all big American cities at the end of the nineteenth century was the general property tax—an annual tax on all forms of property held by state residents. Cities and towns levied the tax without distinction on nearly all forms of property. In Boston, the annual circular announcing the beginning of the assessment season specified that the property tax would be levied on: "Real Estate; Money at Interest; and other debts . . . shares and stock in banks, wherever located, and in insurance, manufacturing, and other incorporated companies . . . public stocks and securities . . . goods wares, merchandise, and other stock in trade, within or without the state, vessels of all kinds, at home or abroad, with their stores and appurtenances, household furniture exceeding $1,000 in value; horses and carriages; income from profession, trade, or employment exceeding $1,000, personal property held in trust or by a wife or minor child."[67] Some form of general property taxation had been in place in the

northern states since the seventeenth century, but its administration, especially in cities, had to be radically bolstered to adapt to an increasing population, proliferating city wards, and new forms of property, as well as the
new scale of public expenditures.[68] The administration of the tax in Boston
during the 1860s and 1870s required a large assessment department of fifty-
seven assessors, assistants, and first assistants, who were appointed annually
by the City Council. Every spring, as city ordinances specified, assessors
would perform "street duty" and "go through the wards." They would visit
the different estates, "appraising the value of the real estate" (land and
buildings) and "estimating the value of the personal property" (all other
forms of property).[69] This approach, with deep historical roots in Massachusetts, aimed to tax each resident with reference to one's estate and "all
other his abilities whatsoever."[70]

Most criticisms of the general property tax focused on inaccurate and
incomplete assessments. Evidence suggests, however, that the appraisal
process aimed not to assign precise valuations for all property in the city,
which would have been nearly impossible, but to arrive at a proportional
rating of property holders and their ability to contribute to public coffers.
Many residents therefore were not assessed anew every year, the assumption
being that their financial position had remained largely unchanged. As
the lingo went among assessors, they would keep the previous year's valuation of an individual with the assumption that they "had him rated."[71]
This pragmatic practice did not preclude the total valuation of property
from climbing from $371,891,000 to $682,723,000 between 1865 and 1872,
helping to keep the tax rate roughly steady even as revenues rose sharply.[72]
The system, in short, might have been imprecise, but it proved remarkably
successful in the underappreciated task of raising resources for the city.
Rather than an undisputed failure, the general property tax should more
appropriately be seen as the period's most important and reliable source of
public revenue.

Like the annexation program, this particular tax regime was associated
with a cohort of urban populists in city government. The individual in
charge of the workings of the property tax in Boston during this critical
period was the city's chief tax assessor, Thomas Hills, whose fervent supervision of the assessment process, by all accounts, made it possible for the
city to raise the necessary revenue to pay for a rapidly growing public
sector.[73] An upholsterer by trade and an active member in the city's mechanics organizations, which offered access to books, elocution classes,

and debating clubs, Hills was no anachronistic neighborhood artisan at odds with the flux of modern life. His life journey, in fact, literally took him around the globe. After graduating from the public schools of Boston and completing his apprenticeship in 1849 at age twenty-one, Hills sailed to California on a gold-digging expedition. He arrived in San Francisco after six months at sea and continued to Sacramento City, where he spent a season in the mines before starting an upholstery, carpet, and furniture establishment. In November of 1850, Hills continued as a sailor to the Sandwich Islands, Canton, and Hong Kong. His journey took him to London, where he visited the Crystal Palace, before returning to Boston in 1852 to resume work at his trade. After his return, Hills's life became deeply embedded in the city's mechanics culture, finding him always living adjacent to other tradesmen (housewrights, printers, grocers, carpenters, painters, masons). He followed the slow migration of middling people out of downtown to the outer neighborhoods of the city, first to East Boston and finally to South Boston, where he became active in the district's charities and religious groups, as well as in its savings bank and trades association. In 1853, Hills entered public life. He initially ran unsuccessfully as a Democrat for the Massachusetts House of Representatives, but left the party in 1854 with the escalation of the controversies surrounding slavery. He served three terms as a Republican state representative in the early 1860s before joining Boston's tax assessors' board, where he remained for twenty-eight years, the last twenty-five as the board's chairman.[74]

Hills's main adversary in the debate over the property tax was David A. Wells, who was best known for his four years in Washington as the special commissioner of revenue. Born in Springfield, Massachusetts, Wells grew up in one of the wealthiest families in the Connecticut valley, as grandson to the owner of a paper mill. He attended Williams College, finishing first in his class, and later graduated from Harvard's Lawrence Scientific School. After pursuing a career as a journalist, publisher, and pamphleteer on issues of science and political economy, he developed a knack for explaining complicated theoretical concepts to broad audiences. His breakthrough arrived when his pamphlet "Our Burden and Our Strength," which touted the fiscal resilience of the Union's war effort, was picked up by the "Loyal Publication Society," a major unionist publicity apparatus run by wealthy New York businessmen. The society circulated 200,000 copies of the pamphlet on both sides of the Atlantic, making Wells a celebrated public figure. With this aura of accomplishment, he arrived in

2.5. Thomas Hills, upholsterer and chief tax assessor for the City of Boston.

Credit: William S. Hills, *The Hills Family in America* (New York: Grafton Press, 1906).

wartime Washington in 1864 and capitalized on his achievement by securing a seat on the Federal Revenue Commission.[75]

Wells assumed his commission as a staunch believer in tariff protectionism, but by the end of his term in 1870, he had become one of the leading proponents of free trade in the United States. Crucial to this astonishing change of heart was the guidance of Brookline resident and cheap-cotton evangelist Edward Atkinson, himself a recent convert to liberal political economy, with whom Wells developed an extensive correspondence.[76] This new policy orientation among wealthy New Englanders was indicative of the region's diminishing importance as a manufacturing center and its growing position as a financial center.[77] Also significant in this context was Wells's increasingly international outlook. As revenue commissioner, he sojourned in Europe many times, studying industrial conditions, "notebook in hand . . . visiting every typical mine, factory, and workshop between England and Russia," as he described it. During one typical visit to London in 1867, he had occasion to enjoy a dinner with the renowned Political Economy Club and to discuss public matters with leading figures in business and government, including William E. Gladstone and John Stuart Mill.[78]

In the years during which Hills acted as the chairman of Boston's assessors' board and supervised the painstaking task of assessing the property in Boston, street by street, ward by ward, Wells was developing a broad view of the American economy in an international perspective from his vantage point in Washington, from the highest echelons of New England's business elite, and from his travels abroad. Hills acquired detailed knowledge of the municipal fiscal system from within. His work revolved around the annual cycle of municipal expenditure and taxation. He knew from up close the distribution of government benefits and tax burdens among the different districts of the city. He became acquainted with the landscape of a small number of large property holders, who held vast concentrations of financial forms of property, and the large number of small property holders, who owned mostly residential property. During those same years, Wells developed an acute sense of the importance of domestic policy on the national, regional, and urban levels as it related to the international economy. As a writer, publisher, reformer, and aspiring public servant, he embraced the mission of rendering fiscal policy congruent with worldwide economic interconnectedness.

Wells had powerful advocates in Massachusetts who emphasized the need to make taxation less political and more attentive to economic "law." Charles Adams, for example, identified taxes as one of the most vital policy questions. "People may say, and legislators may enact, what they please," he argued, "the stern logic of taxation will at last convince us that there is a science of revenue; that the careful adjustment of taxes has something to do with the healthy development of trade; that the good old rule which directs the legislator to impose a tax of one per cent on everything, and, if that is not enough, to make it one and a half, and if he can find any foreign capitalist creeping into the State, to scalp him,—this rule does not, after all, express the whole science of revenue."[79] Ultimately, it was the state of New York that seized Wells to propose a wholesale reform of its laws of taxation. At the time, the commissioner was considered one of the leading American authorities on public revenue on the federal level, and his attention to local taxation reflected the growing urgency of the issue. Wells explained that the growing scale of public spending after the war, especially on the municipal level, made taxation in the United States "larger per capita . . . than any modern nation has ever before been subjected to, continuously, in time of peace." He enthusiastically offered his expert opinion in an attempt to address the multiple "crudities, irregularities, and absurdities" of the existing system. His proposals quickly became conventional wisdom among elite reformers.[80]

Wells was not a man of small ideas, and his two reports about state and local tax reform advocated not incremental change or a way to mend the current system but a complete overhaul of state and local taxation in the United States. His report mocked the inadequacies of the current system, focusing in particular on the incompetence of local authorities in finding and fairly assessing personal property. "Can the present imperfect system be done away with, and personal property at the same time be made to sustain its equitable and proportionate share of the public burdens?" was the question he posed. His answer was "unqualifiedly in the affirmative."[81] The way to do so, he explained, would be to terminate the general property tax and raise revenue exclusively from a tax on owners of real estate and their tenants. Following this basic idea, he formulated two alternatives for legislation. Plan A would, for the purposes of valuation, count land at 50 percent of its assessed value and the building on the land at full value. The more ambitious Plan B would assess real estate (both land and buildings) at full valuation and then tax the occupier, "be he owner or tenant," on a valuation of three times the rental value of the premises. Under both plans, Wells explained, "personal property not embraced under one of the above systems"—most notably "intangible" forms of property held in financial instruments—was "to be entirely exempt from all taxation."[82] The report could not have been more enthusiastic about this proposed system, which not only rested on sound theory but also promised to streamline the assessment process, equitably distribute tax burdens, and promote economic development in cities and states that adopted it.

To support the plan, Wells pointed out that real estate, unlike other forms of property, was impossible to hide and easy to value. His system would focus the attention of assessors on property that was *"certain, visible, and tangible*... disregarding that which is *invisible, incorporeal,* and *intangible,"* especially financial forms of property, which were becoming increasingly widespread among the moneyed classes.[83] Additionally, the value of the real estate one occupied offered a perfect index of one's personal property. An economic rule observed by experts in England, France, Belgium, and Holland, he explained, had it that "the rental value of houses or other occupied buildings is the most certain index of the value of the personal estate of the owners or occupiers, and is also the best measure of an individual's income and ability to pay taxes." By valuing the rental value of one's residence, the state could arrive at a more precise measurement of one's capacity to contribute to the public coffers than by attempting to assess the property in full. With that in mind, Wells went so far as to project that by exempting all forms of property except real estate, total valuations would in fact rise and tax rates would decrease, "affording all the revenue that may be needed at an average rate much less than the rate now prevailing."[84]

Beyond achieving nearly perfect precision and proportional distribution of the tax burden, Wells presented his scheme as also advantageous from the perspective of economic prosperity. In making this point, he elevated the logic of the fragmented metropolis, which protected the autonomous political status of small towns in metropolitan areas, to the status of economic law. Disregarding efforts to politically unify metropolitan areas, Wells explained that individuals and businesses had the liberty to leave a city with high taxes and remove their property with them. Property escaping taxation "in all or in degree, through a change of residence of the owner... the law is powerless to prevent." He pointed in particular to the migration of wealthy citizens from inner cities to escape high property taxes, which was especially pronounced in the case of Boston.[85] Tax policy had to be formulated with this migration in mind. It could not afford to be so onerous as to drive property and resources away from the city.

Wells's response was to narrow city taxes to property that could not be transferred or moved. Since the value of land was, at least in theory, nothing more than an index for the property that it was able to attract to it ("the market value of real estate [being] always proportional to, and dependent on, the amount of personal property, or rather productive capital, placed upon it"), a tax on real estate would put the state in its proper place, rewarding it with revenue only when it promoted conditions hospitable to economic activity.[86] Wells associated such hospitable conditions not with generous spending, as was the working assumption within city government, but with fiscal restraint, which would put "production of every kind, agricultural, mining, and manufacturing . . . upon the most favorable conditions . . . [leaving] shipping fostered; trade and commerce . . . untrammeled." He also hoped that a tax on real estate, and especially on rents, would encourage the citizenry to limit government spending by forcing them to "see and feel in a consolidated form the proportion of the public burden" and directing their attention "to the manner in which the revenues raised by taxation are disposed of."[87]

Overall, the enactment of Wells's recommendations would signal a fundamental reversal in the state's position vis-à-vis private market forces. Currently, city government, by virtue of its political sovereignty, held sway over private actors domiciled in the city. It set developmental priorities and expected private actors to follow suit. A reformed tax system would overturn this hierarchy. Under the proposed plan, city government would yield primary authority to investors. The urban state would not become less important for economic development—not at all—but it would allow capitalists to prescribe desirable policy. State action would have to align with their needs and desires.[88] This new thinking in the realm of political economy was embedded in a new cosmopolitan spatial imagination. The existing system prioritized Boston as the focal point of economic life. Codified in law and bolstered by years of court decisions, it sanctioned a tax on property owners as members of the community, based on their ability to pay, regardless of where they held their property. The property of Bostonians was taxed in Boston "wherever located . . . within or without the state." A merchant's ship was taxable "at home or abroad." It mattered not whether it was currently anchored in Boston harbor.[89] By contrast, Wells's reform program would decenter the city, so to speak, repositioning it not at the core but as yet another node in a larger network of commerce in the overall business activities of its enterprising citizens. It set the city up to compete entrepreneurially for commerce and economic activity against other cities.

Wells's report resonated with tax reformers throughout the United States and in Europe but nowhere more so than among elites in Boston, which he singled out as leading "the civilized world" in the "extent and weight" of its taxation.[90] The Brahmin *Boston Daily Advertiser* drew its readers' attention to the report, explaining that although the document was commissioned by New York, "much of it bears upon the rights, duties, and privileges of every taxable community." The *Advertiser* took special delight in quoting the *London Daily Telegraph's* reaction to the report, which expressed hope that those who "love to count the cost of monarchy, should read, mark, learn and inwardly digest the figures which democracy submits for our inspection."[91] Wells's presentation of the dire situation in the United States led some to believe that the costly whims of a tyrannical monarch were much preferable to the insatiable demands of popular sentiments in a democracy.

Before long, Wells's report became a staple in local municipal politics, as opponents of government spending cited its findings to fight off this or that initiative. It was not uncommon, for example, for Wells's name to creep into the debate over the abolition of tolls on the East Boston ferry, a proposal that aimed to facilitate transportation between the neighborhood and the rest of the metropolis at a considerable public expense. Echoing Wells, opponents of the measure explained that the plan would "impose upon the tax-payers of this city—the most heavily burdened tax-payers . . . in the world,—a burden . . . never assumed by any municipal corporation in the world."[92] To "retain within our borders the taxable property and the wealthy men who contribute to the treasury," they explained, "we must so conduct our municipal affairs as not to drive them away by the pressure of taxation." This was evidenced by "an examination of Hon. David A. Wells' report upon taxation to the legislature of New York." The report thus helped enshrine the logic of capital migration as a guiding scientific principle in politics and as a counterlogic to the expansive public vision that guided elected officials in city government.

Wells's ideas achieved such wide currency in Boston that Hills, in his capacity as chief tax assessor, felt obliged to compile a detailed public reply. In the midst of the annexation battles of the early 1870s, as taxes prompted landowners to subdivide their rural estates and more and more Bostonians came to own homes within the expanded boundaries of the city, the proposal took on particularly regressive implications. The push to exempt some forms of property from taxation, Hills charged, came from those "public-spirited citizens" who would be "found to be in some way or other either directly or indirectly, connected with that portion of the community, which is to receive the immediate benefit of the exemption."[93] He conceded that the existing system had limitations, but disposing of it altogether because it could not be perfectly enforced was too dogmatic a step in his opinion. No legislation is ever infallible, he explained, yet tariffs should not be abolished because smuggling is sometimes successful. The use of money should not be stopped because of the existence of forgeries. In the end, Hills wrote, "no intelligent legislator expects that when a law has been enacted . . . that it will successfully achieve the whole object for which it was framed." "Personal property," despite the shortcomings of the current system and the various evasion schemes, "can be reached in sufficient amount to cause it to bear a very considerable share of the public burdens."[94]

More specifically, Hills argued that it was not sensible to use the difficulty of taxing one form of property as justification for shifting tax burdens onto other forms of property, penalizing "those who find it more difficult to evade the assessment." Here, he moved away from speaking of taxpayers in general and referred directly to the "capitalists of the community" and the difficulty of compelling them to "submit to full taxation." This was indeed a difficult task, and Hills understood it firsthand. However, in asserting "the impossibility of compelling capital . . . to submit to uniform assessment, and that the assessment of such property would be . . . detrimental to the best interests of the community," the New York commissioner went too far. Wells's position, Hills explained, amounted to a direct challenge to the state's "power to tax," undermining "one of the undoubted attributes of sovereignty."[95]

To demonstrate the flaws in Wells's proposal, Hills offered information from the assessment department's ledgers, "stepping from the field of statement and theory, to deal with facts and figures," which he was confident were on his side. Whereas Wells sought to enhance equality among individuals of similar means, Hills thought of fairness in terms of equality between social classes. He therefore started with a sample from the assessments of real estate owners in the city, verifying the impact Wells's tax system would have on them. The sample started with a few property owners in

Location.	Area. Sqr. ft.	Value of Land.	Value of Building.	Total Valuation.	Per cent of building to total value.	50 per cent value of land.	Taxable valuation including building.	Per cent of tax value to total value.	Tax on full value at 15.30.	Tax on reduced value at 34.60.	Increase of Tax.	Per cent of Increase of Tax.
Commonwealth Av.	15,375	$92,000	$58,000	$150,000	32	$46,000	$104,000	69	$2,295 00	$3,598 40	$1,303 40	57
Beacon Street . . .	5,185	77,800	70,200	148,000	47	38,900	109,100	74	2,264 40	3,774 86	1,510 46	67
Beacon Street . . .	7,442	43,400	27,200	70,600	38	21,700	48,900	69	1,080 18	1,691 94	611 76	57
Beacon Street . . .	3,900	25,500	31,500	57,000	55	12,750	44,250	80	872 10	1,531 05	658 95	76
Mt. Vernon Street .	3,528	19,500	20,500	40,000	51	9,750	30,250	76	612 00	1,046 65	434 65	71
W. Cedar Street . .	950	2,800	7,200	10,000	72	1,400	8,600	86	153 00	267 56	144 56	94
Florence Street . .	1,030	2,000	5,200	7,200	72	1,000	6,200	86	110 16	214 52	104 36	95
Broadway	2,666	2,700	6,500	9,200	70	1,350	7,850	85	140 76	264 69	123 93	88
K Street	1,990	800	5,600	6,400	87	400	6,000	91	97 92	207 60	109 68	113
Hancock St.,Wd. 16	5,596	500	1,600	2,100	80	250	1,850	88	32 13	64 01	31 88	99

2.6. Thomas Hills's analysis of the effects of David A. Wells's reform proposal to tax land at 50 percent and buildings at full value. Large property owners in the fashionable Back Bay would disproportionately benefit from the plan at the expense of small property owners in the peripheral neighborhoods of the city. Credit: City of Boston, *Auditor of Accounts' Annual Report* (Boston: Alfred Mudge and Son, 1871), p. 274.

the fashionable Back Bay and Beacon Hill neighborhoods and moved outward to the peripheral neighborhoods of the city, with the idea of "represent[ing the different] classes in the community" (see figure 2.6). As expected, the numbers clearly showed that the farther out from the downtown area one went, as land became cheaper, the larger the relative share of buildings in the overall value of the property. Separating land from buildings, taxing the former at half its value and the latter at its full value—as Wells had proposed—downtown real estate owners would see only a 50 percent increase in their taxes, whereas homeowners in peripheral neighborhoods would see their increase reach about 100 percent. The owner of a residence on Beacon Street, whose land represented 62 percent of the overall value of the real estate, would face a tax increase of $611.76, or 57 percent, and enjoy full exemption from taxation on all other forms of property. The resident of K Street in South Boston (where Hills himself lived), whose land represented 87 percent of the overall value of the real estate, would see a tax increase of $109.68, or 113 percent. The lower down on the scale, the larger the increase in taxation would be, adding "to the weight of taxation, in proportion to the *inability* of the owner to bear it." With 70 percent of dwelling houses in Boston at that point worth under

OCCUPATION.	Total tax under Mass. system, rate $15.30.	Total tax by first plan, rate $34.60.	Total tax by second plan, rate $31.50.	Decrease of taxes.				Increase of taxes.			
				By first plan.	By second plan.	Per cent 1st plan.	Per cent 2d plan.	By first plan.	By second plan.	Per cent 1st plan.	Per cent 2d plan.
Merchant . .	$10,712 00	$3,598 40	$3,780 00	$7,113 60	$6,932 00	66	65				
Capitalist . .	17,566 40	3,774 86	3,729 60	13,791 54	13,836 80	78	79				
Lawyer . . .	7,202 18	1,691 94	1,779 12	5,510 24	5,423 06	76	75				
Merchant . .	4,699 10	1,531 05	1,436 40	3,168 05	3,262 70	67	69				
Do.	4,515 50	1,046 65	1,008 00	3,468 85	3,507 50	77	78				
Cashier . . .	185 60	297 56	252 00	. . . .	. . . .	.	.	$111 96	$66 40	60	35
Clergyman . .	127 46	214 52	181 44	. . . .	. . . .	.	.	87 06	53 98	68	43
Lawyer . . .	173 36	264 69	231 84	. . . .	. . . .	.	.	91 33	58 48	53	34
Public Officer	122 87	207 60	161 28	. . . .	. . . .	.	.	84 73	38 41	69	31
Mechanic . .	34 13	64 01	52 92	. . . .	. . . .	.	.	29 88	18 79	88	55
Bookkeeper	9 65	. . . .	47 25	. . . .	. . . .	.	.	. . . .	37 60	.	389
Clerk	5 06	. . . .	37 80	. . . .	. . . .	.	.	. . . .	32 74	.	647
Foreman . .	2 00	. . . .	28 35	. . . .	. . . .	.	.	. . . .	26 35	.	1,317
Journeyman	2 00	. . . .	23 62	. . . .	. . . .	.	.	. . . .	21 62	.	1,068

2.7. Thomas Hills's analysis of the effects of David A. Wells's proposal to exempt personal property from property taxation. "Merchants," "capitalists," and "lawyers" would get a tax cut whereas "cashiers," "mechanics," and "journeymen" would see a tax increase.

Credit: City of Boston, *Auditor of Accounts' Annual Report* (Boston: Alfred Mudge and Son, 1871), p. 281.

$5,000 in value, the tax load would primarily shift to the "middle and poorer classes." "From those dwellings," Hills poignantly asserted, "come the vast majority of those who create the property that others use, and who in time of danger are called on to protect the wealth that others enjoy."[96]

Given that the shift of taxation from all property to property in real estate would relieve large quantities of property from taxation, Hills produced another table to demonstrate the overall effect of the Wells plan (see figure 2.7). Again, this table revealed a dividing line between the high bourgeoisie and the rest of the urban population, showing how different types of property owners would be affected by the proposed reform. The first proposal, by eliminating taxes on personal property, would reduce the tax levy on merchants, capitalists, and lawyers (of the high-paying type) and pass on the burden to property owners lower down on the economic scale. The second proposal, by introducing taxation on rents, would penalize those on the verge of acquiring some property who paid only a poll tax under the existing rules. A "capitalist" would enjoy an overall tax decrease of 78 percent ($13,791) or 79 percent ($13,836), whereas a mechanic would see a tax increase of 88 percent ($29.88) or 55 percent ($18.79). As

Hills put it, the plan extended "lower down in the social scale" and "seize[d] upon classes heretofore nominally taxed, or wholly exempt from personal taxation": "It would seem impossible, that schemes that thus but nominally tax the wealthy and prosperous, and would transfer their share of the public burden, so that it would fall with terrible force upon the great middle classes, and with crushing weight upon all who are just starting out in life, or who have no accumulated property, could be seriously proposed to an American community." The mere proposition of such a plan, from Hills's perspective, seemed preposterous in a democratic American context.[97]

Hills's most comprehensive contribution in the debates over taxation came about in 1875 in his capacity as the chairman of the Massachusetts "Commission on the Expediency of Revising and Amending the Laws Relating to Taxation and Exemption Therefrom." Rather than deferring to erudite authorities in the study of political economy, the Massachusetts commissioners instead reached out for advice to the local assessment bodies throughout the commonwealth. "We desire not only the statistics from your assessment books," the commission's circular explained, "but the opinion of gentlemen who, as officers, have had experience in the administration of the law we are called upon to consider." The hands-on knowledge of tax assessors—about a thousand of them—unambiguously endorsed and defended the general property tax.[98] In contrast to the New York proposal authored by Wells, the Massachusetts report offered not an indictment of the current system and recommendation to overhaul it but a favorable appraisal and recommendation for better enforcement of the existing tax laws. It recommended that the existing system remain intact with only a few minor changes. Predictably, unlike Wells's report, which won praise in distinguished circles, the one authored by Hills was quickly discredited by elite commentators, including by the genteel *North American Review*. The document was written off as "a disappointment . . . the embodiment of all that is mean, petty, and short-sighted in the administration of tax-laws."[99] Wells himself authored a scathing review, explaining that the report's views had never been supported by any "writer of repute (jurist or economist)" and were "difficult to consider . . . from any other standpoint than the ridiculous."[100] The report fully earned these scornful assessments from elite observers because it indeed went far beyond a perfunctory defense of the status quo. The commission's report was a blatantly ideological document not merely in its policy recommendations but in its articulation of a philosophy of taxation and property relations for the commonwealth. Wells and other educated commentators at the time defined taxation as "the taking of private property for public uses," undergirded by the idea that the government in turn reciprocated and provided services for its citizens. Whereas they recognized that a proper tax system was indispensable, they nonetheless conceived of it as a form of "deprivation." They posited that individuals had "instinctive resistance" to taxation, possessing an inherent "antagonism" toward the state in this regard. In trying to overcome this resistance, the state was prone to use "personal inquisition and restraint as is incompatible with a free government."[101] The enforcement of the property tax was a case in point. Its administration threatened liberal institutions, placing the state at odds with the individual liberties of its citizens.

Faced with this framework, Hills was pushed to explain in more general terms what legitimized the urban state's extraction of ever more resources from its citizens.[102] It was in his discussion of these fundamental tenets that he departed most profoundly from the scholarly consensus. The right of the state to tax, Hills explained, is "often supposed to rest on some implied contract, whereby the subject is bound to render some service to the state, as a recompense for the service which the state has rendered him." Citizens are thus assumed to support the state with tax money in return for protections and benefits that the state offers them in return. "In this view the state stands to its citizens in a relation somewhat like that of an insurance company to its policy-holders. Pay me so much money, and I guarantee you so much protection." Hills dismissed this Lockean formulation, which was espoused by leading experts like Thomas M. Cooley.[103] A man's relationship to the state, Hills argued, is fundamentally different from that of a consumer to a provider of services. He is therefore taxed "not to pay the state for its expense in protecting him, and not, in any respect, as a recompense to the state for any service in his behalf." He did so because his membership in society preceded his right to property. He paid taxes "because his original relations to society require it."[104]

Hills's discussion of taxation pushed him to address the question of property itself, which he saw first and foremost as the domain of society, not of individuals: "Cut off from all social relations, a man's wealth would be useless to him. In fact, there could be no such thing as wealth without society." Perhaps inspired by his season of digging for bullion in the mines of California, Hills inserted into his treatise the deeply political observation that "gold and silver to any amount is not wealth till it is put into the hands of some member of society." In the era of the gold standard, the minerals presented themselves to Hills in disenchanted form as malleable instruments in the hands of human society. Political economy more broadly, Hills suggested, was not governed by natural scientific laws but was itself socially produced.[105]

Hills deduced that all individual wealth was thus inseparable and indeed entirely reliant on social prosperity. "But not only are the enjoyment and even the existence of wealth wholly a social creation; not only would they cease entirely if men were only individuals, living each one alone or apart from others," he argued, "but in like manner all social progress gives an increasing value to wealth, and a man's possessions grow in worth as he grows in the intimacy, and perhaps, also, in the intricacy, of his relations to his kind." This view of wealth legitimized the state's demand to tax individuals to the extent that "the true interests of society may require." The "law of [each individual's] own well-being or perfection summons him thus to do."[106] The laws of nature, in this sense, did not pose restrictions but in fact authorized the state to tax citizens to the extent it deemed necessary.

Hills's views dangerously dissented from expert legal doctrine of the period and in themselves caused an uproar.[107] Hills, however, did not leave things at that. Against the position of the two other commissioners (both of whom hailed from the western and more rural part of the state), he included a minority report that elaborated his worldview even further. This minority report provides a glimpse into the political views of urban radicals during this period. Hills not only supported the continuation of the property tax as it existed but also proceeded to push for the extension of the existing system's authority into the domain of civil society, into the cherished sphere of charitable, educational, and religious institutions, which until then had enjoyed a tax-exempt status. This was a particularly sensitive point for the Boston elite, whose cultural authority rested heavily on their grip on the commonwealth's influential civic institutions. Over the first half of the nineteenth century, Boston's merchants and industrialists had endowed these institutions with immense resources. Even as the endowments reached gigantic proportions, estimated at that point at well over $50 million (at a time when a large-sized textile mill was capitalized at less than $1 million), they remained untaxed and were managed by private boards of trustees, purposely insulated from public sentiment. A conservative assessment showed that Boston alone had over $7 million in charitable, literary, and scientific institutions and $11 million in church property. The crown jewel of all elite institutions in the state, Harvard College, had at that point in 1875 an endowment worth nearly $7 million, including vast properties in Boston and in Cambridge.[108] Strapped for tax revenues to support a bold metropolitan development program, these large assets would be obvious resources the government could tap into.

This, however, was not Hills's intent. He meant not to squeeze tax revenue out of these institutions but to modify and broaden their definition of public objectives. Hills proposed that, given the public purpose of those institutions, they ought to be brought under closer government scrutiny. In the case of "literary and charitable groups," Hills explained, the only way to justify the exemption was to demonstrate that those institutions carried out functions that properly belonged to the state. They deserved their special status only if they operated as "agents or instrumentalities of the state, doing the work which but for them the Commonwealth herself must do, and doing it as well and at as little cost as the officers or agents of the government would do it."[109] This interpretation was striking for its expansive definition of government responsibilities. Hills explained that "few will be found who are not ready to admit that it is the duty of the state to provide for the sick in body or in mind, the poor, and all others whose necessities demand that relief which we call 'charity,'—and few who will not agree that among the highest obligations which the Commonwealth owes to her children, is an education limited only by the capacity, the ambition, and the opportunities of each seeker after knowledge." The provision of social aid to those in need and of higher education to those who qualified for it (grammar school and high school education was already nearly universal) were, in this view, not a form of "charity" but the proper responsibilities of the government. They were "duties and obligations" that "belong[ed] to the state, not to any individual or association." Accordingly, the state had the right to choose its agents, oversee their finances, and enforce limits on the exemption: "The state gives immunity from taxation to property used in her service, and it should not be granted in advance of that use."[110]

In essence, Hills argued that the tax exemption gave the state the right to regulate the operation of universities, literary societies, aid organizations, and other civic institutions. Since many of those institutions came into the possession of valuable land and property, the power to police their holdings and potentially tax them had vast implications. Large amounts of property endowed by private donors would be subject to government oversight. How much property did these corporations need to perform their functions? The "state should be the judge," Hills answered, "the question as to the amount of property necessary for the duties to be performed, the efficiency and economy manifested in the work, and the nature and character of the investments, would all be open to legislative inquiry and discretion."[111] The resting of this authority with the legislative branch—in essence defining the regulatory power as inherently a political question, not an executive or legal one—made the proposal even more intensely controversial.

Hills envisioned regulation that would go far beyond the financial operation of those civic bodies. He claimed for the state the right to assess the purpose of a charitable or literary corporation's actions, to decide whether their work was at all desirable: "The state has the undoubted right to know how all who claim to represent her are doing the work they assume to perform. She has an equal right to accept services, and to reject or discontinue them."[112] To facilitate this type of oversight, he called for annual reports to be made to the state's board of education and the board of charities by all institutions requesting tax-exempt status. Hills's position on these issues continued a long line of democratic efforts to assert control over the region's cultural institutions. One notable precursor was the controversies of the 1850s surrounding the campaign to remove Harvard College from the control of what was referred to in those debates as the "dominant sect in Cambridge" and reassert the legislature's control over its governing corporation.[113] The rapid rise in city government spending in the 1870s and 1880s brought such special tax exemptions under ever-stricter scrutiny.

The case of church property was a somewhat different matter, since the Church did not operate at the behest of the state. Hills did not support the full taxation of religious institutions, which would have entirely removed state support for church property. Rather, he proposed a limited exemption that would tax the wealthiest churches and excuse the poorer ones. Hills agreed that the state had no right to police or intervene in religious practices. The exemption in their case was a more passive recognition on the part of the state of the benefits religious organizations provided to the community. Still, as churches' holdings grew at a rapid pace, the exemption became increasingly onerous to the taxpayers, who had to shoulder the fiscal burden. The exemption in some cases was simply not proportional to the benefits that the community as a whole derived. Hills presented a simple calculation. Over the previous two decades, the number of churches in the state increased from 1,475 to 1,764, a 20 percent increase. The valuation of church buildings grew from about $10 million to $24.5 million, a rise of almost 140 percent. The valuation of church property as of 1874 stood at over $30 million. This was a clear indication of the growing wealth of the state's religious organizations.[114]

In Hills's view, the escalating wealth of some congregations was not evidence of their growing utility to society. Rather, their utility stayed constant, even as the lavishness of their facilities rapidly increased. "It requires neither statistics nor argument to prove the extravagance of some of our modern church buildings," he argued. Just as he did not shy away from referring to the capitalists of the state as a distinctive class of taxpayers, Hills was not vague about the congregations he had in mind, focusing his critique on the luxurious churches that had recently emerged in the exclusive neighborhood of Back Bay. It called for special reevaluation of the tax benefit, he explained, "when, within ten years, seven churches are placed within a circle not exceeding a half-mile in diameter, the valuation of which is reckoned by millions."[115] Upon completion, the seven churches in Back Bay, four Unitarian and three Trinitarian, represented an estimated combined value of $2 million. These structures were not open to the great mass of believers; they remained the exclusive domain of a small group. "While all of the public halls are crowded on the Sabbath and Tremont Temple and Music Hall frequently turn away hundreds from their doors, the Back Bay churches are restricted to special congregations, which are usually small and thin." Whereas other congregations, such as Park Street Church, were always crowded, Hills observed, "the Back Bay churches seem to stand aloof from the people and to be as far removed from their hearts as they are separated from them by geographical position."[116] In exempting those churches from taxation, the state was subsidizing not groups providing a public service but insular class institutions, which were removed from the larger population. Hills recommended that any church property valued above $25,000 would be subject to taxation, allowing poor congregations to operate freely, while requiring wealthier ones to contribute to public needs.

Thomas Hills's discussion of tax policy therefore articulated a robust definition of the public sphere and of state power, which quickly attracted sharp criticism. One such criticism, not surprisingly, came from none other than Charles W. Eliot, president of Harvard College, who engaged in the debate to defend the exemption charitable, educational, literary, and religious institutions enjoyed under the existing provisions. Whereas Hills saw the state as primary and the tax-exempt institutions as instruments of the state, Eliot saw government mostly as a hindrance for the purposes of benevolent donors. He concluded that the state must not stand in the way of private benevolence. The state, he explained, would be better served by "promising not to divert to inferior public uses any part of the income of the money which these benefactors devote to . . . noblest public use."[117]

Eliot denied that tax exemption was a form of "state aid," and instead presented it as a wise policy aimed at encouraging private individuals to contribute from their own means to public purposes. He insisted that the common practice of using an appointed board of trustees, rather than a popularly elected body, to manage these institutions, did not hinder the public purpose of the institution: "the mode of administration does not alter the uses, or make the property any less property held for the public." This was a system, advantageous for providing much-needed public services, while limiting the scope of the state, avoiding what Eliot defined as "the vicious tendency to centralization of power in government." In general, he tended to think new sources of revenue would be squandered by government officials. "Give the cities and towns of Massachusetts new resources and instantly they will make new expenditures which will more than absorb these resources." Rather than searching for new revenues, Eliot observed, efforts should be made to address the root cause of the problem—extravagant public spending: "The one real remedy for the evils, which cause the eager search for something new to tax, is reduction of expenditure."[118] In the view of Eliot and his cohort, social needs were better met by private means, not by government.

Overall, faced with a political system that refused to recognize limits to its power of taxation, it is no wonder that elite Bostonians in the decades after the war were increasingly alarmed and exaggerated the severity of their situation beyond all proportion. How much longer, William Minot Jr., former leader of West Roxbury's petitioners against annexation, asked in one typical pamphlet, could he and his peers be expected to live in a city where "the extravagance of public expenditures, and of consequent taxation, seriously embarrasses business" and where "labor of all kinds . . . is almost wholly exempt from taxation and the whole burden is placed on capital"? Existing laws in Massachusetts, he explained, "formed no obstacle to the wholesale appropriation of private property to general public uses." In other words, the tax system was the "most thoroughly democratic system ever devised, if, indeed, it [did] not border on communism."[119] To protect Boston's future prosperity, it was necessary to guarantee that "capital be left as free as possible, and receive every encouragement." This goal, Minot explained, echoing Wells, could best be obtained by "establishing the system of taxing visible property only, or, still better, real estate only, and this, too, under such provisions as would secure an approximation, at least, of the estimated value to the fair market value of the property."[120] The efforts to address the situation from the state legislature had reached a deadlock, but the existing system simply could not be allowed to continue. Business leaders like William Minot Jr. and his son William Minot III looked for other methods to make sure it would not.

CHAPTER THREE

Brahminism Goes West

H enry Davis Minot's untimely death made national news. On a foggy November night in 1890, this member of one of the wealthiest and most prominent New England families was riding the Pennsylvania Central's *Western Express*, sound asleep in the rear of a luxurious Pullman car. When the train slowed down as it approached the town of New Florence, a second train traveling on the line missed a red-light signal in the darkness and crashed into the *Express* from behind, throwing it off the rails. A "scene of indescribable terror ensued," the next day's papers reported. The shrieks and cries of the "panic-stricken" passengers were heard from the blazing coach.[1] A few broke the windows and tried to climb out; others remained buried underneath the wreckage. In all, two passengers lost their lives and eighteen sustained injuries, some of which would "with little doubt . . . prove fatal." Minot died instantly upon contact, "his head being crushed into an unrecognizable mass."[2]

Before long, as information traveled on the nation's telegraph network, word about the accident and the death of the "railroad man and capitalist" reached readers across the land, from Oregon and California to New York and Maine. Minot was thirty-one and had grown up in Boston, the New Orleans *Daily Picayune* explained. "He lived in St. Paul for some time past . . . but came east frequently."[3] Ever since he resigned from the leadership of the Eastern Minnesota Railroad and ended his association with the St. Paul, Minnesota, and Manitoba Railroad, Portland's *Morning Oregonian* added, "there has been much speculation as to whose interest he was working in."[4] Allan Manvel, president of the Atchison, Topeka, and Santa Fe Railroad, revealed himself as Minot's last employer, on whose behalf the young man had secretly relocated to San Francisco. Speaking to the *New York Times*, he said, "I expected him in Chicago to-night. I thought a great deal of that boy for he was only a round, rosy cheeked boy, but with a will power and ability for work that I have rarely seen equaled.

Minot was very bright and witty, but at business he was all business."[5] The tragic irony was not lost on commentators, who noted that since Minot had "done so much to promote railway enterprises, it hardly seems fair that he should have been killed by one of them."[6]

The most intense reaction to Minot's death came not from his home community but rather from the cities of the Old Northwest, where he had his most extensive engagements. "What sad, sad news comes to us today!" Superior's *Daily Leader* mourned, "Cruel blow! Our friend will never more appear in our midst again." St. Paul's *Daily Pioneer* sang Minot's praises as "a gentleman of fine education and unblemished character," whose death came as "a severe shock to his numerous friends in this city."[7] The Chamber of Commerce in Superior debated how best to express the city's grief. Senior member George D. Moulton called for "floral offerings" to be procured for the funeral and delivered by representatives who had already left for Boston on their own accord. W. B. Banks insisted that "it would be a good plan for all members of the chamber to wear a black band on the left arm tomorrow." W. D. Dwyer proposed that "together with all other flags on public buildings," the flag on city hall will "be kept at half-mast until after Mr. Minot's funeral." These steps aimed to ensure that Superior's grief would not be overshadowed by that of any other western city, hopefully preserving the special relationship these men had cultivated with Minot and with his moneyed colleagues in Boston.[8]

The end of the nineteenth century has long been associated with the displacement of established wealth in American life. Richard Hofstadter offered the most eloquent articulation of this pervasive view when he argued that in this period the "newly rich, the grandiosely or corruptly rich" had "edged aside" members of "the old gentry, the merchants of old standing . . . the old-family, college-educated class that had deep ancestral roots" in their communities.[9] It may, therefore, seem odd to find a son of New England of impeccable social credentials traveling so far from Harvard Yard, doing business and making friends in the remote cities of the West. Minot was hardly a crude upstart or new to wealth and privilege. He was nevertheless emblematic of the new geography of American capitalism in the mostly prosperous 1880s. A State Street financier and a self-described expert on railroad properties, he was a student of the stock market first and foremost. He spent much of his career, however, journeying in the vast expanses of the country's western regions. He worked incessantly to expand the scope of Boston investments and to forge the

3.1. Henry Davis Minot, Bostonian man of capital.

Credit: Henry D. Minot, *The Land-Birds and Game-Birds of New England* (New York: Houghton, Mifflin, and Company, 1895), Plate 1.

business connections that made possible a truly continental flow of capital from the Bay State. His life trajectory reveals not only the inner workings of Boston's business elite, highlighting this group's long understated entrepreneurial, energetic, even aggressive role in conquering the West, but also the mobilization of old wealth into new fields of investment as a driving force behind North American economic development in those decades.

Minot's meteoric career took him from his genteel adolescence in suburban Boston to a position as a stock broker and analyst, a financier, and, finally, vice president of one of the largest railroads in North America. Minot and his associates in Boston, like established elites in other eastern cities, did not passively observe the emergence of a continental railroad network as the inexorable unfolding of a technologically determined development. Nor did they readily delegate the supervision of the process to an emerging class of salaried managers. Rather, they embraced continental economic integration as a project of monumental magnitude, fitting for their own time-tested commercial abilities and skills. They came to see themselves as the architects of the emerging corporate-dominated economy, whose very creation rested on their ability to leverage their privileged access to capital and move investments toward bold new business frontiers.

Men like Minot—men of *capital*—became key agents in the formation of the new continental order.[10] As commercial pioneers, they moved through the landscape on trains, steamboats, coaches, and on foot, studying the terrain, inspecting old rail lines and projecting new ones, assessing the potential for future traffic, and evaluating business associates and investment opportunities. This was but half the job. Reliable and up-to-date information about, access to, and close familiarity with the workings of capital markets back east, where the financial resources that facilitated railroad expansion came from, proved equally crucial to this project. Capital flows were controlled not by countless independent economic actors but by financial middlemen such as investment bankers and securities brokers. These middlemen had the ability to purchase entire issues of new securities before "retailing" them to individual investors in their network or community. They made wholesale decisions for large pools of investors and therefore enjoyed immense influence over railroad financing. The ability to effectively wed eastern capital markets to western ventures gave such intermediaries vast power in promoting and managing economic development throughout the continent. Together, these men inaugurated a wave of capital migration of unprecedented scale, from the capital-rich

Atlantic seaboard to capital-poor regions of the Great West, and beyond to Mexico and Canada.

By all accounts, this was an exciting time on State Street in Boston's business district, and the Minots were well situated to partake in the buoyancy on the stock exchange. They were by no means new arrivals to the scene. The family's roots in Massachusetts extended back to the earliest colonial settlement. In the eighteenth century, Stephen Minot (Harvard class of 1730) accumulated a small fortune as a merchant and entered New England's select circles. His son, George Richards Minot (Harvard class of 1778), became involved in the high politics of the commonwealth, serving as the secretary of the convention that ratified the U.S. Constitution. He was also a founding member of King's Chapel and of the Massachusetts Historical Society. Described as too gentle for the rigors of public office, George instead focused on his work as a private counsel, which, as one obituary observed, allowed "others to profit by the soundness of his judgment."[11] This became the family's motto, and George became the first in a dynasty of five generations of Minots, who, starting in 1782, occupied the same downtown office address on Court Street and specialized in the management of wills, trusts, and estates.

The preservation of Bostonian wealth across generations became the Minots' family business, thrusting them into one of the most controversial political and legal questions of the early national period. Most Americans at the time considered the dynastic concentration of wealth to be incompatible with republican institutions. Departing from "Old World" customs that safeguarded the integrity of family estates and passed property (usually land) to a single male heir, they adopted the principle of partible inheritance, which authorized the equal division of property among descendants. Observers expected this practice to divide and subdivide family estates over time, making lasting concentrations of wealth impossible.[12] Alexis de Tocqueville saw partible inheritance as one of the defining features of a democratic society, inexorably "divid[ing], distribut[ing], and dispers[ing] both property and power."[13]

New England's affluent merchants in the early nineteenth century conceived of trusts as an effective way to counteract this democratizing movement. As these men amassed great fortunes, they embraced trusts as a vehicle for preserving accumulated property in consolidated form as it passed to the next generation. Trusts, they thought, would not only keep inherited wealth intact and safeguard it from misuse by descendants, but

3.2. George Richards Minot, founding father, jurist, trustee, and historian of Shays' Rebellion.

Credit: From a portrait by Christian Gullager in possession of the family. Henry Davis Minot Papers, Massachusetts Historical Society. Ms. N-2244.4.

also facilitate more expert investment of the funds over time, allowing heirs to live comfortably off the generated income. Property managed in a trust would not simply remain idle—"locked up in mortmain"—but also not be lost in the blind vagaries of the market.[14] These elite Bostonians thus rejected both the aristocratic emphasis on the preservation of landed estates *and* the unencumbered circulation of property in a competitive marketplace. They instead put their confidence in the sagacious hand of a trustee, who they thought could best mobilize family property as investment capital, allocating the funds to generate income, managing risk, and adapting to changing conditions.

Lawmakers in Massachusetts associated testamentary trusts with feudal tenures and refused to extend to the judiciary the authority to enforce them.[15] It was only through vigorous lobbying efforts by the commonwealth's leading families, most notably through the avid advocacy of Justice Joseph Story, that the legislature finally gave in in the 1820s.[16] The legalization of trusts opened up a set of contentious questions, which the courts answered incrementally over the next several decades: What were the limits to the immunity of trusts from the creditors of improvident heirs? In what cases could trustees deem some uses of the funds inappropriate and thus withhold revenue from the beneficiaries? How long could trusts persist before they would be dissolved? Most fundamentally—and most urgently for the Minots—was the question of the scope of the trustee's discretionary power over investments. The advocates for trusts expected trustees to manage the property more sensibly and more proactively than individual family members. It remained unclear, however, how the trustee's own investment decisions would be regulated, and the extent to which the beneficiaries of the trust would be allowed to challenge those decisions. The issue hinged on the extent to which trustees would be held liable in cases where investments soured or, worse, were completely erased. The pivotal question became what in fact counted as a sound investment in a dynamic and inherently volatile market economy.

The court addressed this question in the landmark case of *Harvard College and Massachusetts General Hospital v. Amory*, which came before the state's Supreme Court in 1829. In his decision, Chief Justice Samuel Putnam reflected on the line that distinguished sober investment from reckless speculation and articulated what became the "prudent man" standard for fiduciaries. The case concerned Jonathan and Francis Amory, who managed the estate of the late Boston merchant John McLean and chose to invest the funds in the shares of two cotton manufacturing corporations. The college and the hospital to which McLean bequeathed the property upon the death of his widow argued that in their zeal to secure high dividends, the Amory brothers had jeopardized the safety of the trust, exposing it to "total loss."[17]

Putnam ruled unambiguously against the plaintiffs. Departing from English precedent that had long considered only certain types of property such as land and government securities to be safe havens, he argued that all forms of property contained a measure of risk. The price of government securities fluctuated with the prospect of war and peace. The value of real estate investment, often "supposed to be as firm as the earth itself," oscillated as much, and sometimes more, than many commercial ventures. "Do what you will," he concluded, "the capital is at hazard." The inescapably precarious state of affairs meant that the dividing line between judicious investment and market exuberance would necessarily remain murky. The trustee's job was therefore "to observe how men of prudence, discretion and intelligence manage their own affairs, not in regard to speculation but in regard to the permanent disposition of their funds, considering the probable income, as well as the probable safety of the capital to be invested."[18] In other words, the court recognized prudence in the marketplace as a profoundly subjective notion, with the balance between the search for high yields and the desire for safety remaining perpetually in flux. There could be no stable definition of prudence in business, no fixed categories of assets or properties that could unambiguously be deemed safe. Prudence rested not on any permanent benchmark but on the ever-shifting disposition of the investment community as a whole. Viewed in this manner, it made sense that investment in cotton manufacturing—a profitable and increasingly widespread investment and yet one that had been uncharted only a few years before—would be considered legally suitable for those who were supposed to be the city's most conservative investors. It likewise made sense that later in the century western railroads in unsettled territories would be deemed legitimate for vigilant trustees, as long as—in a circular type of logic—these investments received the blessing of the investment community as a whole.

The decision in *Harvard v. Amory* drastically widened the discretionary authority of trustees in Boston, making them into key financial intermediaries over the following decades. The ruling both institutionalized and collectivized the management of old wealth. The Minots, and the few other families that specialized in this line of business, came to oversee enormous pools of capital. By the second half of the nineteenth century, it was rumored that "no man in Massachusetts had the management of a larger

3.3. The office of William Minot in Boston from which he managed the very large properties of his clients.

Credit: Minot-Rackemann Family Photographs, Massachusetts Historical Society. Photo. Coll. 136.

amount of trust funds than the elder Mr. Minot." He, by one calculation, held "more property in his own office and in his single control than any financial institution in Boston, and equal in amount to a hundredth part of the assessed value of all the property in the city."[19] Justice Putnam's decision protected trustees from the lawsuits of disgruntled clients in case of losses but also allowed them—indeed impelled them—to manage estates in a dynamic way, always revising, updating, and moving from declining ventures into more promising ones. Over time, the ruling enshrined in law a deep-seated dynamic that drove old Bostonian wealth into new investment frontiers. The Minots embodied this creed. They became known as particularly adept at balancing caution and drive, supplementing "careful prudence" with "great sagacity, very actively used."[20]

This complicated legacy was Henry Davis Minot's heirloom when he was born in 1859. The sixth of seven siblings, he grew up on Woodbourne, the family's thirty-acre estate in Jamaica Plain, a rural district on the city's outskirts. Henry's grandfather, William Sr. (Harvard class of 1802), had acquired the property in 1845 and passed it on to his two sons, George and

William Jr. (both Harvard class of 1836). William Jr., Henry's father, married Katharine Maria Sedgwick, who was from a distinguished New England lineage herself, and the two made Woodbourne their permanent home, even as they continued to maintain residences downtown, first on the fashionable Beacon Street and then on Marlborough Street.[21] Descriptions of Woodbourne, named after an estate in a novel by Sir Walter Scott, portrayed it as a romantic retreat from the city. The property had a view of the Blue Hills, a grove of white pines, and a meadow stretching to Stony Brook. The grounds, Henry's brother longingly recalled years later—after annexation prompted the selling and subdivision of the land into small house lots—were "laid out with so much landscape art and taste, knowledge of the effects, habits, and periods of perfection of trees, shrubs, and flowers, that the effect was harmonious and beautiful throughout the year."[22] Woodbourne testified to the Minots' cultivated aesthetic sensibilities. Like many such rural estates around Boston built in the 1840s and 1850s, it reflected a wistful aristocratic sentiment among elite Bostonians, who sought to transcend crude materialist values and their own commercial origins.[23]

Henry at first appeared to be best suited for a life of leisure, not one of entrepreneurial pursuits. On the estate and in the family's annual summer retreats around New England, he dedicated himself to the study of the natural world as well as to music and poetry. His brother recalled that "the sensitive and imaginative side of [Henry's] nature, showing itself in his musical and poetical talents, his sympathy with nature, and his abundant and caressing affection, held a threatening predominance in his temperament, and many of those who knew him doubted his fitness for the practical side of life."[24] While his older brothers William (Harvard class of 1869) and Robert (Harvard class of 1877) were training to take over the family business, Henry's energies as a teenager mostly went into his interest in ornithology, which took him to practically every forest, brook, and meadow in the region. At age seventeen, his efforts culminated in the comprehensive 450-page guide *The Land-Birds and Game-Birds of New England*, which he wrote and illustrated with drawings from his own fieldwork. The book opened with a plea to end the period's rampant hunting of specimens by amateur naturalists. The Minots, especially William Sr., were avid hunters, but in the case of birds, Henry implored his readers "never to fire a gun" and instead recommended the use of close observation and reference books.[25]

Like his ancestors, Henry Minot proceeded to attend Harvard, where he befriended the young Theodore Roosevelt. They shared a passion for birds and even collaborated on a short publication on the topic.[26] During his first year in Cambridge, Minot developed a severe depression that forced him to withdraw from school. His agony reached its nadir that summer. Seeking medical advice from Dr. Charles F. Folsom, Boston's leading expert on mental illnesses, he described his condition. "I began to lose my powers of absorption and enjoyment," he wrote, "I have developed morbidly . . . I lost my appetite, slept poorly, always waking early, and sometimes lying long awake, became skeptical, took no interest in life, and after long speculation had that forlorn feeling of being lost in infinity." One crucial issue in his mind was his lack of manliness. He confessed, in a letter to a physician, that he "suffered from dislike to the rougher boyish sports and . . . from a certain timidity, and from want of manliness."[27] He was sent to recover at an institution in Litchfield, Connecticut, where he mostly read books and reform magazines like the *Nation*, wrote letters, played piano, painted, and rode horses. The area offered "almost everything that one could ask for," he wrote in boredom after one ride, "except distance and grandeur: These were wanting everywhere."[28]

Minot spent six months at the asylum and showed no sign of improving. Gentlemanly ease in daily life and freedom from worldly concerns seemed only to throw him deeper into his malaise. Relief finally came from an unexpected source. After an aborted attempt to open his own preparatory school, and with his father's assistance, Minot secured employment with the newly established but well-connected brokerage firm of Jackson and Curtis, situated just blocks from the family's downtown office. Charles Cabot Jackson, the senior partner, gave Minot an opportunity to enter the company as a clerk without pay in training to become a stock and bond analyst. Serving a mercantile apprenticeship had long been a popular substitute for a Harvard education among elite Bostonians. Likewise, for many in Minot's generation, the banking and brokerage firm, as one Bostonian recalled, became a "sort of educational institution, to which the Boston gentlemen crowded to secure admission for training their sons."[29] In Minot's case, the timing could not have been more perfect, just as the economy emerged from the depression of the mid-1870s into an almost uninterrupted, decade-long prosperity (before plunging again in the 1890s). Entering work in the fall of 1881, he seized the opportunity and launched into the new career with a renewed sense of purpose. Within months, he was a changed man.

"My days ship along pretty pleasantly," Minot reported to his father that summer in an upbeat letter unimaginable a few months earlier. "I am at the office by nine or half past, and work till tired, usually about three, when I take the 3:15 for Woodbourne, the piazza, and the tennis ground." He clearly liked his new environment, and he dedicated himself to his new position. He considered Jackson and Curtis to be, in his words, "among the best established and most respected of all the younger firms (the two chief partners are I suppose about 35 years of age) . . . its members . . . thoroughly gentlemen, with whom intercourse is easy and pleasant." He plunged himself into his new responsibilities, reporting that "the immediate and prospective movements of the market have become to me a very absorbing study." "Mr. Jackson keeps telling me it is hot and that I work too hard," he wrote, "but I am much interested in making the office a bureau of information, and in all the problems that come up."[30]

A few months later, Minot himself was in need of a private corner in the office that would give him some measure of confidentiality and in need of a clerical assistant to free him for the more analytical aspects of the job. He now made a salary and used his knowledge to invest some of his own money. Letters from Minot to his father, who eagerly awaited investment advice, began to be filled with analyses of individual stocks and of the market as a whole. The details of Minot's letters reflected his new way of imagining the continent through the prism of the stock market. Exuding optimism, Minot reported in the summer of 1882 that over the first six months of that year 4,415 miles of railroad had been built, 9,477 miles were under construction, and 3,356 miles were "surveyed, located, or projected." The numbers seemed staggering "but need not, I think, give any alarm now." "We have very reasonable assurance of a good crop (in some ways, magnificent), and the prospect of a demand for it abroad," another letter noted. "Except in the event of a specific disaster, I foresee no reasons for any decided check or set back." Upon "careful study," Minot recommended the Northern Pacific Railroad to his father as a good investment, boasting of his increasing knowledge of the ins and outs of railroad investments: "Its completion is looked for within a year. . . . To cover 6% on the Common, about $10,000 gross earnings a mile will be needed. Last year the Atchison earned $6,500 and the Union Pacific about $13,000. The Preferred Stock (8%) is already owed its dividends, which may reasonably be expected next year. The stock now is nearly 90, and might then be 115 to 120. The Common Stock runs from 38 to 43 points below, now almost touching 50. . . . Should you trust my discretion, I should sell at 55 (or if the market really turned), and trust to buying back . . . if a second plunge should seem desirable."³¹ Minot's father was clearly proud of his son's recent recovery and success. He urged him to continue to "accumulate knowledge and experience . . . they are your best capital." "I shall be much interested in your conclusions," he added.³²

Minot's responsibilities included monitoring changes in the price of railroad securities and estimating future trends through careful assessment of a long list of parameters or, as he put it, "determining the probabilities and the opportunities of the market."³³ He evaluated the performance of particular railroad stocks, taking into consideration internal company issues such as revenue per mile, pace of construction, level and structure of debt, possession of government land grants, quality of management, and ability to raise additional capital. External factors such as the prospects for settlement and growth in a particular region, which were usually connected with agriculture and the availability of natural resources, also figured into the assessments. Clearly, each parameter entailed endless complications and involved multiple unknown or unreliably known components. Who could tell for certain the completion date of a particular railroad line under construction; which might encounter engineering difficulties, legislative "meddling," or labor "unrest"; or the continuing access to cheap coal that a particular line enjoyed; or the quality of a crop in some western county, even if the rainy season seemed favorable, not to mention its ability to compete with Indian or Russian harvests in the world market? Despite the clear shortcomings of any prediction, Minot was apprehensive about seeing himself as a speculator and distanced himself from the worst connotations of that label. Echoing Justice Putnam's language more than fifty years earlier, Minot explained that he concerned himself with the "problem of investments, and of speculation . . . [a term] which I use in a restricted, respectable sense. [However], in no place are the lines more difficult to draw." He insisted that his work did not involve any "rash or dishonorable business."³⁴

Indeed, brokerage firms exerted vast amounts of time and energy to gather, process, and evaluate information. Despite the efforts of firms like Jackson and Curtis to base investments on accurate information, however, the project of constructing a continental railroad system remained fraught with contingencies and difficulties. It proceeded less like a top-down projection of sound logic than an ongoing battle to make sense of a bewildering array of factors and forces that defied sweeping generalizations. Minot spent his days trying to grapple with the maps and figures that flooded his desk, in a desperate effort to absorb the multiple issues that were involved. In trying to make sense of such an intricate and dynamic process, Minot felt like a participant in a monumental trajectory of unprecedented proportions. "The great difficulty it seems to me in comprehending the bigness of the day is in multiplying one's personal experience of weights and forces to an adequate conception of great proportions. I sometimes think this necessary stretching of the individual mind, is a large factor in to-day's progress of humanity."[35] The historic scale of the project and the truly heroic analytical powers it demanded infused the enterprise with an exhilarating sense of grandiosity.

Minot's career took a significant leap forward in the spring of 1883, when Jackson and Curtis sent him on a three-month western expedition.[36] This was the first of many such trips he embarked on with the goals of inspecting properties where Bostonians had staked their capital and surveying opportunities to broaden their investments. The ability to undertake such a journey across the continent and back was itself derived from the expanding scope of economic undertakings by eastern businessmen, who became the first generation of American entrepreneurs to move freely throughout the continent and do so many times over. The first nationwide railway guides and hotel directories started appearing in the 1870s, replacing the previous generation of handbooks that focused on single cities. Equipped with such pocket-sized guides, Minot could depart from Boston with an indefinite itinerary and still navigate large swaths of territory with fairly good information about transportation and about adequate lodging facilities along the way. He could calculate the length of each leg of the trip, plan for train transfers (sometimes telegraphing in advance to reserve a sleeping berth), and even pick hotel accommodations for the night.[37] Using telegrams, he could also stay in regular communication with his employers and his family, to whom he also sent weekly letters describing his whereabouts. With some measure of confidence, he could give his contacts in the East the city and hotel where he could be reached.

Despite the relative ease of going on such expeditions, it is important not to overstate the perfect operation of this developing system of travel and communication. Minot traveled during the peak years of railroad construction, which meant service was incomplete in many of the regions he journeyed to. This made his trips erratic and at times strenuous, which Minot liked to emphasize in his letters. He was often drawn to newly completed lines and to the more peripheral, treacherous parts of the railroad network, and so his travel arrangements spanned the full range from luxury cars to steamboats, carriages, horseback, and walking. Lodging and food could also vary from first-class hotels in the big cities to quite miserable shacks along the way, from elaborate meals to road provisions and some fruit.[38] The schedule of trains was routinely disrupted, and accidents were not uncommon. Minot's letters home could be expected to arrive with regularity, but that was less true of letters to him on the road.

Ultimately, the single most important factor that made such business expeditions successful was not new technology but the assistance of western hosts, many of them transplants from the East, who welcomed powerful visitors like Minot with open arms, providing guidance and information at every turn. His experience on those trips (at age twenty-four) reveals the superior position that he held over the general managers of railroad lines and other western businessmen in his capacity as an agent of eastern financiers. In an era of rapid railroad construction, access to capital translated into the ability to control expansion policy, which represented the most important strategic decisions for railroad corporations.[39] The western executives and businessmen Minot dealt with on his journeys understood this hierarchy and behaved accordingly. From Minot's copious notes and reports, it is clear that he did not settle for a secondary role but rather saw himself as a planner and a leader in the creation of the railroad system. He attended to the minutest of details along the way, recording the wide range of factors that might affect the profitability of the railroad and its ability to expand successfully. In his memoranda, the quality of the railroad's management was one relevant issue, and not the most important one, alongside numerous others.

Launching his one-man western campaign, Minot departed from Boston in early April of 1883. He first stopped in New York and then continued on the newly constructed Nickel-Plate Road to Chicago, where he stayed for several days. While there, he traveled along with a group of Bostonian brokers to visit the town of Pullman. He enthusiastically approved of the town's reformist experiment in urban planning and its reflection of its founder's noblesse oblige: "It is a place of more meaning than any I have yet seen . . . product of one man's fertility, a whole township beautifully built . . . I wish I could know the measure of the influence of all this elegance and art, thus thrown into [the] daily life" of the five thousand workers. He continued with the same party to Kansas, spending a week around Kansas City, Topeka, and Atchison, where Boston capitalists had already entrenched themselves since the war. Conditions on this part of the trip were superb. Traveling in an official private car, courtesy of "various railroad corporations," Minot wrote home that "the luxury is magnificent. The parlor, furnished with lounges and cozy chairs, is in the rear, with a glass back to look out from, and wide windows. Meals are a la Delmonico—the society [of fellow brokers] was pleasant."[40] From Kansas, he continued on the Kansas Pacific to Colorado, visiting Denver and several mining towns in the Rockies, accompanied by David C. Dodge, the general manager of the Rio Grande system. Next, he continued west to Salt Lake, Ogden, and on to Stockton, California, where he paused for a few days to travel to Yosemite. It was the middle of May when he arrived in San Francisco, and from there, by a steamboat up the Columbia River, to Portland.

"My opportunities here for a wide exploration of the Northwest have become so favorable that I cannot sacrifice them to my home affections and desires," he wrote his father at the end of May. "I am undertaking much more investigation than was ever intended in dispatching me hither." Upon arrival in Portland, he was received by Charles H. Prescott and Paul Schultz, the manager and the land agent, respectively, of the Oregon Railway Navigation Company. Minot explained that the two executives' help, together with the letters of introduction he had brought with him from Boston, "put me in the way of learning much that is worth knowing."[41] He surveyed Portland and continued south on the Oregon and California Railroad to the Willamette, Umpqua, and Rogue valleys. He then moved north to Tacoma, Puget Sound, and up to Seattle and across the border to Victoria, British Columbia.

All along the way, Minot did not limit himself to the perspective of a passive visitor and recorded every relevant detail. It was his firsthand observations of these details that made them reliable and valuable back home. He inspected the quality of construction of each railroad and its access to terminal facilities. He tried to anticipate the lines that would soon need to be expanded and improved. Which railroads were still ill equipped for heavy freight? Where would wooden trestles need to be replaced with iron ones? Which local line would become a through line or even a trunk line? Minot learned much about the climate and agriculture of the different regions. What counties in the Northwest were too cold for corn and grapes but perfect for grain? How was Kansas livestock different from Dakota livestock, and why was one of the breeds more expensive to raise or cheaper to transport? How would sandstorms or heavy snow affect maintenance costs of the engines and rails? Topographical conditions influenced settlement patterns and determined the costs of railroad construction and operation. Where would bridges and tunnels be needed for a new line north of Portland, and how quickly could they be completed? Which town had the better prospects for growth, Farmington or Lewiston? How would elevation affect energy costs of one line, and how would it compare to the competition?

In his free time during long hours on the train, as the landscapes of the West flew by, Minot translated much of this raw knowledge into financial terms, trying to estimate costs of construction, expansion, and maintenance. He plugged the figures into a projected ledger to see if it could be balanced. The information he recorded about the climate, the quality of the soil, the density and pace of settler movement, or the amount of land brought under cultivation was factored in to evaluate local and through traffic both for passengers and for freight, which determined revenue. The features of the terrain (the need for bridges or tunnels), the proximity to cheap coal, and pending congressional action in removing Indian tribes boiled down to the expected expenditure. Minot's experience allowed him to assess a railroad company's ability to raise capital through bond issues back east. The company's present financial condition and its ability to mortgage existing properties against new debt figured into the rates of interest and the quarterly payments that would have to be made to bondholders. The capacity of a railroad to make the payments made the difference between a viable development and one that quickly descended into bankruptcy.

Heading east from Portland to Walla Walla and the Great Columbia Plain, travel conditions significantly worsened. "Yesterday I drove thirty miles across country," he wrote as he pulled into the town of Dayton in Washington Territory, "the fine dust was saturating . . . induc[ing]in the afternoon a little shower, and in the night a heavy one, [but I expect] this afternoon my stage ride . . . to be pleasant."[42] He continued across the northern plains, making stops in Pomeroy, Spokane, Lewiston, Farrington, Missoula, Deer Lodge ("Montana air is delicious and not as yet too warm"), Helena, Billings, and Moorhead. He had intended to spend June back in Boston, but his own diligence kept delaying his return. "I am given opportunities every day for gaining knowledge that is worth sacrifice," he explained. "Here a chance to meet a well-informed cattle-dealer, there a chance to be escorted over some of Dakota's finest farms, and again a chance to be with some official, all interpose themselves between myself and home, besides all the country and important points that I wish to examine."[43] It seemed like everywhere people were eager to host and entertain him. "Yesterday I was seized upon by an energetic citizen of the young city of Fargo," he related to his father. "Having learned from some traveler that I was going over the Northern Pacific," the man "insisted on driving me about town and introducing me to the mayor, the chief banker, the chief editor, and to some other prominent men, as a representative of Boston's Capital!" The arrivals in Duluth and St. Paul marked a return to better accommodations. While there, he also became acquainted with James J. Hill, the president of the St. Paul, Minneapolis, and Manitoba Railroad, a personal connection that would have great significance for him. He then returned home and composed comprehensive reports about his findings.

Minot did not wait long to leave home again. Before he even regained his footing in Boston, he was called on by the president of the Flint, Pere, and Marquette Railroad, who wanted to attract a new infusion of capital and pleaded with Minot to visit Michigan: "[President William W.] Crapo expressed a desire to have Boston represented and more largely interested in his road. J[ackson] and C[urtis]'s interest is chiefly in the Common Stock, but if my report is favorable, an increased holding of the Preferred Stock among our customers, or in our own hands, may ensue."[44] Soon enough, in September, Minot was deep in the forests of northern Michigan, enjoying the benefit of the comfortable Director's Car, riding through East Saginaw, Harrison, and to Marquette.[45] Upon his return to Boston, he reported favorably that the road "gives abundant evidence of great recent improvement": "The ballasting, the ties, and the 'lay' . . . are excellent. A good deal of trestle work needs to be filled up, several bridges to be rebuilt (some with stone and iron to replace wood), and some grades to be economically reduced." He estimated the costs of those and other necessary improvements. Management was competent and reliable, "the general officers . . . thoroughly interested in efficiency of maintenance and of operation, and there seems no reason to anticipate any unwise expenditure." The State of Michigan did not threaten hostile legislation or regulation. Overall, Henry determined that "certain extensions within five years, for the protection of territory, the enlargement of independence, or the increase of profitable business, may be reckoned on with some confidence."[46]

These first western journeys enhanced Minot's reputation in Boston and nurtured his self-confidence. They had taught him a great lesson, which he was not shy about sharing with his colleagues, namely, the power that firsthand knowledge brought with it: "I now feel so strongly the superiority of being a field naturalist rather than a closet naturalist that I am much inclined to hold my tongue about the properties that I have only studied in my office work."[47] Signaling Minot's transformation from an ornithologist to a financier, this principle continued to guide him in his career as he continued to insist on firsthand inspections of railroads and other investments. Furthermore, if he had once yearned for "distance and grandeur," his wish was certainly granted. Traveling far beyond the New England landscapes of his childhood and adolescence, he embraced the empowering role of Boston's business envoy and became comfortable in all corners of the continent.

The flow of Boston capital pushed beyond the borders of the United States, and so did Minot's journeys. His next major assignment, in the spring of 1884, sent him to inspect the Mexican Central Railway. Stretching for 1,225 miles from El Paso to Mexico City, the railroad was a Massachusetts-chartered corporation, organized under recent legislation that authorized the formation of corporations for the purpose of constructing and operating railroads in foreign countries. Controlled by the same Bostonian investment group that owned the Atchison, Topeka, and Santa Fe Railroads, the company's principal office was in downtown Boston, as were the residences of its president and the majority of its directors (nine of thirteen).[48] The railroad became the single largest foreign-owned company in Porfirio Diaz's Mexico and the largest private enterprise in the country.[49] As was the custom in many places in Latin America, the company enjoyed generous "concessions" from the Mexican government, including complete exemption from local and national taxes for fifty years, protection from duties on imported construction materials, and a hefty subsidy for every mile built.[50]

The power of investors in Boston to control economic development in Mexico, wrest enormous benefits from the Mexican government, and structure trade on favorable terms was not perceived in Boston as in any way coercive. The completion of the first phase of construction was heralded by the *Boston Advertiser* as a benevolent endeavor: "Not the desire for territory, not fanatical zeal, nor the hope of pillage, inspires the movement of today. Not only are the swords beaten into ploughshares and the spears into pruning hooks, but the cannons are rolled into railroad iron and spun into telegraph wires. The new-comer brings his treasure with him and lays it through the mountain passes and plateaus of Mexico, asking only a share in the prosperity he seeks to establish."[51] In contrast to earlier invasions, elite Bostonians thought of their engagements in Mexico as entirely founded not on an imbalance of power but on transformative cutting-edge technologies, altruistic financial investment, and mutually beneficial free trade.

Minot was one of the first envoys from Boston to travel on the railroad. No longer with Jackson and Curtis, he now worked on behalf of Lee, Higginson, and Company, the financial home of the Calumet and Hecla copper mines and by then one of the two largest investment banks in Boston. Minot was at the helm of a party of three, with a private first-class car, fitted for this particular journey and designed to make them comfortable and independent. "The number of persons put in motion to equip us," he reported from Topeka, where they stopped for two days of preparation, "makes me very sensible of the gravity of my work." On the trip from Topeka to El Paso and into Mexico, sitting on the open platform in the rear of the car, he enjoyed the "delicious spring air of the Southwest, gazing over the irrigated fields of the Pueblo Indians to the snow peaks beyond, or noting the gay Indian dresses, flocks of cranes, . . . and other interesting bits of landscape." Minot was excited by the novelty of the trip and eager to come to "know of what I meanwhile guess at."[52]

The expedition proved much more difficult than had been expected. Minot based himself in Mexico City and began weekly excursions to remote districts east and west of the Mexican Central's trunk line. Among other places, he explored el Salto, Guanajuato, Zacatecas, Jalpa, Córdoba, Cuernavaca, Morelia, and Fresnillo.[53] He was experienced in the work of gathering information about regional prospects for economic development. The party's daily life consisted of "calls on station agents; of interviews and correspondence with merchants, manufacturers, miners, farmers, and travelers; of topographical surveys, railroad inspections, and so on, through an active round of duties."[54] This routine was the same as in his previous travels, but it proved more complicated to carry out south of the border. When forced to leave the comfort of their private car, the group discovered that lodging conditions did not match American standards. Minot found the food adequate but complained about bedbugs inside his mattress: "In a Mexican hotel, one cannot have a bed to himself; the permanent lodgers are always there."

Political conditions in Mexico became a more substantial obstacle. At first, Minot dismissed the risk of rebel forces. "Should there be any occasion for self-protection," he assured his father, "I am in a position to secure it." Fierce opposition to Diaz outside of the capital was all too real, and Minot started to take various precautions and avoided unnecessary interaction with the local population. The governor of Cuernavaca, who lavishly entertained Minot, attached a military escort to the party, which Minot attributed to hospitality, an expression of "Spanish politeness . . . they are to be not guards, but guides." Minot was genuinely afraid for his life, but he was determined to complete his mission. Luckily, the worst act of real violence against his party was a minor act of sabotage by the local population when rebel forces placed a rock on the railroad tracks. The engine hit the rock and was derailed, tumbling to its side (according to Minot: "lying there piteously like a wounded bull"). The passenger cars fortunately remained standing. The train was not moving at full speed, having just left the station, and a worse accident was avoided. After that, Minot could not wait to complete his duties there. "How cheerfully shall I look upon Mexico when it lies behind me!"[55]

One of the foremost dilemmas that hovered over Minot's visit to Mexico was the advisability of constructing branch lines for the Mexican Central Railway. The Bostonian investors prioritized the trunk line from El Paso to Mexico City, where the Mexican line connected across the border with the Atchison, Topeka, and Santa Fe Railway. This first phase of construction, which made the Mexican Central into a tributary of an American railroad and provided access to populated urban centers, was completed within the company's first four years. The construction of branch lines— shorter lines that would serve particular regions and feed traffic into the railroad's main line—proceeded at a much slower pace. The first feeder lines extended to silver mining zones that offered quick and assured profits. Non-mining branch lines were built to only two agricultural regions in the west and north. This sparse feeder network meant that trains carried only freight that could be accessed directly, which was normally confined to sites located less than ten miles from the road. Like other railroads in Latin America, the Mexican Central therefore lacked depth and density of traffic at the regional level, limiting its overall impact on the Mexican economy.[56]

Minot's report reflected the perspective of the investors and warned that the construction of branches "may easily prove a most unjust financial burden to the Main Line."[57] He was pessimistic about the potential for a rise in the volume of traffic. Conventional metrics such as "gross income per mile" showed that the Mexican Central compared unfavorably to that of the Atchison, Topeka, and Santa Fe. Provincial towns had a miniscule manufacturing base. Minot cited one example, the city of Leon, which was "reputed to have over 100,000 inhabitants, represents less industrial activity than many a railroad town of 5,000 people in the United States." The "general poverty of the people" meant that they were "scarcely consumers at all," which was similarly a "serious drawback to the development of traffic."[58] It seemed perfectly judicious for him to affirm the prevailing view that further construction would produce excess capacity and hurt the overall profitability of the Mexican Central.

Minot's judgment against the development of short branch lines was shared by other American railroad entrepreneurs in Mexico. This was not merely a financial issue but also a legal and political one. The construction of regional lines proved exponentially more difficult than building trunk lines under the auspices of the national government. Land titles in the provinces were less secure and legible to outsiders, who could never be certain as to whose cooperation needed to be secured. Construction efforts easily became entangled in legal disputes with local authorities, who were less consistently friendly toward the Americans than the national government was. Large rural landowners and urban populations often resisted the railroad's encroachments, which disrupted established trade routes, favored some locales over others, and flooded the Mexican market with cheap American goods.[59]

These circumstances meant that routes to Mexico's provincial areas remained underbuilt, leaving the majority of the population to use dirt roads.[60] The patterns of railroad construction instead tended to favor the export of American goods into major Mexican cities and the importation into the United States of Mexican primary commodities, primarily minerals. These patterns of trade across the border indeed increased rapidly between 1880 and 1900.[61] With these priorities in mind, Minot pointed to the strategic significance of the main trunk line and predicted its continued viability. "In the event of any outbreak or revolution," he explained to his audience back east, "the main line of the Mexican Central will be one of the most important properties for the Government to defend, and for insurgents to attack." Investors, however, could rest assured that the Mexican government would protect American interests. "Diaz . . . being familiar with revolutions . . . understands thoroughly how to deal with them."[62]

The St. Paul, Minneapolis, and Manitoba Railroad marked the next phase and the apex of Minot's career. The Manitoba, as it was commonly referred to, had a rocky beginning before his arrival. The railroad had been reorganized in 1879 out of the ruins of its predecessors, the St. Paul and Pacific. The territorial government chartered the company in 1856 and endowed it with generous land grants as part of an effort to build up regional transportation. Those initial assets allowed the company to raise capital in New York, London, and Amsterdam. For the first twenty years of its existence, however, settlement in the region continued to lag behind optimistic projections, and traffic remained insufficient to support debt payments. The company's financial condition thus remained tenuous, and it fell into bankruptcy and receivership in the 1870s. Prospects turned for the better in June of 1878 when a new group of investors renegotiated the firm's debt (freeing the company from burdensome interest payments, largely at the expense of the Dutch bondholders) and acquired the property, giving it new life. As the national economy rebounded from a prolonged slump at the end of the decade, the railroad controlled prosperous territories of increasingly dense settlement. Standing at a key traffic junction, it linked Minnesota's urban centers to the state's agricultural heartland and connected north of the border to the wheat markets of Winnipeg.[63]

Like the railroad network more generally, the development of the Manitoba rested on an axis of investment that connected East and West. Under the new ownership, two men assumed key positions in the company: President James J. Hill, a St. Paul entrepreneur and a member of the new ownership group, and Vice President John S. Kennedy, a New York banker who had helped broker the acquisition and gained an ownership stake in the company. Although the two men were usually a thousand miles apart, the collaboration between them worked remarkably well. Hill oversaw the railroad's operation and expansion into the Northwest. Kennedy acted as the company's financial agent back east. Hill's construction projects and acquisition of local lines proceeded successfully, enjoying the favorable fiscal foundation that Kennedy provided as he marketed the company's bonds to investors in New York.[64] Between 1879 and 1883, the synergy between the two turned the Manitoba into one of the major railroads in the

Great Plains. The company's miles of rail had more than doubled from 500 to more than 1,200. Its workforce had expanded to 5,800 employees, and it was in possession of a growing fleet of locomotives, cars, and stations. It had evolved from a local railroad to a prominent regional system.[65]

The two leaders of the Manitoba faced a potential crisis when the Canadian investors turned their attention to the Canadian Pacific and began to sell blocks of their holdings on the open market. The company's ability to raise additional capital relied on the long-term stability of the stock and on the reputation of the stockholders, both of which were threatened by the dispersal of ownership. To ensure the continued success of the railroad, Hill and Kennedy searched for a reputable group of investors who could purchase the Canadians' shares and enter the company as large stockholders. They identified the Bostonian leaders of the Chicago, Burlington, and Quincy Railroad as potential partners who would not only bring in the necessary capital and hold the stock long term but, if friendly to the Manitoba's interest, could also provide their system with a connection into Chicago. The confidential negotiations with the Boston group, headed by John Murray Forbes and Charles Elliot Perkins of the Burlington in addition to Henry Lee Higginson, continued for two years, concluding in the summer of 1885 with an agreement between the parties. Under the agreement, the Bostonians acquired, as a first step, 20,000 shares of Manitoba stock, or about 10 percent of the company. The Bostonians wanted two seats to represent their interest on the board of directors but settled for the time being for one director who would also serve as vice president. They chose Henry Minot to be that person. At the end of August, he relocated to St. Paul to assume his new position.

Minot's selection was a reward for his catalytic role in the consummation of the deal. Over the previous year, he had been working at his father's office but continued to inspect western railroads for Boston's financiers. In 1885, he conducted a thorough investigation of the Manitoba.[66] His favorable report was circulated to the parties involved and helped ramp up support for the transaction in Boston. Minot followed up with direct correspondence with Forbes, Higginson, and Perkins to answer questions and clarify details. In addition to an assessment of the property itself, he offered information about power relations within the firm, other investor groups who might make competing offers, propitious timing for the final negotiations, and prospects for future increases in holdings (possibly to a "controlling interest").[67] He enthusiastically urged them to move ahead with the deal and received a broker's fee per share as a reward when it eventually went through.

The Manitoba could not be a more different railroad from the Mexican Central, highlighting the divergence between development patterns north and south of the Mexican border. The Manitoba was also fundamentally different from the transcontinental Northern Pacific, which was its chief rival in the region.[68] Unlike in the case of the Mexican Central, where branch lines seemed to undermine the financial viability of the main trunk line, the Manitoba's expansion in the early 1880s proceeded via "branch[ing] about generally."[69] The road reached into regions in Minnesota, Manitoba, Wisconsin, and Dakota Territory with multiple and relatively short lines— Alexandria to Barnesville, Morris to Brown's Valley, Breckenridge to Durbin, Grand Forks to Ojata, to name only a few. This regional focus allowed the Manitoba to foster settlement and in turn tap into heavy and profitable traffic from the wheat regions of the Northern Plains. While the resources of the Northern Pacific were perpetually worn thin by its costly campaign to expand west to the Pacific Coast through sparsely settled territories, the Manitoba's entrenchment in the lakes region and the Upper Mississippi valley put it on a much firmer financial footing. This foundation provided the means for gradual expansion west, from Dakota into Montana and beyond in later years.[70]

In his new setting in St. Paul, Minot began to assume executive responsibilities as the second vice president of the Manitoba. The transition from a financial to a managerial role seemed to him a perfectly natural one. Financial imperatives dictated a constant search for order, system, control, and accountability within the corporation. Ownership and management did not seem at odds but rather fully aligned. "My chief usefulness here at present," he reported, "seems likely to be in the way of organizing . . . hitherto the administration has been unmethodical and insufficient; with needless friction and irregularity."[71] Minot took on administrative tasks and authored the company's "Code of Organization." Aiming to rationalize corporate operations, the new code delineated the functions of the various departments, the relations between them, and channels for the authorization of expenditure. It also strengthened the requirements for reporting and record keeping.[72] A financier in search of profit rather than a salaried technocrat, Minot nevertheless championed managerial principles and efficiency within the bureaucracy of the firm.[73]

No less important than promoting orderly business operations was Minot's task of keeping his associates in Boston informed of developments within the company in addition to scoping out opportunities for investment in other western ventures. Beyond regular mail and telegraph communication, he now played the role of host to eastern financiers who came west to study the property. After one ten-day trip over the road, he reported that he "had great pleasure in the companionship of Tucker Burr" of the Boston brokerage firm Peters and Parkinson (soon to be Parkinson and Burr). A few months later, an even more distinguished delegation arrived, composed of Forbes, Perkins, and two other directors of the Chicago, Burlington, and Quincy. The party traveled a total of about 1,600 miles, and on one of the new extensions of the system reached the "verge of civilization," the town of Minot, North Dakota, recently named after Henry. "It would shock the quiet dignity of my forefathers—the use and advertisement of their name for an ungodly encampment on the Northwest plains," Minot wryly commented. "It is to be regretted that the prohibition party has so very light a vote in the new Garden of Paradise."[74]

Over the next few years, as he permanently established himself in the old Northwest, Minot developed a strong allegiance to the Manitoba. He was enthusiastic about further expansion of the railroad across the high plains in Dakota and Montana territories that would allow the company to diversify its freight beyond wheat to include livestock, wool, minerals, and timber. He decried the size of the Blackfoot Indian Reservation that stood in the way of this growth. He explained that the "great Indian Reservation" had become "the Promised Land" for the Manitoba. "A tract of twenty-four million acres, or nearly forty thousand square miles, given over by the Government to a band of four or five thousand Indians, who probably have not as many acres under cultivation." Writing from the mouth of the Marias River, the site in 1870 of one of the worst massacres of Indians by the U.S. Army, he expressed little doubt that this land would soon be "thrown open," allowing the railroad to connect across it and reach the Rockies.[75]

But like other eastern transplants who found a new home in the West, Minot's connections in Boston were never attenuated. His mere presence on the board, coupled with his firm faith in the future of the railroad, facilitated a gradual increase in stock holding in Boston. By 1888, the Boston interest in the company stood at 65,000 shares out of 200,000. The Bostonians now occupied two of the seven seats on the board of directors. The following year, they gained yet a third seat as Minot was joined by his brother William Jr. and by William H. Forbes. Ownership in Boston spread beyond a narrow group of investors to a large number of families. Members of the eminent families of Forbes, Higginson, Cabot, Lawrence, and others owned stakes in the line. Henry Minot's father controlled 6,500 shares, and he held them in trust for sixty-three estates under his management, including those of members of the Thayer, Lee, Appleton, Perkins, Gardner, and Coolidge families, to list a few prominent names.[76] Under the management and oversight of Henry Minot and his father, and in accordance with the doctrine of prudence articulated by Justice Putnam, those families mobilized their savings—earned over generations of entrepreneurial activity in trade and industry—into lucrative, cutting-edge investments, keeping their portfolios competitive and earning them remunerative dividends. Rather than eroding over generations, capital that had been saved in earlier decades helped finance the railroad boom and western economic development of the late nineteenth century.

Minot's position reflected the formation of a crucial alliance that shaped continental economic growth. Within this alliance, the axis that guided the flow of capital across the continent also mediated between social and regional differences, bringing together the established elites of eastern cities and rising westerners of no social pedigree. The union of interests was celebrated and shored up at numerous meetings and private gatherings. On one expedition in preparation for a new trunk line from the lakes region to the Rockies, to cite one illustrative example, Minot and two visiting Manitoba directors from New York, Samuel Thorne (a banker and financier whose family credentials surpassed even those of Minot) and Smith Weed (adviser to former governor and Democratic presidential candidate Samuel J. Tilden), could be found mingling with Montana's rugged leadership. Members of the local Board of Trade in Helena, whose fortunes would be secured if the line terminated in their town, hosted an event to woo the eastern visitors. Minot sardonically characterized it as a gathering of "some two hundred distinguished citizens, to drink about two hundred bottles of wine, and listen to about two hundred speeches, more or less." Minot noted his misgivings about this type of social mixing, explaining to his father that "it shows the strangeness of life that I, with my temperament, and bringing up, and associations, should be knocking about among the Rocky Mountains, bunking with strange bed-fellows, and eating the uncouth victuals of the hardy mountaineers."[77]

It is not difficult to decipher the general tone of such festive evenings. Cities like Helena vied for eastern capital, and the local business community used any opportunity to showcase their economic potential. "Helena is a city of boundless possibilities," one publication by the local Board of Trade explained. Over the course of two decades, it had "been metamorphosed from a rude mining camp into a metropolitan city." The town's population had indeed increased from 3,600 in 1880 to about 13,000 by 1890 (the Board rounded the number up to 20,000). Future prospects, however, were impossible to assess with any precision, which gave the Board license to greatly exaggerate. Montana, in their view, was no less than "an empire to be," and Helena, "with the vast country tributary to it; with its enterprising business men; with its economical but progressive city government . . . cannot be stopped from taking the place to which it aspires—the leading city in the Northwest." If there was any doubt, members of the Board pointed out that, "Eastern capitalists have become aware of the advantages Helena offers for investment and are placing their capital there."[78] Businessmen who questioned the manifest destiny of the town risked being left out of a bona fide bonanza.

Minot learned how to overcome qualms he might have had about social intercourse with men of questionable backgrounds. He adapted to his newfound intermediary role, most notably in his relationship with Hill, his boss, who came from a modest background. Observing from up close the American entrepreneur who rose from rags to immense riches, the scion of Boston's old wealth found a lot to admire, even as he never questioned his own superiority. "He is a first rate type of the American pioneer," Minot wrote in a moment of reflection. "His start in life I imagine was without any considerable advantage of birth or breeding, but he had in him a native, original force that backed by a tremendous physique and by a rough strong intellect and by ready shrewdness of observation and action, has promoted him to the front rank of practical success." There was always the risk of excess embodied in such a man, who was "undoubtedly . . . self-absorbed and over-reaching," but being "good hearted . . . and remarkably temperate in all his ways of life," he had redeeming qualities as well. There was always more than a touch of condescension in Minot's view of Hill: "His quickness to see everything about him, and the meaning of it, is very pleasing. And he has tasted, relished & digested a good deal outside of business and home-life; and surprises me now and then by a common sense familiarity with English literature and modern art. As a sportsman, he rather fails from want of opportunity and study, but he is a capital shot, having learned to shoot left-handed of recent years, after an injury to his right eye. With all his want of training and refinement, I have enjoyed his society not a little."[79]

Minot offered a less generous assessment of Hill in 1889 when their friendly relationship reached an end. The Manitoba had then launched a construction campaign that would eventually make it into the transcontinental Great Northern Railroad. Minot, who had by then supervised several line-extension projects, most recently from St. Paul to Superior, Wisconsin, saw himself as more than fit to supervise the system's grand transcontinental line. When Hill refused to put him in charge, Minot resigned, angry and disappointed. He was quickly scooped up and was offered the vice presidency of the Atchison, Topeka, and Santa Fe, a position he held when he met his death soon after, in November 1890.

Henry Minot's premature death denied him a greater role and consideration as a leading figure in American economic development. His career, however, highlights the historical links between the accumulation of wealth through investment and reinvestment and the trajectory of American capitalism in the late nineteenth century. By and large, elites in Boston during this period celebrated these connections. They associated the amassing of great wealth not with unfair economic disparities or undue power in a democracy but with the promotion of national progress and widespread material comfort for all. The immense power of finance, they argued, was ultimately a force for good. They viewed financiers not as reckless speculators or illegitimate profiteers but as daring visionaries, gentlemen whose prudent judgment made them indispensable to general welfare and prosperity.

One of Minot's contemporaries on State Street, private banker Nathaniel Thayer, inspired some explicit reflections on how growing concentrations of wealth, rather than being malevolent or regrettable, were in fact deeply intertwined with social and economic progress.[80] At the time of his passing in 1888, Thayer left behind the largest single fortune in the history of Boston. Thayer's eulogist used the occasion to applaud the virtues of great riches. In a period when most Americans ascribed prosperity to productive labor, the tribute to Thayer's life made the case for the necessary relationship between the accruing of "towering fortunes of individuals" and the "economic progress of this section of our country in its relations to the whole of which it is so prospered a part."[81] This relationship first became manifest in the age of sail when New England's "most prospered individuals" facilitated advantageous trade of "the products of the wilderness and the fisheries" for "those of the West Indies," and in time promoted "world-wide traffic over all oceans." That was at the time "the only agency for our development and improvement." This tradition continued with the rise of "the great manufacturing enterprises, promoted by joint capital." These industrial ventures provided "comfort and luxury among the whole community," even as "the largest gains of wealth from them accrued to a comparatively few favored individuals."[82] These earlier modes of accumulation paled by comparison to great riches made more recently in "the vast operations of the banking and brokerage business consequent upon the introduction of the railroad system for travel and traffic over the ever-extending expanses of our territory." The movement of financial resources from the East made possible railroad construction in the West, allowing both sections "to be alike benefited by the opening of the intercourse and traffic" between them.[83]

Boston's moneymen, as the eulogy affirmed, never relinquished their dominant position in the American economy. Thayer and his colleagues were not a group in decline but among the primary creators of contemporary economic expansion throughout the continent. More than mere material resources, these bankers and brokers also provided vital intellectual leadership. They possessed, in this view, an almost superhuman capacity to mobilize resources across *space* and across *time*. They were able to connect distant locales, making "what is of value here available in any part of the globe, either through the medium of a piece of paper or by a message sent under the ocean currents." They were also able to anticipate the future. "Furnish them with a seed that has life in it," he argued, "and they will anticipate for you its deferred harvest." Like a "system of water-works, with its contributing springs and water-courses, its reservoirs and its distributing and service pipes," these men were able to efficiently allocate resources in ways that benefitted the community and the nation at large.[84]

Far from predatory or exploitative, the pervasive sentiment among elites in Boston cast Thayer and his associates on State Street as essential social and economic actors. The Bostonians, of course, acknowledged that the financial system was not free from fraud and corruption. It was also prone to bouts of dangerous volatility. To the extent that these themes overshadowed more systemic inequities of power, these foibles were lingered on at great length. The custom on State Street was to attribute these darker aspects of finance not to prudent businessmen in their own city but rather to other, less qualified men, "elements neither judicious nor legitimate." This rhetorical distinction, which has since been reified in many historical and literary accounts, became ever more paramount to the Bostonians' sense of themselves. As captured by the eulogy, it effortlessly shifted responsibility away from established wealth and toward upstart elements, "avaricious or reckless," that were blamed for concocting "sharp schemings and unscrupulous or hazardous maneuvers." It was these lesser figures that "came in to pervert, embarrass, or bring under distrust [what was otherwise an] honest and safe method of business." By contrast, the Bostonians were always assumed to be "largely, intelligently, and profitably concerned" in "legitimate and wise enterprises."[85] This discursive distinction allowed elite investors in Boston and elsewhere—despite their deep involvement in new ventures far and wide and in close collaboration with "new men" like James J. Hill—to retain their reputation as seasoned and ultimately benevolent stewards of modernity.

CHAPTER FOUR

The Contest over the Common

In January 1877, the Massachusetts Charitable Mechanic Association, Boston's organization of craftsmen, master artisans, and small manufacturers, petitioned Boston's city government for permission to hold its thirteenth triennial exhibition on Boston Common. The petitioners reasoned that Faneuil and Quincy halls, the venues of the previous twelve exhibitions, had become too small to house the ever-expanding array of objects intended for display. Having outgrown their previous accommodations, the mechanics sought to hold their exhibition of "industry and art" at a large temporary building that would be constructed on the Common. The event aimed not only to advertise Boston's preeminence as a hub of American manufacturing but, more critically, to inspire a new generation of skilled workers who would sustain the city's economy in the future. It was envisioned as a celebration of the contributions of craft production to the region's industrial development. The response from the elite citizens of Boston—financiers, merchants, industrialists, and lawyers—many of whom lived in close proximity to the proposed location, was forceful and decisive. They saw the idea of holding a mechanical exhibition in a space meant for quiet recreation as offensive and crass. In a barrage of letters and petitions, and at two prolonged public hearings that stretched deep into the night, they made it clear that this "attack on the Common" would not go unchallenged.

The campaign to hold a mechanical exhibition on the Common reflected a new level of assertiveness among urban producers in Boston. The determination to occupy the most prominent public space in the city signaled the ascendant clout of these small manufacturers, tradesmen, and petty dealers within the metropolis as well as their command over its politics and its economy. The developments of the previous two decades gave credence to this self-assured outlook. The turmoil of the 1850s had displaced the all-powerful cotton magnates of the Bay State from their hegemonic position and strengthened the plebeian grip over city government. Under the control of skilled workers, or mechanics, most noticeably after the Civil War, the municipality assumed broad new responsibilities, drastically expanding public resources for infrastructure, education, and health. With the support of massive government spending and a favorable tax code, new neighborhoods emerged in the city's peripheral districts. A diffuse metropolitan economy of urban producers enjoyed a period of rapid expansion, and a class of small businessmen, shopkeepers, and craftsmen, deeply embedded in this process of metropolitan expansion, began to swell. The recession of the 1870s dampened the optimism of the immediate aftermath of the war, and the flow of capital to the West alarmed many observers, who feared the long-term consequences of this trend for Boston and New England. Nevertheless, on the whole, the period was a golden age for the urban industrial economy and those who were involved in it. The proposed exhibition aimed to herald their achievements and their vision of free labor in an industrial society.

The city's business elite experienced the period very differently. The antislavery fervor that had enveloped Boston before the war overwhelmed their conciliatory attitudes toward the South, sweeping them out of office and undermining their moral leadership. Although they were able to regroup and stabilize their financial position (indeed, their economic prospects never seemed brighter), their authority in Boston—the hub of their financial, social, and cultural power—drastically eroded. The annexation of extensive territories into Boston proceeded against their prudent warnings and against what they perceived as the region's tradition of small, fiscally responsible towns. That and other seemingly misguided priorities among policymakers plunged the municipality into ever-growing expenditures and rising property taxation. These conditions (so it seemed to these elite observers) threatened the status of the metropolis as an attractive place for business. City government appeared impervious to reason and good leadership, while reform proposals, which had the enthusiastic backing of leading experts in political economy, met stubborn opposition. Led by a City Council populated by working-class and lower-middle-class representatives, Boston risked losing its standing as the "Athens of America." Instead, it was fast becoming a city of mechanics, shopkeepers, and small businessmen, whose rapid increase transformed the old, compact port city into a sprawling and grimy metropolis.

The confidence of the mechanics was buoyed by a sea change in the industrial economy of Massachusetts in the 1860s and 1870s. This shift allowed Boston's diverse manufacturing economy to supersede the earlier dominance of single-industry towns around it. Before the war, the center of gravity of the commonwealth's manufacturing economy resided decidedly in the towns that orbited Boston, in places like Chicopee, Lynn, and most notably Lowell. As late as 1860, Boston, which served as the political, financial, and cultural hub for the region, remained marginal as a site of manufacturing. The county where Boston was situated ranked a distant fifth in the state in the total number of people employed in manufacturing. It ranked a distant fourth in both the amount of capital invested in industry and total amount of value produced.[1] This situation changed drastically over the next two decades as Boston emerged as the state's topmost center of manufacturing. By 1880, Boston's county ranked first in the state in the total value of manufacturing product. It came a very close second (and soon after became the leader) in total capital invested and total employment in manufacturing.[2]

Boston's industrial base grew not only in magnitude but also in a fundamentally different manner. Unlike the towns surrounding it, Boston had no one dominant industry. It industrialized via the proliferation of relatively small producers in a wide range of economic sectors. Cities in Boston's orbit such as Lowell, Lawrence, Fall River, and Lynn, for example, were overwhelmingly dependent on a single industry. At Lowell, Lawrence, and Fall River in 1880 more than 80 percent of manufacturing capital was invested in textiles. Approximately 80 percent of the workforce was employed in textiles, which amounted to nearly 80 percent of the overall output of the town.[3] At Lynn, nearly 90 percent of all industrial capital was invested in boot and shoe manufacturing, which employed more than 90 percent of the workforce and produced more than 90 percent of the overall output.[4] Whether through capital-intensive growth of textile mills in the case of the textile centers or through the conglomeration of medium-sized factories in the case of Lynn, these towns specialized heavily in one line of business.

In Boston, by contrast, no single industry became prominent. Urban manufacturers increased in number and ranged widely, from stationery goods, saddlery and harnesses, soap and candles, brooms and brushes, and bookbinding to photographic equipment, trunks and valises, spectacles and glasses, and shipbuilding, and so on and so forth. The city had a total of 3,665 manufacturing establishments in 225 different categories, the vast majority of which were small unincorporated companies. The largest industry in terms of capital investment, "foundry and machine shop," employed 6.5 percent of the overall workforce and produced less than 4 percent of the overall amount for the city as a whole. The largest sector in terms of value of products, "sugar and molasses," produced less than 13 percent of the total amount for the city and employed just over 4 percent of the workforce. The largest industry in terms of the number of workers, "men's clothing," employed less than 16 percent of the overall workforce, produced just over 12 percent of the overall value of products, and added up to less than 9 percent of overall manufacturing capital in the city.[5] Boston's remarkably diverse industrial base was made up of many hundreds of manufacturing establishments that were capitalized at a modest average of just under $13,000 and employed an average of 16.2 workers. These urban businesses sustained large swaths of the city's population, but they were rarely platforms for the accumulation of significant and lasting wealth.[6]

Boston's metropolitan industrialization proceeded outside of the purview of the business elite, whose gaze and resources were directed in entirely different directions. The small manufacturing establishments that drove industrial growth were poor vehicles for financial investment. They were too diffuse, too eclectic, and too numerous to absorb the enormous capital reserves of the city's major banking institutions. Moreover, the rapid spread and growth of manufacturing in the city created a labyrinthine urban terrain that elites struggled to control and navigate. This emerging industrial geography—a belt of mixed-use neighborhoods that stretched from the peripheral districts of South and East Boston to the annexed districts of Roxbury, Dorchester, Brighton, and West Roxbury—proved an anathema to their sensibilities. Affluent Bostonians literally and symbolically turned their backs on this landscape. As their city became a center of manufacturing, they mobilized to extend their investments across the continent, triggering large-scale industrial development elsewhere. They came to regard Boston as first and foremost a site for the cultivation of a refined and cohesive upper class, grounded economically in the financial district on State Street. The city was where they forged the common culture and tight-knit social bonds that enabled them to mobilize in concert and preside over national development.

The linchpin of the elite urban vision in those years was the neighborhood of Back Bay. Historically a shallow and stagnant body of water west of the Boston peninsula, the area was filled in and developed during the 1860s as an upper-class residential enclave, adjacent to the Common and within walking distance of the financial district. Unlike urban growth in the annexed neighborhoods, which proceeded under the purview of Boston city government, the development of Back Bay was managed by the Commonwealth of Massachusetts via an unelected commission whose members were closely associated with the elite. Free from political involvement, the commission denied the city land rights in the area and defeated initiatives to use part of it as a commercial dock. It instead designated the neighborhood—a sizable tract of 450 acres—for high-end residential development and auctioned off the land in a deliberate process that ensured demographic homogeneity.[7]

The urban planning principles that guided the development of Back Bay set it apart from the rest of the metropolis. Modeled after the West End neighborhood in London, the commissioners laid out a grid of long, wide boulevards, flanked on both sides with rows of uniform housing blocks. The terms of sale prohibited manufacturing and commerce and reserved a generous 43 percent of the land for avenues and parks. They specified the construction of first-class dwellings of uniform height, set back from the street in the front and with generous service passageways in the rear. The residents, who moved into elegantly designed domiciles inspired by a sequence of fashionable European styles, consisted of wealthy families whose members filled the pages of the Social Register, populated exclusive clubs and churches, and studied at Harvard.[8] This pattern contrasted sharply with development that took place at the same time in the annexed districts, which proceeded gradually and in small patches in the absence of overarching grid patterns, producing a multiplicity of overlapping land uses and diverse populations in close proximity. Unlike this granular pattern of development, Back Bay—orderly and homogeneous—opened to the world at large. It looked visually and stylistically to the capitals of Europe. Its inhabitants' financial investments pointed overwhelmingly to out-of-state properties and assets in the Great West. Within a few years, Boston's wealthy residents, who previously congregated on Beacon Hill, moved into the new neighborhood in large numbers. Back Bay became the embodiment of their shared hopes and sensibilities.[9]

In this context, the idea of holding an exhibition of steam engines, greasy machines, mechanical instruments, and other new inventions on the Common was an immensely loaded proposition. It signaled the collision of two competing urban trajectories. The residents of Back Bay envisioned the Common as a barrier against the industrial city, which they saw as an encroachment on their genteel domain. For them, the open space marked the beginning of an uninterrupted beautified stretch extending from the Common, through the graceful Commonwealth Avenue in the Back Bay to the suburban Brookline. This graceful urban environment paid tribute to their affluence, wisdom, and refined taste—the very qualities that made them fit to wield power and influence. The mechanics, in turn, sought to seize this space to commemorate the growth of the city as a hub of manufacturing. If sanctioned by the city, the exhibition would allow them to wrest control of the Common from the wealthy individuals who lived in its vicinity and incorporate the space into the surrounding industrial metropolis. For the duration of their event, they would use the Common to celebrate not the sage leadership of a small elite but men of humble backgrounds whose industry, know-how, and ingenuity, in their view, had contributed to the city's prosperity and sustained its democratic institutions. At stake in this political contest was not simply the occupation of the foremost public space in Boston but the ideological underpinning of an urban industrial society. The confrontation was a battle for the symbolic power to guide the city into the future and shape its political economy. It is no wonder that a seemingly trivial petition sparked a highly passionate and wide-ranging debate that positioned class sensibilities and ideologies in direct conflict.

The premonitions of controversy over the mechanics' petition had already surfaced when the city government's Joint Committee on Common and Squares held its first hearing on the issue at the beginning of February 1877. A few days after the official request was submitted to the City Council, the upper-class bellwether *Boston Daily Advertiser* noted a flare-up of letters about the matter from concerned readers: "Not one of our correspondents is in favor of the plan, but they all oppose it in earnestness." It conveniently concluded that "popular opposition to the project of using the Common is radical and thorough."[10] Against the mechanic association's request, which was endorsed by three petitions in aid from "citizens and business men of Boston," the opposition submitted a letter of protest from "citizens and tax-payers in Boston," which was signed by some of the city's most distinguished names, including Jackson, Lawrence, Abbott, Shaw, and Coolidge.[11] These eminent rivals of the exhibition hired official counsel to formally represent them during the hearing. As the proceedings commenced on a Saturday afternoon, some of Boston's most notable gentlemen arrived thoroughly prepared, armed with legal treatises and painstaking research on historical precedents.[12]

Despite this well-organized opposition, Joseph F. Paul and Charles W. Slack, respectively the president and the secretary of the Massachusetts Charitable Mechanic Association, who appeared in person to make the case for the exhibition, had good reason to expect a favorable decision. City government was familiar terrain for both men. Paul, a carpenter who had built up a substantial lumber yard business, had been a councilor for two terms and an alderman for three. Slack, printer and editor of the Radical Republican *Commonwealth* (and a veteran of the antislavery and annexation battles), had served for two terms as an alderman, the second of them as chairman of the board of aldermen.[13] Another reason for optimism came from the social profile of the committee on the issue, which resembled that of the petitioners, consisting of two grocers, one clerk, one insurance agent, a silk goods trader, a machinist, and a crockery seller. This plebeian makeup suggested that the mechanics could expect a sympathetic hearing. Confronted by the remonstrants' barricade of lawyers, Paul began the hearing by mocking his opponents' legalism. "I did not know that it is a case that requires a large array of counsel on either side," he confessed. He instead struck a distinctly populist tone. "We appear on behalf of the citizens of Boston. . . . I do not know what is the practice in the courts myself, but we want the practice of the people, and want to hear plain straight stories."[14] Indeed, in claiming to speak for "the people," the mechanics exhibited a remarkable level of self-assurance. They thought of themselves as much more than one interest group among many within the urban polity. They expected the committee to acknowledge their unique status by granting them a special privilege. Since the charter of Boston specified that the Common, or any portion of it, could not be sold or rented out for private uses, the mechanics' exhibition, if allowed to take place there, would be formally endowed with a public mandate. Rather than an appropriation by a small group, the exhibition would signal an acknowledgment that the petitioners stood broadly, as Slack insisted, "for the benefit of the City of Boston."[15]

Convinced of the crucial contribution of craft production to Boston's economy, the mechanics defiantly identified themselves not only as faithful Bostonians in the civic sense but also as the city's true men of business. Slack explained that "our petition speaks for itself. . . . 'We, citizens *and* business men of Boston.' It does not say 'citizens' alone, but 'business men' as well, who come here from various localities, and labor and toil, adding to the aggregate wealth and honor of the town." In this view, the mechanics' welfare as urban producers—a collective identity that combined small businessmen and skilled workers—were aligned with the economic well-being of the city. They did not play second fiddle to the authority and wealth of the leading men who presided over the city's banks and financial institutions. "Seven-eighths of the prosperity of Boston, to-day, depends upon the mechanical industry of our people," Slack asserted. "Everything of this kind that promotes and fosters that industry should [therefore] be favored." Boston's small producers deserved full support from their government. "If there is any remaining love for Boston here, and of the men that have made it what it is and who have maintained its commercial activity," Slack contended, referring, not to long-haul merchants or large industrialists, but to his fellow mechanics, "every Bostonian, believing in the prosperity of his city, will say—. . . take those grounds."[16]

Despite the focus on the direct economic benefits of the exhibition, the petitioners emphasized that their gatherings contributed to the welfare of the city in much more profound ways. True, the exhibition would bring direct financial rewards by advertising Boston-manufactured goods and attracting to Boston thousands of visitors, whose "knowledge may in time be turned into desirable orders." Far more significant, however, was the edifying impact of those events on the region's own population. "From the lowest of motives, . . . we have consideration for the exhibition. But, higher than this, all our witnesses have testified to the elevating influence of such exhibitions." In this view, the celebration of mechanical ingenuity had a profound enlightening effect on the city's inhabitants. In honoring the ideal of craft work as a moral and intellectual activity, Slack argued, the exhibitions inspired the population to greater achievements in the future. He pointed to the crucial role of mechanics' exhibitions in nourishing these essential features of the region's industrial culture. "We have gone forward in our long career," dating back to the American Revolution, Slack explained, "fostering all new thought, favoring inventions and development, and giving constant examples of those attributes that make up the glory of a people."[17] The next exhibition on the Common would be another rung in this distinguished tradition.

The opponents of the exhibition summarily dismissed both the moral and the economic arguments of the mechanics. They began by declaring their superior authority in the realm of business. In their capacity as prominent financiers, merchants, and industrialists, they challenged the mechanics' pretense of representing the industrial interests of the region. Sugar merchant and treasurer of the Milan Mining Company of New Hampshire William H. Whitmore led the charge, stating that the petitioners were "not authorized to speak for the manufacturers of New England." The list of petitioners and endorsements for the exhibition included no "responsible capitalists or great manufacturers." To remove any doubt that the "real" businessmen of the city opposed the petition, the region's large textile manufacturers publicized a letter reprimanding the mechanics. The treasurers of New England's largest cotton and woolen firms (including the Boston, Lowell, Dwight, Nashua, Chicopee, Amoskeag, Lyman, and Lawrence manufacturing companies), which had their offices in Boston, signed the letter and expressed strong "disapproval" of the mechanics' "impolitic" initiative. Foes of the exhibition portrayed the mechanics as careless men who rushed to secure a space for an event that enjoyed little support from the economic leaders of the commonwealth. These small businessmen and urban producers, they argued, "set out with a light heart to ask the city to grant them an inestimable boon . . . with as much nonchalance as though their pockets were crammed with credentials." They argued that the petitioners lacked crucial backing for their endeavor and little ability to carry it to successful fruition on their own.[18]

Clearly, the opposition argued, the mechanics lacked the clout to mobilize and lead Boston's industrial interests. Whitmore explained that as a result, the exhibition failed to secure the participation or support of the economic leadership of the region. There were "no preparation[s] by the various industries of New England . . . no trade-meetings, no trade-committees, no canvassing for exhibitions, no commissioners from other States, no pledge of the necessary funds." He addressed the mechanics' president Paul directly during the hearings, asking him to verify the breadth of support for the exhibition. "Are you aware," he asked, "that any large manufacturing interests, other than the glass and boot and shoe trade, have expressed any desire to go down on Boston Common?" Paul responded that only a handful of industries, primarily those associated with cotton and woolen manufacturing, announced they would not participate in the exhibition if it was held on the Common but added: "I thanked God that those [few] did not make up the City of Boston. We have had a great many say they desired us to hold the fair there." The support of hundreds of urban industries might have seemed sufficient to the mechanics, who thought of their city primarily in terms of its myriad small-scale manufacturing establishments. The remonstrants, however, found the mechanics' perspective easy to dismiss: "Until they can come before you with responsible backers; . . . with the cordial co-operation of the great branches of our manufactures; . . . until they can show a reasonable chance of success, they have no right to ask for a hearing."[19] Until then, permission to use the Common was clearly unwarranted.

The two sides in the debate understood the urban economy in different terms and disagreed about the sources of its industrial strength. As articulated in the annexation debates several years earlier, authorities in the field of political economy had it that wealth came from long-haul, or at the very least interregional, trade. They associated economic strength in manufacturing with specialization in a few major industries that could compete in national and international markets via economies of scale. Whitmore assuredly explained that the economic prospects of the city could only advance through the expansion of national and international markets for Boston-produced goods. This was not likely to be served by an exhibition that attracted mostly local audiences: "They must hope that this fair will attract the great merchants of the distributing centres South and West. They must hope that foreign buyers will come here, and then commence to send our manufactures to new and foreign markets. But what chance is there of this? . . . What probability is there that the Boston fair will so attract the world? . . . These local exhibitions, what great influence can they hope to exert?"[20]

The mechanics in fact had little such false hope. They welcomed national markets for their goods and were by no means opposed to long-haul trade. Their conception of prosperity, however, revolved emphatically around their own metropolis, whose population, at nearly 360,000, exceeded that of many western states several times over. The rapidly growing metropolis, with an ever-increasing number of city dwellers—consumers and producers—provided a solid domestic foundation for industrial development and growth. This type of metropolitan industrialization had several key advantages. It avoided an overreliance on a single industry as economic engine, of the sort that plunged the region into crisis when cotton manufacturing faltered in the 1850s. It also distributed economic power more evenly, keeping it out of the hands of a small cohort of wealthy men. Finally, as the mechanics pointed out, it rested prosperity on the mechanical aptitude of the urban population, on the virtues of "labor and toil," ingenuity and skill, not commerce, investment, or even entrepreneurship. They insisted that metropolitan industrialization, contrary to Whitmore's argument, could in fact benefit tremendously from opportunities to stir and educate workers, in ways that the mechanics' exhibition promised to do. Instead of conceding hegemony to rapidly growing urban centers such as Chicago, which elites attributed to the laws of political economy, the mechanics thought of economic change as malleable. They intended their exhibition, in Slack's words, to "lift up this ancient domain, that it shall be the pride of all the cities of our country." As they had successfully done with annexation, they were determined to continue to mold the metropolitan industrial economy along democratic and sustainable new lines.[21]

The mechanics were not the only Bostonian patriots in the debate. As they extended their economic horizons and invested in locales far beyond Boston and New England, members of Boston's business elite saw themselves as no less loyal to their hometown than the mechanics. However, they articulated their devotion to their city very differently, not by looking for ways to revitalize their city as an industrial center, but by defending what they perceived to be its venerable traditions. They denied the material benefits of the exhibition, but irrespective of that, they felt very strongly that holding an exhibition on the Common would be a blatant violation of an almost sacred ground. They insisted that the peaceful, pastoral atmosphere of the Common must never be disturbed. John D. Bryant, lawyer and resident of Back Bay (who had the leisure and expertise to look into the matter), found that sweeping resolutions passed in 1634 and 1646 decreed that "no part of Boston Common should be leased, sold or let for any purpose whatsoever." The Common, he asserted, was always "to be kept open." Robert D. Smith, who was hired to represent the opposition, explained that the Common "has always been kept a green place—the one green spot in the centre of the city. . . . [It] has been kept an open space for 200 years." Whitmore argued that the exhibition would amount to a "curtailment" of the public's "ancient rights."[22]

Since they saw themselves as the custodians of public good in the city, it was easy for those who were opposed to the exhibition to overlook competing notions about communal benefits that might be derived from the event. They saw their own uncompromising public spirit as the only defense standing between the Common and an atrocious onslaught. They consistently took the high ground rhetorically and painted their adversaries as narrowly self-interested. The *Advertiser* pointed out that the exhibition would save the mechanics the cost of renting space elsewhere. It informed its readers that the "only argument that has been, or that can be, presented is, that by securing the Common for the purposes of its exhibition a large saving in ground-rent can be affected."[23] Curtis Guild, editor of the mercantile *Commercial Bulletin*, echoed this sentiment at the hearing, attributing the lowest of motives to the mechanics. "That, sir, is human nature; for anyone of us are willing to get good quarters rent free. I should go to you very readily and ask you for your store for three or six months if you would let me have it gratis, because I am public-spirited." What could only be "natural" in the economic sphere was potentially disastrous if brought to bear in civic affairs. If we allow the exhibition to proceed, we may as well "go the whole figure," Curtis mockingly proposed. "Let us put rows of streets on Boston Common, cover it with magnificent warehouses; let us remove the trees and put magnificent dwellings there. . . . Then when every sentiment shall have given way to trade and business, you may be sure that when you strike upon men's breasts you will get, instead of the sound of true patriotism, the rattle and ring of the Almighty Dollar."[24]

Faced with these accusations, the petitioners cried slander. Slack protested the characterization of the mechanics as cynical profit-seekers and emphasized that the association was "not a set of predatory individuals, designing to monopolize any of the public parks." "Not a cent of the receipts goes into the private pocket of anyone," he emphasized. "All who work in the cause do so without salary."[25] In return, the petitioners struck back at Whitmore, Guild, and their cohort and questioned *their* motivations. One proponent of the exhibition argued that the opposition emerged from a "class of gentlemen living in the vicinity of the Common, who . . . have lived there so long, and become so accustomed to the beauties before them, that they really believe that they themselves own the fee of Boston Common." Another one added, stressing the nature of the mechanics' exhibitions as more than a commercial venture: "There are some gentlemen whose heads are so round that it is painful to see that they don't know the difference between an exhibition of the Mass. Mechanics' Association and a dog-show. . . . What is the Common for? Is it so sacred that we cannot cross it or step on it?"[26]

The mechanics' response did little to appease the opposition. To more scrupulously protect the Common from the exhibition and from similar threats in the future, the remonstrants sought to enshrine this public space in a higher order above political wrangling. To this end, aside from the debate over the desirability of the exhibition, expert legal opinions were brought forth to declare that the issue was in fact not under the jurisdiction of the City Council. These legal authorities explained that regardless of the event's potentially positive effects, the matter could not be decided based on the benefits it would bring to the city as a community. City government did not actually have the authority to allow the gathering to take place because it would infringe on the rights of the public *as individuals*. In this view, the public good rested not on any benefits to the majority of the population but on the inalienable rights of each and every citizen of Boston. Lawyer Samuel M. Quincy stepped forward to explain the "fallacy" in the minds of the committee in charge of the issue. The Common, members of the council say, "is in our hands to be devoted to such purposes as we honestly and firmly believe will be for the highest or best interests of all the citizens." "Not so, Mr. Chairman!" "It is not the City of Boston as a corporation which has a right to this particular use." Rather, "the right is every citizen's in his individual capacity." This fracturing of the community in its collective capacity was derived in Lockean fashion from the "perpetual and irrevocable" seventeenth-century dedication of the Common to the public by its original private owner, a dedication that was later codified in the charter of the city.[27]

In this expert view, Quincy elaborated, "city government cannot legally say to the humblest citizen, you must give up your use of such and such portions of the Common for the enjoyment of air, exercise, trees, grass and foliage, and accept in return something far better, if not for you individually yet for the community at large."[28] From this perspective, the community as a whole was a suspect entity, a threat to the rights of individuals and to public order. Richard Olney, a prominent legal voice, concurred. He determined that "it is not within the province of the city government to grant the petition, [even] if it were convinced that it would be wise to do so." The city held the Common "not merely for the general public benefit, but for the benefit of the public in a prescribed and particular way." The council had "care and custody" of the Common not to determine how it might best be used but merely to make sure the prescribed uses were "not encroached or depredated upon."[29] The role of city government, so it seemed to these commentators, was not to actively promote collective prosperity and welfare but rather to serve a public interest by protecting the individual rights of Boston's citizens.

This line of argument against the exhibition somewhat unexpectedly drew particular attention to the rights of the poor and disadvantaged. Years later, Olney would enter the history books as the attorney general who allowed federal troops to break up the strike in Pullman, Chicago. On the issue of the exhibition, however, he appeared to side solidly with Boston's least fortunate citizens. "Those most interested against this petition," he waxed poetic, "are not represented here, except by proxy; they are those whose daily labor must earn each day's bread; who have not gardens and playgrounds and lawns of their own; who cannot take wings and go to the seashore in the dog-days, and to whom this public Common gives the only glimpse of the bloom of summer, and . . . it is their only chance for fresh air."[30] Others among the opponents also invoked the plight of the city's poorest citizens and cast themselves as their charitable protectors. Reverend Joshua P. Bodfish explained that "if you would go down into one of those crowded streets, and up to the fourth story, where there is a widow with five children, working hard all day long to obtain bread enough to keep life in their bodies; and when you ask her where are her little ones, she will say she has put the younger ones in the charge of the older ones, and they are all out on the Common." These children's rights would be violated by the exhibition. "It is all very fine for those people who can go to the opera and the theatre, and have every kind of recreation and enjoyment all day long, but for them it is very hard to be deprived of their only place for recreation."[31]

These arguments in the name of the city's poor were met with ridicule from the mechanics, for whom that form of paternalism seemed grossly disingenuous. "[There was] one good thing after all," Paul commented on those claims, "and that was to hear men basing their opposition on the fact that they were the best friends of the working men! Who ever knew it before?"[32] Indeed, the humblest citizen, however prominent in rhetoric, did not seem foremost on Quincy's mind when he associated individual rights with the inviolable rights of urban landowners who acquired property near the Common. He explained that "it is obvious that individuals acquire vested rights in such a dedication [of the Common for certain uses]," since they "purchase and build in the neighborhood upon the faith of it." There was no question that stabilizing use of the Common for a narrow set of activities would also enhance the value of residential property in its vicinity, but at least publicly, the opposition mostly steered away from that reasoning.[33] To give additional weight to his and his cohort's legal arguments, Quincy instead surmised that "any attempt to override or defy the law is sure to be checked by the appropriate tribunals."[34] The implication for the committee in charge was clear: a favorable decision in this case would be challenged and probably reversed in the state's highest courts. It was better for the committee to avoid public embarrassment and rule against the petitioners in the case.

Altogether, opponents of the exhibition made a powerful case that the public good was in better hands when founded on the doctrine of individual rights and in the responsible jurisdiction of the courts, rather than being left to the vagaries of a democratic political process. The mechanics held a radically different approach, retaining full faith in political institutions and in the people's elected representatives. Paul asserted that he had "confidence in the committee to abide by their judgment whether it is proper to have a fair there, or not." Slack reinforced the point: "You, Mr. Chairman, are at the head of the Committee on Common and Squares. . . . You and your associates of the Aldermen are the accredited representatives of the . . . citizens of Boston. Had they confidence in your judgment, or did they think you were without balance, to be moved hither and thither with every popular gust? I will not belittle your position by suggesting that your constituents can be gratified by a swerving from a straight line of right and propriety."[35] Unlike the opposition, who aimed to narrow the mandate of city government, the mechanics continued to see it as an esteemed representative and deliberative body, fully able to institute responsible and steady policy.

At the end of two protracted hearings, as he stood up to present the petitioners' closing arguments, Slack was palpably exasperated with the arguments presented against the exhibition. Although the request was not a trifling matter, the level of acrimony in response to the mechanics' initiative far exceeded expectations. The mechanics proposed to use less than three acres out of the Common's forty-nine, yet their exhibition was portrayed as a total "occupation." The length of the proposed temporary structure, projected to be 500 feet, was reported in some places to be 1,200 feet. The area the mechanics asked for was empty, "not a seat upon it, not a shade-tree or any growth upon it." Nevertheless, the opposition propagated the notion that the Common's beauty in its entirety would be compromised. Moreover, they depicted the exhibition building as a health hazard that would spread disease and defile "the purity of the atmosphere." The forebodings were repeated so often that the warnings began to resonate as if they were true. Many in Boston became convinced that the Common's "greensward and pleasant paths and umbrageous trees were all to be denied to the citizens while this exhibition was being held," even though "nothing could be more fallacious." Every possible claim was advanced to "fill the public mind with apprehension of great danger to the Common."[36] Slack found this extreme reaction incomprehensible.

Indeed, the language of the conversation revealed that ultimately it mattered very little how big the exhibition building would be or how minimal the damage to the Common. The mere holding of a mechanical exhibition on the Common was offensive to the upper classes regardless of its magnitude. The proposed exhibition infringed on some of the basic tenets of the bourgeois vision of social order, which was increasingly organized around the segregation of industry and leisure, home and work, production and consumption, fine art and commerce, and, most fundamentally, mental and manual labor. Like business classes elsewhere in the industrial world during this period, elites in Boston sought to enshrine a set of physical and ideological dichotomies, reorganizing society around separation between different uses of urban space, as well as between human faculties, visual aesthetics, and metropolitan populations. In planning to bring machines into the Common, the mechanics clearly pushed back against this prescribed system of classification. They rejected the hierarchies implicit in elite-sanctioned dualities and instead championed amalgamation and integration. They insisted, along with labor radicals in other cities, that mechanical work was intellectually enlightening, that machines and other everyday artifacts could be beautiful, and that the life of the mind was not the province of a select few but rightfully belonged to working men and women. They argued that the mechanics' intricate skills, power of invention, practical experience, and commitment to technological progress deserved to be recognized among the region's best accomplishments.[37]

Elite opponents of the exhibition utterly dismissed these ideas. Steeped in an exclusive and learned domain in literature, theology, law, and art, they sneered at the suggestion that a display of an assortment of mechanical devices and miscellaneous goods should be honored in such a way. For them, the exhibition symbolized the uncouth materialism of a democratic society and, if validated by city government, the sway of populist politics. Whereas the mechanics, as mentioned, envisioned their exhibition as bestowing "elevating influences" on the city, their elite rivals saw it as utterly vulgar. They opposed any public gatherings on the Common, but to "this class of exhibitions there particularly," as Julius Adams put it. "The use [the Common] is proposed to be put to," said lawyer John D. Bryant, expressing conventional wisdom among his cohort, "is the lowest that can be thought of." These commentators were willing to acknowledge the edifying effects of exhibitions in other cases, when art or music were presented for the appreciation of a refined audience, but this certainly did not apply in the case of a mechanical display. "This is not to be a show to benefit, improve or educate the spectators, such as we have had in Boston before," Whitmore explained. "It is not to be a musical festival, a picture-show, nor a flower-show."[38]

The opposition thought of the exhibition not as an important civic gathering or even a grand display of consumer goods, which would have been seen as less harmful, but essentially as a manufacturing facility. "Now, what is a Mechanics' Exhibition?" lawyer Thomas J. Gargan asked. "It is an exhibition where machinery of all kinds is shown; it is but a large workshop." Adams continued: "It is an exhibition which entails smoke and noise. There must be an engine there, and that must have fire and smoke and if they are to carry out the exhibition they have heretofore, there must be shafting and all the multifarious machinery which go to make up that class of buildings." Wealthy Bostonians were no strangers to engines, shafting, and heavy machinery, to which they owed the profits of their mills, factories, mines, and railroads. In the context of the Common, however, the deployment of such technology was unthinkable. Appalled by the very suggestion of the idea, they greatly exaggerated the damage to the turf of the Common. Gargan and Adams warned that "deep entrenchments will have to be made; the whole parade ground will have to be upturned."[39] Despite such gross exaggerations, the notion of the exhibition as a manufacturing space was not conjured. Steam, water, and gas were in fact provided during the exhibitions to power and run through the machinery. The presenters were encouraged to display their inventions and equipment in operation. The space of these exhibitions indeed throbbed with the sounds of machines that demonstrated the manufacturing of various products.

The introduction of this manufacturing environment into what they conceived of as a space of leisure caused special distress to the opposition. Their metaphoric language portrayed the Common as a parlor—a temple of bourgeois domesticity and refinement—at risk of being violated. "Now,

4.1. Scenes from the mechanics' exhibition of 1881.

Credit: *Fourteenth Exhibition of the Massachusetts Charitable Mechanic Association* (Boston: Alfred Mudge and Son, 1881).

4.2. Scenes from the mechanics' exhibition of 1881.

Credit: *Fourteenth Exhibition of the Massachusetts Charitable Mechanic Association* (Boston: Alfred Mudge and Son, 1881).

sir," Bryant lectured to the committee, "I fancy you would be a little hurt if, having left your private house in the care of a faithful steward, you should find that, in your absence, your parlor had been made a shop." This production facility "might not hurt the carpets—I think it would in this case [of the exhibition], but when the owner came home and found that that use had been made of his house, I think he would think his steward had not been faithful to him."[40] Just as manufacturing activity could not properly take place within a domestic space, especially one adorned with expensive carpets, city government—imagined in this view to be a servant in a private elite domain—should not neglect to uphold the strict separation between residential and industrial spaces in the city.

Failing to grasp or even acknowledge the mechanics' goals and ideals, men like Whitmore, Olney, and Quincy projected ideas onto their opponents. Quincy surmised that "the mechanics of this City of Boston, after having worked through the week . . . in the shop, using the hammer or attending to machinery, . . . when the Sabbath comes, or if they desire to take recreation in the evening, do not care to be disturbed by the noise of machinery. . . . They desire to look upon the green grass, and flowering trees, and hear the singing of the birds; and, further yet, they desire to have some young lady companion and hear her noise rather than any triphammer, or anything of that sort."[41] The tone of the comments revealed the wide gulf between the remonstrants' sheltered environment, which was completely alienated from labor, and the mechanics' immersion in the city's industrial landscape, where they were most at home. The separation between work and leisure seemed so natural and necessary to the critics that they could not conceive of why anyone would like to attend an exhibition that encroached on the divide between the two.

Another tendency among those opposed to the exhibition was to translate their class perspective into aesthetic terms, casting the mechanics' exhibition as irredeemably unsightly. As Olney put it, the exhibition would "deface the most ornamental part of the city . . . by a structure which, however well adapted to its particular purposes, cannot be anything but a blotch and disfigurement in that place."[42] A building constructed for a manufacturing facility could not possibly be aesthetically pleasing, let alone when placed in the middle of a public park. Slack articulated an idea that kept being lost on his opponents. "We do not propose to erect 'barracks,' as some have intimated; but a building . . . tasteful and beautiful in itself. . . . We certainly are not to have anything disagreeable at that time upon or around the Common." In Slack's mind, there was no contradiction between visual beauty and functional utility of a structure. He articulated an essential modernist sensibility. The exhibition, he summarized as an alternative aesthetic principle, was an opportunity to celebrate "the highest perfection of skill and industry, and make it an incentive and a pleasure to everybody that looks upon it." He insisted that the event could be useful, have enlightening value, and provide aesthetic pleasure.[43]

The battle of the Common was one critical episode in a long history of contestation over the premier public space in the city. Viewed in this perspective, the elite's staunch defense of the Common in the name of tradition was profoundly ironic, as the space had gone through a radical redefinition only a few decades earlier. It was only through vigorous reform efforts in the 1820s and 1830s that the Common, previously a communal resource, a place where work, recreation, and resource extraction intermingled, became a landscape for quiet leisurely activities. The Common had indeed been in the possession of the city since 1640, but the treeless expanse was situated north and west of the core of the town for most of the seventeenth and eighteenth centuries. Endowed with little symbolic significance, the Common had housed public institutions such as the town's almshouse, a prison, and a granary over its long history. Ordinary Bostonians came to the Common to graze animals, draw water for washing, and cart off stones for construction. Hardly pristine, the turf was trampled, covered with animal droppings and muddy watering holes. During holidays, the public would gather for festive celebrations. Stalls, booths, and tents were set up by various vendors to sell beverages and candy. "Why we did not all die of the trash which we ate and drank on such occasions, I do not know," one elderly Bostonian recalled years later.[44]

The movement to remake the Common into a space exclusively for quiet leisure was intertwined with the process of bourgeois class formation in the nineteenth century. As transoceanic trade and industrial growth enriched elite Bostonians, they developed Beacon Hill, previously a remote "hamlet" adjoining the western side of the Common, into an elegant new neighborhood. The Common not only provided the wealthy residents of the neighborhood with picturesque vistas, which they could enjoy from their houses up on the hill, but also served as a barrier from the more commercial and industrial neighborhoods of the city.[45] In 1825, in an effort to remake the Common into a more pastoral landscape, the City Council, in the days when a cadre of elite citizens controlled it, explicitly restricted the dumping of refuse, the "injuring" of trees, the taking of gravel, sand, or dirt, and the pasturing of animals other than milk cows. In 1830, against much protest by the city's laboring population, a committee chaired by Mayor Harrison Gray Otis (a resident of Beacon Hill as well as a real estate developer there) added cow pasturing to the list of prohibited activities. The removal of the cows cleared the way for a quick remaking of the park's landscape. The wooden fences that had separated the cows were removed, the cows' watering hole ("Horse Pond") was filled, the land was graded and planted with over two hundred trees, and a decorative iron fence was constructed around the Common to shield strollers from horse and carriage movement in adjoining city streets.[46]

This quite recent wholesale transformation did not prevent opponents of the mechanics' exhibition from portraying the event as a violation of ancient customs and traditions. In part, this was because by the latter decades of the nineteenth century, the pastoral past of the Common had become a historical verity in the minds of many. "A few of us can remember that much of our childhood's pleasure was gathered from the Common," an "Old Lady of Boston" wrote to the *Advertiser* in 1869, painting the Common in nostalgic terms as part of an enchanted preindustrial world: "We remember the days when the cows ate clover, and brought home the supper for the children; when on Wednesday and Saturday afternoons we went joyfully to the 'Wishing Rock' and felt assured that some fairy would fulfill our wish whispered to the rock; when the Frog Pond looked as broad as the Atlantic. . . . Alas that the spot should not always be 'Holy Ground.'"[47]

This ingrained vision nevertheless did not go unchallenged. In response to the "Old Lady," the *Boston Post* wrote that the Parade Ground (the area of the Common later sought for the exhibition) was a "quagmire, avoided by all people." One reader reminded others that the area not so long ago had been a "swamp-hole . . . a filthy, slimy bog, upon whose surface rested 'the green mantle of the standing pool.' . . . The little 'tip-carts' of the day . . . dumped their contents of swill, which was lightly covered . . . and so for years this land was a festering mass of decay." Clearly, "if cows sought their food there, they must have yielded 'swill milk' for the children's suppers."[48] These memories discredited the idea that the Common had always been sacred and could therefore not be intruded upon. Among the mechanics, memory of the public events that took place on the Common in previous decades, even after their official prohibition, remained strong. Slack could name many precedents since the 1840s—political meetings, horticultural exhibitions, mass carnivals on various occasions—some of which required construction of log cabins, wooden barracks, large tents, fences, seating stands, and board floors (the latter being a particular sore point for the opponents who shuddered at the notion of trampling the terrain of the Common). The charitable mechanic association itself had held some of its earliest presentations on the Common in the 1810s and at one point even received permission to use part of the grounds to launch a display of fireworks. Rather than establishing a dangerous precedent, the mechanics in fact continued a long tradition of using the Common for communal gatherings. Slack argued that the history of the Common revealed "repeated instances of the occupancy of the Common," showing that "it was the common custom of the people to go there." The all-threatening "entering wedge"—the precedent the opposition to the exhibition kept warning against—had long been at work and "the Common is not yet split!"[49] The doomsdays scenarios drawn by opponents of the exhibition had clearly blown the situation all out of proportion.

Despite the long history of communal uses that the mechanics pointed to, the main challenge to the Common's newly installed pastoral qualities came not from deep-seated traditions but from much more recent aspirations and political mobilization. The conflict derived not from a campaign to reclaim the space for traditional uses but from a mechanics' exhibition celebrating a particular view of modernity, industrialization, and progress. The mechanics' effort did not intend to pay homage to a mythical pre-industrial artisanal world but rather to embrace the democratic possibilities of a forward-looking industrial society. Their goal was not to preserve the customary subsistence- and use-oriented functions of the Common but rather to convert the Common to a *novel* purpose. More generally, the mechanics' exhibitions themselves in this period revealed no nostalgia for the craft prerogatives of a preindustrial age. Ironically, just as powerful intellectual currents among elites in Boston and elsewhere began to romanticize the medieval artisan, rendering craft production noble yet irredeemably anachronistic in the world of big business and mass production, the mechanics' exhibitions included no heroic portrayals of traditional ways and no fatalism with regard to the economic destiny of skilled work.[50] Against upper-class wistfulness for precommercial times, the mechanics positioned themselves as leaders in the building of a modern, technologically advanced society.

Always upbeat, the mechanics maintained a consistent celebratory tone. Rather than lamenting the impending decline of skilled work, the mechanics regularly touted the spirit of material and intellectual improvement as expressed in the city's workshops, warehouses, and production floors. The circular for their exhibitions called for participants, in what was a deliberate mix of human faculties, to bring forth "the best results of the thought, labor, skill, and taste, in the production and multiplication of whatever will add to the convenience, comfort, and education of mankind."[51] The displays were demonstrative of the mechanics' contribution, "in industry and art and in the application of science," to the economy of the region. "Behold here," exclaimed honorary guest Governor John D. Long at the exhibition of 1881, "another exhibit of her [the Commonwealth's] fertility of resources," which was clearly not rooted in the rocky soil but in "her genius of invention, the labor and intelligence and enterprise of her people!"[52] The mechanics positioned themselves as the representatives of all those human traits.

They viewed their exhibitions as opportunities to sustain the region's "fertility." Their circular announced their events as venues for "the diffusion of much useful knowledge, and the means of inspiring renewed efforts for the advancement of mechanical skill." This seemed to be of crucial significance, especially as Bostonians faced growing competition from the cities of the American west. "Hitherto we have had the field of manufacture to ourselves almost without rivalry," one speaker explained in a typical vein, "but the future threatens an earnest and active competition: not the competition of transatlantic nations . . . but the competition of our own countrymen; domestic competition." Faced with competing cities' easy access to natural resources and boundless potential for growth, Boston could only survive by resting on the mechanical capacities of the region's population, precisely the capacities that the exhibitions aimed to nourish.[53] This issue came up during the debate over the Common, giving Slack the opportunity to exalt the exhibitions as nothing less than a "great university . . . cultivating the taste of our young people, stimulating their brains in the healthiest manner, and quickening and developing in them . . . inventive faculties."[54] The analogy to an institution of higher learning presented hands-on education as an alternative to the academic mode of learning.

The mechanics betrayed no sense of being at odds with modernity. One address, delivered by Governor Charles H. Bullock, who paid tribute to the mechanics during their tenth exhibition in 1865, captured the historical narrative that was pervasive among them. Entitled "The Mechanic Arts Favorable to Liberty and Social Progress," the speech associated the mechanics with progressive social change. In this conception, ancient and medieval times were not friendly to artisans and their craft. "The medieval landed proprietor held his artisans under the limitations of a quasi-white servitude," Bullock explained. Their status was no higher than that of the mechanics of Greece and Rome, "who were slaves." Whereas the achievements of their skills at times rose to "sublime" heights, their social standing remained held in check; their craft was not yet an instrument for social change. In those historical epochs, there were "no considerable and enduring manufactures which were popular in their origin, popular in their uses, and popular in their relations." As a result, according to Bullock, "productions of genius and art" did not come within "the circuit of golden links which in our day bind the productions of genius and art to the welfare of human kind." This situation began to shift not in the countryside, which the mechanics generally cast as a feudal domain and expressed little nostalgia about, but in the growing metropolitan centers, the breeding ground of mechanical labor—"in urban life, in the smoke of cities, in the din of ports." Skilled workers were the epitome of this process, not its hapless victims. "By the click and whirl and thunder of the arts," they awakened humanity from the Middle Ages into the modern era.[55]

This worldview was not hostile toward commerce as such. Rather, it envisioned parity between the status of mechanical labor and trade as engines of change that evolved alongside each other. Nevertheless, two key ideas separated this view from liberal conceptions of civilization and progress in this period. First, skilled work, in this narrative, produced highly politicized subjects. "There was something more in their occupation," Bullock explained, "as creators in the system of political economy and in the domain of art," namely, in the combination of skills as producers and participants in the marketplace, "which elevated them to lofty conceptions of manhood and made them fit for earnest service in the struggle for liberty." The mechanics' amalgamation of those two roles in their capacity as commodity producers was at the core of this political consciousness. The mechanical trades were thereafter deeply associated with "the democratical interest . . . running in even flood with ideas of equality and independence."[56] The mechanics' support for the democratically elected officials of city government in the debate over the Common was not opportunistic but rather was fundamental to their worldview. It was precisely this deeply politicized consciousness that the elite wanted to keep away from the Common, and more generally from public life.

Second, craftsmanship, as celebrated by the mechanics, was not a passing phase, doomed to be replaced with alienated work, but rather one of the essential, animating forces behind industrialization. The mechanics emphasized the critical connections between the worker's mind and his hands. One speaker who commented on the vast diversity of machines and goods on display explained that "as the eye takes in all the suggestive kaleidoscope of this Exhibition, it discovers something more than is embraced within its immediate vision. It discovers the education of the mind and the faithful labor of the hand, of which all this is but the type and expression."[57] Intellectual development and manual skill did not stand as separate but rather fed into one another. Slack presented the mechanics' exhibitions as tributes to this relationship. He argued that the "well-built and educated brain, the constructive intellect, and the skilled hand of New England, besides being themselves our staple articles of export to other regions, are our principal stock in trade for home business, filling our bleak and sterile territory with smiling plenty."[58] Free labor, in this sense, was less about some romanticized notion of proprietary independence, than about the joint work of head and hand—an ideal shared at the time between the mechanics of Boston, the communards in Paris, and curators at the South Kensington Museum in London—and an embeddedness of economic life in a democratic state.[59]

Whereas bourgeois conceptions worked to segregate and classify certain realms of human endeavor, the mechanics kept them fully integrated. They sustained a vision of skilled work as intellectually elevating and aesthetically inspiring. Bullock argued that the exhibitions were evidence that mechanical production was "alive with the higher taste and sentiment which becomes a part of aesthetic culture." Against notions to the contrary, they maintained that skilled work ennobled its practitioners: "These are the works,—but whence has come the conception? These are the arts,—but who are the artists? Is it according to the analogies of our knowledge, that they who perform these things can be coarse and rude in their natures,

unresponsive to taste, and sentiment, and humanity?" Bullock and the mechanics insisted that they could not and offered a different dialectic. "The
soul of mechanism," they observed, was "animate with poetry."[60]

This was the very idea rejected in the Common dispute by the remonstrants, who embraced a cultural hierarchy that separated high intellectu-
alism from debased materialism. Bullock elaborated further and described
deep linkages between intellectual development and physical labor, the
production process leading from one to the next: "The ideals first exist in
the mind of the mechanic, and are next transferred to wood and metal,
and then are applied under the laws of time, and space, and fluids, and at
length are invested with a perpetual life of motion that finds its type in
the revolving spheres of the heavenly world." The process then came full
circle to elevate the mind of the mechanic: "can these things be so and
not awaken all the capacities of his nature to the pleasures of culture, and
refinement, and sensation?" In this view, the mechanics were not merely
providers of labor power but also "authors of most useful inventions." Their
inventions were the product of ongoing engagement, a "thoughtful experiment" that combined mechanical ability and creativity, "skill and
fancy."[61] Much higher than vulgar utilitarianism, the result was a transcendent achievement. Instead of marginalizing and removing them
from open view, the "aesthetics of the mechanical arts," as Bullock put it,
deserved to pervade "the social life of our time."[62]

The ability to develop a dialogue with the natural world through work
remained central to the mechanics' view of free labor. The elite view approached nature as a set of scientific principles from which social, technological, and political-economic laws could be derived. They pleaded with
their fellow men to defer to the immutable power of those laws. The mechanics, on the other hand, marveled at the ability of humans to mold the
natural world for their purposes. Over against the deductive approach of
the bourgeoisie, the mechanics advocated a gradual reciprocal process that
required active and enduring engagement with the world of matter. Bullock
celebrated the mechanics' "toiling and patient philosophy of induction and
experiment, of investigating, step by step, and process by process . . . the
laws which guide mankind in their efforts to subdue matter and combine
[natural] forces." This relationship with nature entailed neither a total-
izing conquest of the kind Bostonian investors sought in industrial sites
such as the mines of Michigan or the stockyards of Kansas City nor complete withdrawal from it in an effort to preserve it as pristine. Rather, skilled

work was a form of communion with nature. "That which was dead in nature," Bullock explained, was "made by skill and art to speak in a language felt and understood by the great circle of humanity . . . the wood, the metal and the ore, so changed as to become a charm to the eye, music to the ear, and an awakening medium to all the sensations which are undying in the heart of man."[63] The mechanic had the ability to unleash the intrinsic qualities of dead matter that otherwise would have remained hidden, triggering a deeply resonant response among humans.

The mechanics viewed this communion with nature in spiritual and religious terms. Governor Long in his address argued that the mechanics' exhibitions were "rich with such evidences of the divine spark of human genius," making the exhibition space itself into nothing less than "a house of God."[64] Slack used his own address at the exhibition of 1869 to quote at length from Theodore Parker, his abolitionist mentor, about this question. "How can the finite mind communicate with the Infinite Mind, and receive inspiration from God?" Parker rhetorically asked. "Aspiration alone," he explained, was not sufficient. Rather, "aspiration with normal work, of head and hand, secures this communion with God." "By learning the mode of operation of the material forces of the world," he argued, we "thereby get communications of material force from God, and share His power over the world of matter. . . . By this process the worker becomes inspired with the material power which God put into the universe." This mode did not culminate in human mastery of nature. Far from it. Rather, even as the mechanic gained new technological capacities, the process constantly revealed the immense powers not accessible or even knowable to him. Even as "mankind goes on, ever aspiring for more, ever working for more, ever inspired with more," the material forces of the universe "stretch . . . away before him and above him, vast treasures of power not yet made use of. . . . There is always this reserved power, which man sees but cannot master, and beyond that yet other power, not mastered and not seen."[65] To the mechanic, work made the limits of human powers viscerally known.

Elite notions of beauty, inspiration, creativity, and physical labor, occasionally presumed to emerge in opposition to the irredeemably commercial urban culture, were formulated in direct opposition to those of the mechanics. The original mission of the Museum of Fine Arts (MFA) in Boston when it was chartered in 1870, to take one prominent example, was not fundamentally different from that of the mechanics' exhibitions.[66] The museum's charter stipulated that the museum "ought to be a popular institution, in the widest sense of the word" and ensured it would be open for free four times a month. Alongside representatives from Harvard College and the Boston Athenaeum, the original board of trustees of the museum included elected government officials, including the mayor, the secretary of the state Board of Education, and the Boston superintendent of schools, whose presence, it was hoped, would allow the museum to be closely integrated into the curriculum of the public schools. At the dedication of the functional, inexpensive museum building in 1876, the superintendent proclaimed the place "not only a museum, but a school—a school in which some of the best and noblest faculties of our nature find their daily, their yearly, their constant claim." The mayor claimed the MFA for the population at large, announcing that "all classes of our people will derive benefit and pleasure" from the institution, labeling it "the crown of our educational system." The urban masses, in turn, readily embraced the museum, overwhelming it in its first year of operation with one hundred and forty thousand free visitors (as opposed to only seventeen thousand ones who paid admission).[67]

The museum's collections reflected the focus on the institution's educational goals. They encompassed not the "private fancies of would-be connoisseurs," as Charles C. Perkins, one of the early trustees and then the director of the museum, publicly explained, but "materials for the education of a nation," primarily casts and reproductions that were used for pedagogical purposes. Perkins looked favorably on the educational activities that took place on the premises. He was enthusiastic about the combination of aesthetic pleasure and educational value that the variety of objects at the MFA offered. "Casts, stuffs, pictures, engravings, are constantly utilized," he approvingly observed, "and a never-ceasing influence for good goes out from them, to charm, to elevate, to instruct, and to delight those who are brought in contact with them, day after day, and week after week." This type of multifaceted way of engaging with objects in the museum seemed to him perfectly consistent with what a museum ought to be.[68]

Over time a few of the trustees became increasingly concerned about education draining resources away from what they perceived to be more suitable uses for the museum. About a decade after the original charter, several members of the board expressed apprehension that "the extensive educational tail . . . [was] wagging the museum's dog."[69] They raised objections to exposing the collections to the design students. As one of the students explained, these board members warned against "the possible depredations of irresponsible young men who, if nothing worse happened, would soil the floors with their paint and charcoal and probably break glass cases."[70] Design students became dangerous invaders rather than valued visitors. This new guard of aesthetes on the board moved the museum away from its educational mission and from its popular orientation. They recast the museum as a sanctuary for the appreciation of art. They abandoned reproductions, which were thought to profane this sacred space, and instead endeavored to collect original work—the "fruits of this exalted and transcendent life," as one of the new trustees explained. Casts and reproductions, which had instructional value for students, were pegged as "mechanical" in nature, a label that was meant to carry pejorative connotations. "The exhibition halls of our Museum," one trustee elaborated, "have the same right to be free of mechanical sculpture as the programmes of the Symphony Concerts have of exemption from mechanical music." Against the mechanics' affirming view of engagement between man and nature through work, the trustees of the museum celebrated a purely aesthetic communion between the viewer and the work of art. They asserted that "the direct aim of art is the pleasure derived from a contemplation of the perfect."[71]

Art at the MFA was increasingly identified with refinement and with insulation from commercial culture and popular art forms. To accomplish this goal, the curators increasingly looked to historical works, marginalizing art by Boston-based and other contemporary artists. They required viewers to appear in full dress, observe new rules of decorum, and appreciate what was in many cases an increasingly austere environment. Whereas the mechanics encouraged visitors to touch and operate the items on display, the new institutions created a conscious divide between art and spectator, performer and audience. The mechanics continued to showcase art alongside agricultural implements, wagons and bicycles, fireworks, upholstery, and sanitary instruments. They displayed "fine art"—oil paintings, watercolors, sculptures, and statues—together with "decorative" and mechanically reproduced art—engravings, lithographs, and heliotypes. Elite cultural institutions like the MFA, however, increasingly defined mechanical invention as the very opposite of artistic creativity. They defined aesthetics and connoisseurship as distinct and inherently superior to ingenuity and hands-on engagement.

The mechanics' exhibitions made a mockery of such hierarchies. They continued to reject the cultural boundaries that became so central to the bourgeois cultural order. In doing so, they did not seek to perpetuate an unthinking premodern landscape. Rather, they articulated their own modernist sensibility. They embraced the chaos of urban life, the eclecticism of mechanical invention, and the mingling of art, industry, labor, and commerce. At the close of every exhibition, they made their tribute to the cacophony of modern life literal in a festive ritual. The contributors to the exhibitions were encouraged to demonstrate their feelings about the event, which they did by cranking up the noise from the machinery. For several minutes, one account reported, "the valves on all the engines were opened, the bells began to ring, the various machinery to clatter, the rock crushers to thump, the whistles to shriek, and the orchestral band by each player to sound a different note; until at last the din was sufficient for the least impressible temperament."[72] Celebration of dissonance, not of universal and seamless harmony; of amalgamation, not segregation; of active self-assertion, not passive observation, was the mechanics' creed.

The exhibition of the Massachusetts Charitable Mechanic Association did not take place on Boston Common. The arguments of the petitioners and those of the opposition were debated by the aldermen and councilmen, who considered the legal dimensions, the history, the commercial impact, and the edifying influence on the population. They accepted, on the whole, the petitioners' argument that the event would be highly beneficial to the city. It would be, as one alderman explained, "an exhibition which will redound to the honor and good name of the community, and be in itself an educator, a stimulant to invention, and a promoter of taste and utility in every department of industry and art." Those opposed, however, had one winning argument to deploy. If the resistance to the event proved one thing, they explained, it was that the exhibition would serve to divide the community. These internal antagonisms would undermine the very goals of the event. "Instead of a united exhibition of all our mills and workshops," the logic went, "it will be a house divided against itself."[73] In the face of such fierce opposition, members of city government became reluctant to rebuff the expressed wishes of the city's most powerful citizens. They reconsidered their decision, and the mechanics' request was denied.

Despite the setback, the mechanics' exhibitions gained a new scale. They held one in 1878 in a temporary building on a space that was provided by the city.[74] They then confidently moved ahead and acquired private land on Huntington Avenue, where they erected a mechanics' hall, which was symbolically located in proximity to cultural institutions such as the MFA, the Boston Symphony, and the Massachusetts Institute of Technology. They solidified their public presence in the city and continued to hold mass exhibitions there through the 1890s, which became major events in the life of the city, attracting hundreds of thousands of visitors and thousands of presenters. Politicians, businessmen, and other dignitaries continued to appear at these events and paid tribute to the mechanics in orations and toasts. For the mechanics, however, this new position was nonetheless a defeat. In losing the special public status they had enjoyed in their years in Faneuil Hall, they became one civic association among many, and one without access to donors with particularly deep pockets. They were forced to relinquish their aspiration to represent something greater than a narrow social group and became one interest in a pluralist environment. This important transition redefined their role as one far less threatening to the hegemony of the urban elite. The mechanics continued to hold a central place in public affairs for the time being. Over time, however, this ostensibly minor setback anticipated the marginalization of the mechanics and their ethos within the urban public sphere.

CHAPTER FIVE

Eastern Money and Western Populism

T he urban politics of industrialization, as manifested in contests over metropolitan space, public finance, and civic institutions, found their analogs in the sparsely settled territories of the Great West. The influx of financial capital from outside the region, from places such as Back Bay in Boston, funded exploration, infrastructure, and development. It facilitated the incorporation of vast western regions into the national economy. These far-flung capital flows also galvanized a forceful political pushback from western settlers. The rights of out-of-state investors to extract the natural bounty of the land, control labor, and ward off taxation and government regulation were not immutable or taken for granted. Nor were they readily bestowed. Rather, they were constituted in law through hotly contested political battles on the state and local levels. In the 1870s and 1880s, the power of these investors moved into the core of regional politics.

Like in the urban East, market integration and state formation were deeply intertwined processes. As eastern capital penetrated the Great West, the settlers of U.S. territories, jostling to position their communities in the emerging commercial system, began to clamor for their territories to gain political autonomy. They sought to free themselves of federal authorities, not by leaving the Union as Confederates had done, but by entering it as new states.[1] Scholars have often associated the integration of a national market with the consolidation of national authority in Washington, DC, but in this context, the integration of the West into the national economy produced the reverse. It greatly energized a proliferation of subnational political units, each of them in charge of large swaths of policy that the federal government had limited capacity to attend to.[2] In a period strongly associated with political and economic consolidation at the national level, the contentious process by which the federal government parceled out its enormous western domain into states unleashed a powerful countervailing thrust of decentralization. As it did on the metropolitan level in Boston, the drive of market integration did not converge toward a seamless whole but rather accelerated a contradictory trajectory of political fragmentation.

The political origins of the process could be traced back to the 1860s, as the unopposed Republican Party opened the floodgates to the rapid creation of U.S. territories. The process carved Dakota (1861) from parts of Minnesota and Nebraska, Colorado (1861) from Kansas, and Idaho (1863), Montana (1864), and Wyoming (1868) from Washington, which had itself at one point been part of Oregon.[3] By the 1870s and 1880s, when the residents of these territories began to lobby for statehood, the economic triggers for this process had become the main focal point. Remarkably aware of falling rates of return on older investments such as cotton manufacturing in the East, settlers realized they had a unique opportunity to attract financial resources to the region. Because of the "utmost difficulty in finding profitable investments" in the older states, members of the chamber of commerce in Denver noted, in what became a common refrain, "a 'plethora of money' must seek employment in the West where there [is] greater need, and naturally greater necessity for the payment of a higher rate of interest." They confidently expected that "all the Eastern capital for which reasonably safe and profitable employment can be found, will be sent here for that purpose."[4] State governments that could launch development—charter corporations, establish a legal regime and a system of courts, build infrastructure, and regulate industrial relations—became crucially important.[5]

The relationship between these new state institutions and corporate vehicles of financial investment raised a long array of controversial questions. Politically empowered as voting citizens, settlers took a hard stance vis-à-vis nonresident investors. They affirmed the primacy of state authorities over corporate interests. They analyzed property rights not as unassailable or natural but as subject to negotiation. They considered laborers' efforts to mobilize in collective ways as desirable and therefore deserving of government support. They envisioned a wide spectrum of possibilities for a capacious democratic state. Despite their general sense of grievance against eastern capitalists, which sometimes took the form of hostile political agitation and belligerent rhetoric, westerners clearly were not impulsive or somehow reckless. Rather, they creatively and thoughtfully tried to translate economic priorities, ideological commitments, and ideas about fairness into policy. Never shy about their desire to spur development, they mobilized politically to structure their relationships with distant investors in ways that would harness eastern money in the service of their own particular vision of balanced regional development.[6] Financial elites and their representatives in the region had very different expectations. In their effort to forge an integrated national market, they aspired to devise political institutions that would be conducive to the rise of a new, consolidated economic order. These men mobilized to orient incipient state governments toward greater focus on their position in a larger, interconnected market system. They sought to subsume the political autonomy of western settlement under a set of general, legible, predictable, and investor-friendly principles.

The conflict over the formation of political institutions raged most visibly as the settler population of each territory seeking statehood assembled their representatives in constitutional conventions.[7] These gatherings resembled one another in tone and content. Together, they constituted a larger regional debate about the trajectory of the American political economy. In contrast to the federal constitutional convention, which had assembled a cadre of affluent elites behind closed doors, western conventions included farmers, workers, miners, local lawyers, and small businessmen and were reported on daily in the press. Farmers and labor representatives went on record to voice the grievances of the region's working population. They placed on the agenda a wide spectrum of policy ideas beyond what was admissible in more polite circles back east. Within these western gatherings, however, these policy ideas had a much wider base of support, even among more upwardly mobile and formally educated delegates. These men dissented from market dictates, reflecting the pervasive sentiments of a broad cross section of the population. They expressed hostility toward corporations that were controlled not by the local political authorities that had initially chartered them but by "foreign" shareholders back east. They were adamant about prioritizing actual settlers over distant investors. Against the financiers' aspirations to shape policy with an integrated economy in mind, they advanced democratic processes over financial imperatives. In ways that echoed simultaneous debates in the urban East, they prioritized relative regional autonomy over the prerogatives of the national market.

Ultimately, the West's peripheral position, which made it dependent on eastern financial resources, proved an immensely powerful counterfactor to these populist aspirations. As they moved to codify their own vision in the legal foundations of the new states, constitution writers faced categorical demands from the representatives of eastern investors, demands they found difficult to disregard. Any deviation from prescribed policies, formulated according to the conventional wisdom back east, threatened to jeopardize their community's access to capital markets, with far-reaching economic consequences. Loath to cripple their economic prospects, the delegates at the time erred on the side of caution. The final drafts therefore included meaningful achievements for the populist agenda but were nevertheless more deferential to the designs of eastern financiers than many participants had initially hoped.

The participants' distinctly regional outlook did not mean that the conversations were somehow parochial or insular. Having moved between regions and between various western settlements, settlers developed a sophisticated and varied purview that was informed by their own migratory experience. Fully aware of a large economic transformation under way across the continent, their arguments routinely drew comparisons between their own territories and other locales. They freely adopted provisions from the constitutions of other states and frequently invoked lessons learned in places such as Pennsylvania, Illinois, Wisconsin, California, and Nevada, among others. The intersection of the delegates' diverse perspectives infused the deliberative process with a sense of open possibility. The law, many reasoned, was not derived from unchanging abstract principles. Rather, it emerged from the everyday practices and collective wisdom of the settlers. William Stewart, a senator from Nevada who addressed several of the conventions, held that the law was "simply a system of principles to be applied to the facts as they are developed." Constitutional conventions should therefore readily welcome pragmatic innovation and a measure of jurisprudential pluralism, resting on "such application of the facts as they exist in the different localities as will inure to the greatest good of the people."[8] This view was shared by many of the delegates who proceeded to shape policy not in accordance with any established doctrine but with conditions on the ground in mind.

This approach flew in the face of legal orthodoxy at the time. Expert authorities urged the settlers to follow the federal model and write short and elegant constitutions that would outline a general legal framework. Chief Justice of the Supreme Court of Michigan Thomas M. Cooley, the era's most prominent scholar of constitutional law, spoke at several of the conventions and implored the delegates to confine themselves to fundamental principles. "Leave what properly belongs to the field of legislation, to the Legislature of the future," he pleaded.[9] Most participants, however, considered state legislatures, in the absence of a detailed constitutional framework, to be too vulnerable to corporate manipulation. The members of the Colorado convention, in a joint address to the people of the territory, explained that legislatures "have, in most cases, been found unequal to the task of preventing abuses and protecting the people from the grasping and monopolizing tendencies of railroads and other corporations."[10] Melville C. Brown, a Maine native who migrated to Wyoming via California and Idaho, warned that any important policy issues left out of the constitution would permit corporations to shape legislation in their best interests. "As you have seen in the past men elected to our legislatures wearing the brass collars of the great railroad corporations," he cautioned, "you will see just such men wear the brass collars of the great monied mining corporations." The constitution should therefore explicitly place some policy issues "forever . . . beyond reach."[11] These apprehensions about corporate power encouraged the conventions to author long constitutions that carefully delineated the authority of state governments, demanding direct state involvement in some spheres and firmly limiting it in others.

The question of water and its distribution called for a particularly creative treatment. The common law doctrine of riparian rights practiced in the East, which bestowed water rights to the owner of the adjacent land, was inadequate in the arid West, where sources of water were few and far between. If settlers were to enjoy wide access to water, water rights had to extend to nonriparians. The alternative doctrine of "prior appropriation," giving ownership to the first mover who diverted water from its natural source, presented its own pitfalls and was similarly questioned. Charles Burritt, a Vermonter who had practiced law in Michigan before settling in Wyoming, denied that "when a man builds a ditch and takes out water . . . he has not the right against his country and all the world to the use of that water as long as he pleases."[12] More threatening than individual users gaining disproportionate amounts of water was the fear that corporations, with the large resources to construct canals and ditches, would create water monopolies and subjugate the rest of the population. George W. Fox, who was raised in Ohio and lived in Iowa and Montana before opening a hardware store in Laramie, Wyoming, pointed out that, in the absence

5.1. Delegates of the Wyoming Constitutional Convention on the steps of the Territorial Capitol, Cheyenne, Wyoming, 1889.

Credit: Wyoming State Archives, Department of State Parks and Cultural Resources. WSA Sub Neg 1671. (CC BY 3.0)

of countervailing legislation, "a corporation may organize a strong company to take out nearly all the water in a stream . . . , and . . . prevent the settlers . . . from obtaining water out of this canal."[13]

To address this challenge in a region where access to water could only be provided via heavy investment in infrastructure, several delegates voiced well-reasoned support for state ownership of water and water infrastructure. Alexander Burns, a Missouri prospector-turned-farmer who settled in Montana, boldly proposed that "the legislature shall provide for the construction and maintenance of a system of irrigating canals and ditches in this state," which will "belong forever to the state and remain under its direct control."[14] Given that the new states lacked the resources to build the infrastructure, other stakeholders proposed more realistic measures that

5.2. Delegates of the state Constitutional Convention in front of the Territorial
Capitol building in Olympia, Washington, 1889, with support personnel, wives,
and local grade school students.

Credit: Inauguration of Governor Ferry Photographs, 1889, Washington State Archives, Digital Archives,
AR-28001005-ph000003, http://www.digitalarchives.wa.gov, accessed March 1, 2016.

would charter private companies to carry out the construction but maintain as public property all water in the state.[15] This approach granted corporations the right to charge regulated rates for delivery of water but not to hoard and monopolize this precious resource. It also allowed the state to regulate how water would be distributed, attenuating the principle of "prior appropriation" with constitutional provisions restricting the allocation of water rights according to the principles of "beneficial use" and of "sufficiency." These provisions limited the right to water to the amount one put to actual use, requiring that water be divided up in dry seasons to provide each user with an adequate amount. William H. Claggett, a Maryland-born lawyer who had practiced in Nevada and Montana before migrating to Idaho, clarified that these clauses aimed to promote a more "equitable distribution"—to serve "the greatest good to the greatest number, bearing in mind constantly the fact of the prior right of the first man as well as the necessities of the second."[16]

Some delegates thought that declaring water everywhere to be public property was too radical. Walter Cooper, a dealer in mining properties and real estate, who was raised in Michigan and arrived in Montana after spending time in Kansas and Colorado, protested that "if this amendment had emanated from that distinguished person, [the heterodox political economist] Henry George . . . I would not have been surprised." Llewellyn Luce, a New Englander who had moved to Montana on behalf of the Department of the Interior, similarly argued for the commodification of water. "A right to use water," he claimed, was "just as much property as is a horse, and it would be just about as consistent for us to declare in this Constitution that every horse in the State should be the property of the State."[17] Most delegates, however, agreed that a failure to depart from precedents on this issue would result in an intolerable situation that would be incompatible with republican institutions. Without the proper constitutional protections, Martin Maginnis, a miner who was born in New York, raised in Minnesota, and later became the editor of the *Helena Daily*, foresaw that "the men who hold the water . . . [would] practically own the country," leading to "a system of landlordism in contrast with which the evils of all other systems of landlordism will be as nothing."[18]

Industrial relations in the new states emerged as another area of legislation that attracted the full attention of the conventions. Clear-eyed about the region's large industries, railroads and mining in particular, delegates foresaw the intensification of class conflict. They anticipated, as Claggett explained in Idaho, that the "great development of the material resources" of their territories would bring about "problems of a very difficult nature relating to labor in its various forms of employments and various exactions that may be imposed upon it."[19] The conventions thus discussed a long list of labor protections that aimed to place the power of the state firmly behind workers. They considered clauses mandating government oversight of workers' safety, eight-hour days, minimum-age restrictions, labor bureaus to study and publicize industrial conditions, employers' liability for injuries, restrictions on the use of convict and contractual labor to compete with free labor, and prohibition of blacklisting of labor "agitators."[20]

Particularly controversial in this context were proposed bans on the use of armed Pinkerton detectives by management during strikes, an issue that was bound up in the question of workers' right to organize. Peter Breen, who was born in Kansas and raised in Illinois before finding work as a locomotive fireman in Colorado, Idaho, and Montana, argued that this provision was absolutely urgent. "We do not want any such class of men as makes up the standing armies in Chicago today to go to any part of the Union where they can be at the call of corporations," he explained. These men "did not come as soldiers, or as officers of the law interested in the welfare of the Territory," but rather, "they came at the bidding of some corporation, that, for a monetary consideration, wishe[d] to crush the manhood of the people of the Territory."[21] Others agreed that in a free society workers should be able to organize without the threat of violence. William T. Fields, a locomotive engineer who arrived from Illinois, declared that no corporation had "the right or power to employ armed bodies of men to shoot down people who assemble and congregate for the purposes of freedom." This use of private militias founded, in effect, "a despotic form of government" that kept workers in a state of "chattel slavery."[22]

Again, as with water, these types of restrictions on the prerogatives of corporate property prompted fierce opposition. Francis Sargeant, who was making his way in the mining industry in Montana, announced that it represented "an abridgment" of his "rights and privileges, guaranteed to [him] by the [U.S.] Constitution," if he could not, at his "discretion, within the law, call upon the sixty millions of people within the United States, if necessary, to preserve [his] life and property."[23] This line of reasoning gained little traction with the other delegates, who were far from eager to further militarize their region. Elliot Morgan, who had moved to Wyoming from his native Pennsylvania, where labor conflicts involving

Pinkertons had already erupted, explained that the importation of "armed men . . . clothed with authority of law" was "one of the greatest outrages ever perpetrated upon any people."[24] Delegates who were even more conservative, such as Luce, agreed that "government should protect private property, not private militias."[25]

One common-law tradition to which the delegates held fast affirmed the supremacy of the state over chartered corporations. Martin N. Johnson, a farmer in North Dakota, explained that "railroads are 'quasi' public institutions. [Their shareholders] don't own their roads as we own our ox carts. They must run their roads in the interest of the public—they cannot stop these arteries of commerce, and deprive the husbandman of the fruits of his labor." Citing the case of *Munn v. Illinois,* Johnson reminded his fellow delegates that the United States Supreme Court itself had "settled that principle once and for all."[26] This decision validated delegates' efforts to endow state legislatures with far-reaching regulatory powers over corporations, including the right to set rates. It sanctioned constitutional provisions that repealed or altered existing corporate charters and declared railroads to be "public highways and common carriers," prohibiting the practice of setting discriminatory rates that gave high-volume shippers and select cities favorable rates over other shippers and other locales.

The debate surrounding the rights and privileges of corporations in the new states became especially contentious as delegates sought to constrict the tax exemption and subsidies that corporations sought and in some cases already enjoyed. Idaho judge John T. Morgan protested against the lax tax regime under the territorial authorities. A "vast amount of money [in the mining industry] has been taken out of this territory and almost no taxes have been paid upon it at all," he argued. Since mines were difficult to assess for a more conventional property tax, he proposed a tax on the net proceeds of mining properties. "While they are becoming wealthy . . . and build[ing] up mansions and rich homes . . . in Boston and New York and other places . . . I desire that they shall pay some little tribute to the government of the state."[27] Others advocated strict limits on direct government subsidies to corporations. Thomas C. Griffitts, a printer who had arrived in Washington via Illinois and Utah, curried favor with his proposal that "no county, city, or other municipal corporation give any subsidy or loan its credit to any corporation or individual."[28] The representatives of the mining, stock raising, and railroad industries maintained that tax incentives and public subsidies were absolutely necessary. Alfred Myers, a

Montana stock grower who hailed from Illinois, explained that the construction of water infrastructure was not remunerative, making government subsidies "necessary in order to induce people to invest money in this kind of speculation."[29] Lycurgus Vineyard, a former superintendent of schools in Oregon, argued that taxing the territory's "languishing" mines would be analogous to "clos[ing] them out" along with the "enterprising mining men who are seeking to develop this industry."[30]

The notion that the region's largest industries in their fledgling phase needed nurturing seemed plausible in the context of competition among states, where any extra costs threatened to put one's particular state at a disadvantage. Louis J. Palmer, a county attorney who was originally from Illinois, explained that taxing extracted minerals would "destroy" Wyoming's mining interests, "for they cannot compete with the Colorado men, if you are going to put a tariff on coal."[31] Most delegates nonetheless objected to these special favors. William Parberry, a Montana doctor and rancher who was born in Kentucky and raised on a farm in Missouri, posed the question that if the corporations receive tax relief, "why in the name of justice cannot a man who is trying to make a living by the sweat of his brow?"[32] Alexander Mayhew, a dealer in mining claims who had come to Idaho by way of Kansas, Colorado, and Montana, similarly spoke against "sacrificing everything in this territory for the purpose of building up these corporations." It was "a dangerous precedent to establish in this territory as we are now budding into statehood, to encourage the railroads in such manner."[33] These sentiments lent support to forceful constitutional amendments that stripped legislatures of the authority to grant corporations special giveaways.

As the various conventions appeared intent on passing significant checks on the power of corporations in the new states, in a range of policy areas, it fell on local compradors—men who had forged relationships with eastern financiers and were therefore attuned to the vitality of interregional investment—to articulate the forceful retort. And indeed, these stewards of eastern financial interests worked tirelessly to resist the conventions' populist tide. They of course harbored no enmity against state institutions per se. They fully agreed that economic development could not proceed without adequate government institutions and wise public policy. Indeed, they interpreted the entire statehood movement as an effective way to attract outside investment. Mark Hopkins, a Pennsylvanian who had spent time in Colorado and Utah before heading to Wyoming as the superintendent of the mines of the Union Pacific Railroad, took it "for granted" that "one of the benefits to be derived from statehood" was the improved ability to "bring outside capital into this state . . . to develop the latent interests of this territory." Lawyer Frederick H. Harvey, who was raised in Iowa and educated in New York before arriving in Wyoming, similarly explained that "we are advocating statehood in order to bring in just as many corporations as we can possibly."[34]

What these spokesmen on behalf of finance objected to most was not robust government institutions as such but the notion that economic policy was the province of democratic politics. Francis Henry, Illinois-born former clerk of the Territorial Supreme Court in Washington, explained that an elected railroad commission, with rate-setting authority, would be incompatible with liberal institutions. He rejected such a body as "discriminatory, arbitrary and unjust in the extreme . . . [a] violation of the fundamental principles of free government."[35] According to Henry and others like him, the forging of government policies should ultimately be determined not via a vote by the people but by educated experts and in accordance with universal laws. These critics were dismissive of provisions such as state regulation of hours of labor or public ownership of water, which threatened to endow what they considered to be ludicrous economic doctrines with firm legal standing. John W. Hoyt, an Ohioan who had previously served as the appointed governor of the Wyoming territory, argued that such policies were "opposed to the great economic law" that "commanded the respect of all statesmen of every land."[36] These "great" principles stood high above any policy that the people's elected representatives could devise.

These defenders of corporate prerogatives proposed that, regardless of the people's preferences or ideological commitments, the ultimate costs of ignoring the universal laws of political economy would forever outweigh the benefits. Any imposition on the rights of investors would be counterproductive, as it threatened to drive capital away and retard future development. This concern about alarming providers of capital crystallize the key dilemma at the very core of those constitutional deliberations, one that came up time and again, in every state and around nearly every question of economic significance. On the one hand, the compradors dangled an alluring "carrot." William A. Clark, a banker and a heavy investor in mining, and among the wealthiest men in Montana, shared with the convention what was the conventional wisdom in elite business circles. Declining profit margins back east and in Europe, he explained—the "very low rate of interest" resulting from "the great accumulation of capital in foreign countries"—created a real opportunity for the fledgling new states to become the next focal points for massive investment. Instead of deterring them, wise legislation should "induce [these capitalists] to come here and build large smelting plants and large mills and other enterprises of that kind."[37] Hoyt similarly dazzled his fellow delegates in Wyoming. "We have extraordinary resources, thirty thousand square miles of coal, endless soda lakes, inexhaustible supplies of oil, mountains of iron that have not yet begun to be developed," he waxed poetic. "What we want is capital, and shall we not keep out capital if we discourage capitalists? Shall we build a Chinese wall around Wyoming and prevent the investor from coming in to develop its resources?"[38] In his view, instead of creating a heavy-handed regulatory apparatus, exacting taxes, and empowering labor, the top priority should be to forge an effective framework for money to pour in from the East and produce broad-based prosperity.

When participants seemed unmoved by these alluring prospects, doubting that wealth would trickle down to the general population, the same spokesmen pulled out the "stick." Ringing the alarm bells, they warned that unfriendly policies toward investors would surely derail the economic trajectories of states that adopted them. Railroad regulation, Francis Henry warned in Washington, would thwart "the investment of capital in the development of the resources of the state, . . . paralyze the great enterprises of improvement which have already been commenced, and . . . prevent the inauguration of others now in contemplation."[39] A tax on mine proceeds in Idaho, Vineyard announced, would deter investors, who would channel their investments to friendlier locales. You could very well "tear down your advertisement to the world that you invite mining men and mine operators into this territory, and tell them that they need not apply to this territory," he added.[40] Similarly, Anthony C. Campbell, who moved from Pennsylvania to Cheyenne, Wyoming, to become the U.S. attorney for the territory of Wyoming and later served as the attorney of the Denver and Rio Grande Railroad Company and Standard Oil, explained that employers' liability for injuries would prove ruinous, making it "impossible for any railroad company or any corporation to do business . . . without going into absolute bankruptcy."[41]

Constitutional delegates responded to these confident arguments in mixed and contradictory ways. Some believed that these doomsday scenarios were vastly overblown. Others objected to corporate encroachment into the domain of political sovereignty, to corporations "com[ing] in and bind[ing] us hand and foot," as Mayhew put it.[42] Several speakers defiantly rejected the very notion that the state had to "coddle and fondle and caress these great capitalists in order to get them to come out here and invest their money," as Charles Hartman, a lawyer who had come to Montana from Indiana, put it.[43] Nonetheless, the threat of alarmed capitalists fleeing their states weakened the resolve of constitution writers on these issues. Not eager to confront powerful financial interests, many delegates conceded their territory's position of weakness. Jack H. Beatty, an Ohioan by birth who had previously practiced law in Missouri and Utah, spoke as an insider when he plainly explained: "You invite eastern capitalists to come in here and build railroads, and they will commence to look over your laws. The first thing they will find is that we have adopted stringent measures to operate their roads for them." Given "how timid capital is," this would prove disastrous.[44] Walter A. Burleigh, a lawyer from Maine, led the retreat in Montana. "We are not working for the nabobs of the east, we are not working for the lords of England, we are not working for the capitalists of New England," he reasoned, and yet, "we do not want a hedge around the development of our resources by any such strict rules of conduct either moral or business."[45] As the deliberations proceeded, these concerns led to the elimination of some of the more restrictive provisions, making the constitutions less radical.[46]

In more general terms, what was at stake in these constitutional debates? Beyond the realm of any particular policy question, and beyond the scope of a contest among different interest groups, the conventions revealed fundamental conflicts over the three fundamental and deeply interrelated issues of distribution, legibility, and spatiality. On the most basic and obvious level, the contests were driven by an effort to determine how material resources would be distributed between employers and employees and between foreign investors and settlers. This was part of a general contest in this period among what political scientist Richard Bensel has termed competing "claims on wealth."[47] Inherent in the process of writing a constitution was the premise that the structure of state institutions, and their relationship to private interests, would ultimately determine how the material bounty of the land would be divided. Delegates were deeply worried about the emergence of a society sharply polarized between rich and poor, a situation they deemed incompatible with a free society. It is with these concerns in mind that they promoted a legal code that prioritized "beneficial use" of resources such as water and allocated them broadly according to principles such as "sufficiency." The distribution of these resources would not be governed by the ostensibly objective laws of supply and demand but rather, as Montana territory justice Hiram Knowles put it, according to "what was reasonable."[48] The same distributional goals similarly motivated delegates to regulate the exploitative tendencies of the labor market, empower labor to mobilize collectively, and tax corporate property.

Delegates, however, were concerned not merely with how wealth would be divided but much more fundamentally with how the modern political economy would be organized and governed. Different parties to the conversation were doing more than battling over the distribution of economic rewards; they thought of development in radically different terms. This came up during persistent skirmishes over the comprehensibility of the emerging state institutions, or their "legibility," to apply political scientist James C. Scott's apt term in a particularly broad way.[49] Corporate investors were not merely immensely affluent and therefore a target of redistribution; they were also absentee investors who shipped their capital across the continent. These men wanted the property regime to be not only secure but also predictable and transparent, especially from afar. Local farmers had full confidence in an institutional framework governed by democratically elected officials, who were answerable directly to the residents of their state. They wanted railroad freight rates and water rights to be allocated, as Maginnis put it in Montana, by "a tribunal that was near the people . . . [and] elected by the people."[50] From an absentee investor's perspective, this was a nonstarter. As Luce explained to his peers, "people do not let their money out from a distance. They will not bring it here or send it here to be controlled by County Commissioners" or other locally controlled bodies.[51] A democratic process that appeared to be most reliable and accountable to the farmers in the region seemed utterly indecipherable to distant investors and their representatives. These investors viewed the democratic political process as an arbitrary infringement on the more predictable laws of political economy and the methodical workings of the private market.

As legal scholar David Schorr has shown regarding Colorado, the entire legal notion of "beneficial use" resulted in what investors considered to be an illegible property regime that placed significant restrictions on the transfer and sale of water rights. Unlike rights based on the physical capacity of each ditch to carry water, which remained constant, rights based on use fluctuated with rainfall and the precise acreage of land under irrigation. These rights were also always set to expire owing to a failure to put water to use. Investors thus could not hold on to water rights while blocking bona fide settlers. Nor could they shift rights from one type of use to another. All transfers rested on the ability to demonstrate conclusively that the quantity of water passed over was indeed applied for a particular use by the seller prior to sale. Any precise measure of this amount required litigation in locally controlled state courts, which affirmed the scope of ownership on a case-by-case basis. To complicate things further, any given water stream had dozens of upstream and downstream users whose intertwined rights, which were not recorded in any central registry, could not be legally interfered with.[52]

Needless to say, in reducing the clarity and certainty of property rights, this notion of "beneficial use" did not make for easy alienability of water. Crucially, this regime tended to privilege settlers over absentee investors. Local users, steeped in this dense thicket of arrangements, enjoyed a clear advantage over prospective buyers from outside the region, who had little chance to make sense of it, let alone navigate it.[53] Scholars have often associated this type of illegibility with premodern or precapitalist modes of governance. This particular legal framework, however, developed through legal decisions in territorial courts and later codified in state constitutions, was not a vestige of an earlier age but a distinctly modern edifice, driven by the commercial, dynamic, developmental aspirations of westerners. It nevertheless introduced highly contextual standards that were relatively transparent for local actors while remaining opaque to eastern investors.

Finally, again transcending mere issues of distribution, the question of organizing space—which historian Richard White has labeled "spatial politics"—became a key theme in the constitutional debates.[54] The struggle to shape the emergent, and extremely unstable, geography of the modern political economy was central to the politics of the era overall. Westerners were not concerned about the volatility of the geography around them per se. Having migrated time and time again themselves, adroitly traveling across and within regions, they were modern actors who thrived in the flux of their dynamic environment. Unlike more elite investors and commentators, for whom instability and risk were constant sources of anxiety, western delegates did not appear to be obsessed with imposing a rationalized order on an ever-changing situation. They instead focused on the economic trajectory of the various states and their position in the broader geography of national and world markets. Preoccupied with fostering a measure of relative economic autonomy for the region, they pushed back against the centralizing tendencies of national corporations and worked to counterbalance them with local and regional manufacturing and trade. "When it comes to a question of corporations and the mechanics, laborers, and business men of the territory," Breen reflected on this conflict, "I think it is to the interest of the people of Montana that it shall be the corporation that will suffer."[55] The ideal was not isolation from national and world commerce but the emergence of overlapping markets of varying geographical scale, with commerce and industry pursued by a diverse array of business forms.[56]

Quite explicitly, delegates were not content with their region's peripheral status as a provider of raw materials, primarily minerals, which threatened to perpetually leave it in a dependent and vulnerable position. They were concerned about their long-term viability and sought to broaden the economic base of their respective states. As Knowles explained in Montana, the "wealth that is created by mines passes away in the next fifty or one hundred years perhaps." It was important for the state to nurture a greater diversity of economic pursuits, in industry and agriculture, which would become a lasting source of prosperity: "If we can settle up our valleys with a thriving farm population we know that here will be permanent wealth . . . property that will remain the property of the country."[57] Pro-corporate delegates played to these sentiments. They argued that heavy capital investment in mining would naturally have a multiplying effect and inevitably flow to other sectors. Clark optimistically proposed that "the expenditure of large sums of money" in mining would "result in the fostering and development of *other* great industries."[58] Hoyt took that to be the main lesson from the experience of Colorado: "Why has Colorado become the great state she is? Because she has welcomed capital, she has not closed her gates, she has opened them wide, and Colorado today is a workshop. Colorado is alive with industry."[59] The sense of urgency around regulating railroad and water corporations suggests that most delegates were not convinced. They associated unbridled corporate power—an unwise opening of the gates—with one-dimensional and ultimately unsustainable development.

The effort to endow the new states with capacious regulatory powers vis-à-vis the railroads, and especially in regard to freight rates, owed a lot to these concerns about long-term sustainable development. Many of the conventions took place in the aftermath of the Supreme Court's decision in the *Wabash* case in 1886, which curtailed state-level authority to regulate interstate commerce. In response, delegates fought to expand the definition of *intra*state commerce and the scope of their jurisdiction over it. They required all corporations transacting business within their states to open offices and appoint representative agents within their state, which would be required to meet the state's regulatory and information-disclosure requirements. Locally chartered railroad lines that were acquired by "foreign" corporations and integrated into larger railroad systems, they declared, would remain under the jurisdiction of state courts and thus subject to local regulation. Most crucially, the "short haul, long haul clause," requiring that rates would remain proportional to distance, prohibited railroads from shifting the costs of long-distance traffic, where profit margins were squeezed by competition, over to local traffic, where competition among railroads was limited and rates could more easily be raised.[60] Low freight rates within states, relative to interstate commerce, nurtured regional manufacturers and discouraged importation of goods from national urban centers like New York and Chicago. This was not a backward-looking initiative, a doomed effort to force freight rates to conform to a seemingly neutral standard of pricing, but an attempt to facilitate the emergence of a more decentralized political-economic geography and countervail the tendency of low long-haul freight rates to build up a handful of mega-metropolises.[61]

One of the most striking features of the constitutional struggles in the different states, despite their many similarities, was their indeterminacy and therefore the heterogeneity of their outcomes. Access to large pools of capital and powerful social networks that spanned across long distances gave pro-finance forces immense leverage. Their power, however, remained far from absolute. The political pushback from farmers, workers, small businessmen, and other settlers enabled them to score meaningful victories, assimilating elements of their own vision into the political framework in the areas of tax policy, infrastructure, social services, government oversight, labor rights, and public control of natural resources. The final drafts of the constitutions, as adopted, were not a clear triumph for any particular interest. They bore the mark of the divides and disagreements that surfaced during the writing process, varying based on the conditions of different industries and economic sectors at the time of the convention and the ability of the respective parties to mobilize and rally support.

In Idaho, for example, the constitution included a strong set of labor provisions outlawing the deployment of private police forces and the hiring out of convict labor. It formed a bureau of "immigration, labor and statistics" and stipulated that eight hours would be the working day for all government work. Mining interests, however, were powerful enough to eliminate the clauses that required regulation of safety in mines, held employers liable for workers' injuries, and disallowed blacklisting of labor leaders. They were also able to escape a clause enforcing a tax on the net proceeds of mines.[62] Farmers in the state proved a more potent political force than industrial workers. The constitution thus subjected railroad corporations to assertive regulation, including government oversight of freight charges and the prohibition of discriminatory rates. Tax breaks and other subsidies to private business interests were made illegal, tying the hands of overeager or pliable state legislators in their future dealings with corporations.[63] The constitution furthermore banned private property in water, prioritized agricultural uses over industrial ones, set firm limits on the transfer of water rights, and explicitly sanctioned the regulation of water rates. However, it did not form a water commission to enforce these policies, leaving that to the discretion of the legislature.[64]

Similar battles in Colorado, Montana, Wyoming, Washington, and North Dakota produced an uneven and unpredictable range of outcomes. The constitutions of Idaho, Montana, and Wyoming, for example, provided for eight-hour days for all government work. This provision failed to pass in Colorado, Washington, and North Dakota.[65] The constitutions of Colorado, Wyoming, and Washington mandated strict regulation of safety in mines. Those of Idaho, Montana, and North Dakota did not.[66] Washington was the only state of the six that failed to restrict child labor in mines. Where age limits were imposed, however, they varied from sixteen years in Montana, to fourteen in Idaho and Wyoming, to twelve in Colorado and North Dakota, which extended this restriction to underage workers in factories and workshops.[67] All six constitutions declared railroads to be common carriers and prohibited undue discrimination between users and locales. However, the constitutions of Montana, Washington, Idaho, and North Dakota explicitly authorized state regulation of railroad freight and passenger rates. In Colorado and Wyoming, this clause was struck down.[68] The constitutions of Montana, Idaho, and Washington included explicit "long-haul, short-haul" clauses, requiring that rates correspond to distance, but those of Colorado, North Dakota, and Wyoming did not.[69] Colorado exempted mines from special taxation for ten years from adoption of the constitution. From the onset of statehood, Wyoming and Montana mandated a tax on gross product. Idaho, Washington, and North Dakota left this tax out of final drafts entirely.[70] Lastly, all states reserved water for public uses, subject to "beneficial" appropriation. However, whereas the deliberations in Montana, Washington, and North Dakota whittled down the issue of water to a single obtuse clause, Colorado, Wyoming, and Idaho included more elaborate articles on this topic. Colorado and Wyoming established permanent state commissions to oversee the allocation of water. Colorado and Idaho prioritized domestic and agricultural uses over industrial uses. Idaho included a special clause subjecting prior appropriation to "reasonable limitations" in dry seasons. Colorado alone explicitly empowered its commissioners to establish "reasonable maximum rates."[71]

The tug of war between investors and populists therefore produced a variety of legal regimes, depending on the contingent progression of each constitutional convention. This is how issues of legibility and spatiality intersected. The comprehensibility of political institutions to investors was contested not merely within each individual state but also within the overall cluster of western states, each with its own property rights regime (under the sovereignty of state courts), regulatory apparatus (controlled by elected state commissioners), and framework for industrial relations (mediated through a democratically elected legislature, courts of arbitration, and labor unions). Constitutional provisions had to be followed up by legislation in state assemblies and then implemented by local officials, leaving the entire apparatus in radically uncertain flux in the years to come. Therefore, the constitutional conventions enacted an uneven regulatory landscape that national corporations would have struggled to traverse. In the absence of measures to the contrary by federal authorities over the next several decades, led by the unelected Supreme Court, the consolidation of the national market, rather than being preordained or necessary, seemed more likely to derail and fracture.[72] Instead of producing a "flat" world market, integration produced a complex new geography, an institutional patchwork that was never fully transcended in the twentieth century.

CHAPTER SIX

The Age of Reform

The growing integration of the North American economy held profound implications for all American cities, and for Boston in particular. The strains of municipal finance, which were incipient in the 1870s and 1880s, became a painfully concrete challenge by century's end. Waves of capital migration across the continent, facilitated by the work of men such as Henry Higginson, Charles Adams, Alexander Agassiz, and Henry Minot, had created a new fiscal reality for American cities. Investments in "foreign" or "out of state" corporations largely escaped assessment in eastern cities, enabling the wealthiest citizens to evade their due share of the tax load. To make things worse, men of means took refuge in the low-tax havens of suburban towns around the major cities, further undercutting the revenues of city governments. In this context, expenses and revenues diverged, and municipal debt reached unprecedented proportions. The fiscal foundation built on three decades of abundant municipal budgets began to rupture.

More than any other factor, this tenuous budgetary situation undermined the ambitious metropolitan development program inaugurated by urban populists after the Civil War. As property held as financial assets escaped taxation, government revenues were raised disproportionately from weaker segments of the population. The increasingly regressive sources of tax revenues diminished the polity's appetite for ambitious public programs, making voters more amenable to a period of "retrenchment." Structural fiscal conditions alone were not in themselves sufficient to affect changes in policy. The sense of urgency around growing deficits, however, gave urban elites an opportunity to organize and reassert themselves in politics. It gave their political action electoral viability that it had not previously enjoyed.

The ascendance to the mayoralty of Boston of Nathan Matthews Jr., the first true member of the elite to capture this office in a generation, demonstrated the newfound assertiveness of the upper class and the politics it introduced. Capitalizing on the opportune moment, Matthews and other members of the city's elite plunged themselves into the political fray. They advanced their reform agenda by innovating in the field of party machinery, overcoming any qualms about collaborating and building electoral coalitions with less genteel social groups. Matthews thus became, perhaps paradoxically, both a reform mayor and the head of a statewide political "machine" of great reach. His well-oiled party apparatus forged a powerful cross-class political network that allowed contributions from wealthy individuals and political propaganda to flow to strategic local operatives, mobilizing voters during campaigns and on Election Days. In this manner, elite private economic resources were translated into public power.

With his newly won mandate, Matthews led the charge against the urban legacy of metropolitan growth. He sought to contain the expansion of urban government and to streamline the existing departments according to managerial business methods. He pushed to shift power away from the legislative branch—controlled by neighborhood businessmen and skilled workers—and centralize executive power in the office of the mayor, an office that had previously been mostly symbolic and that lacked operative authority. Additionally, his municipal finance program aimed to shift the burden of taxation away from downtown businesses and wealthy taxpayers onto working-class and lower-middle-class homeowners in the peripheral neighborhoods of the city, the very neighborhoods that had for decades had been supplied with an abundance of public improvements and services. In this manner, Matthews effectively undermined the ambitious program of using public resources to shape the political economy of the metropolis. With its access to revenues cut off, city government lacked the ability to affect economic conditions in a meaningful way, a situation that in turn only reinforced support for elite-led reform.

The fiscal dilemma facing cities was best captured by Richard T. Ely, professor at Johns Hopkins University and the most heterodox of the new wave of progressive political economists. In 1888, Ely set out to elaborate his own groundbreaking philosophy of local and state taxation, confronting the liberal doctrine that characterized the established authorities on the subject, such as David A. Wells and Thomas M. Cooley. Educated in Heidelberg, Germany, and flush with new continental ideas about property, Ely broke with previous conventions in the field and did not portray taxes as payments in return for government protection or services, or as part of a contract between the citizen and the state.[1] He rejected the formulations of laissez-faire economics and dismissed the notion of taxes as market-like "payments in exchange."[2] When he turned to devising a new foundation for his own doctrine, however, he found little need to innovate or transplant collectivist European ideas in an irredeemably individualist American soil. There was no need because the ideas about the social foundations of taxation and the morality of taxing citizens based on "ability to pay" had long pervaded the political system. Ely acknowledged as much when he grounded his treatise not with passages from scholarly treatises on the issue but with the words of Thomas Hills, Boston's chief tax assessor, the autodidact upholsterer whose report only thirteen years earlier had been dismissed by educated authorities on the matter as petty and ignorant, if not a form of "communistic" propaganda.[3]

As noted, Hills had never formally studied law or economic theory, let alone at a prominent German university. His political education took place in the gold-molding shop of his father-in-law, in the charitable mechanics' apprentice library, and in the tumult of urban politics. Nonetheless, Hills's ideas, particularly the emphasis on the organic unity of individuals in society and their social interdependence, resonated with Ely's—to the letter. "The correct doctrine of taxation," Ely explained, "is ably stated in the 'Report of the Massachusetts Commissioners relating to Taxation,' made in 1875," the one headed by Hills. He quoted directly from the report's assertion that "a man is taxed not to pay the state for its expense in protecting him, and not in any respect as a recompense to the state for any service in his behalf, but because his original relations to society require it." Taxes were part of the obligations "man, as a human being, owes . . . to his fellows," making "civilization possible." Ely's firm intellectual commitments stood with this view, which Hills and hundreds of other tax assessors in Massachusetts (and elsewhere) had long endorsed as common sense while erudite tax reformers had struggled to discredit for a generation. This position in theory justified and legitimized far-reaching taxation powers limited only by "what the true interests of society require."[3]

These were consequential statements, especially from a credentialed intellectual. Ely, however, shied away from the radical measures that this theory of taxation made room for. On one hand, Ely used this social reasoning to introduce a truly trailblazing proposal into the conversation, a state income tax that he thought would raise much-needed public revenue and promote greater fairness in taxation. Ely softened the blow as much as possible. He reassured wealthy taxpayers that the tax was preferable to the "merciless" property tax that was levied regardless of the revenue a taxpayer derived from his property in any particular year. He added that the tax "need never exceed one per cent," which would make it much lighter than the prevailing urban tax rate on property. The shifting of tax administration from the contentious city level, where it was handled by motivated assessors, to more dispassionate bureaucrats on the state level was also advantageous from the perspective of large property holders. The proposal was nevertheless an important progressive breakthrough.[4]

On the urban level, however, Ely's proposals were considerably less ambitious. Whereas Hills emphasized the social underpinnings of taxation to bolster the general property tax, Ely invoked these principles to argue against it. Ely's policy recommendations in the field of urban taxation, primarily as they related to taxation of "personal" property, closely resembled those of his laissez-faire predecessors. Fundamentals aside, his book echoed the policies that had long been advocated by David A. Wells, Hills's bitter opponent, who had called for a tax exemption on financial forms of property.

Ely bridged his socialist tenets and liberal legislative proposals with an appeal to sober pragmatism. Changes in the realm of political economy, he argued, made taxation of "personal" property—namely, stocks, bonds, and other financial instruments—extremely perilous for city governments around the country. The formation of a national financial network, and the mobility of investment capital limited the taxation power of city governments, which consequently had to adjust their spending agendas. In essence, Ely explained that, regardless of the urban populations' political agendas and ideological commitments, the taxation of highly mobile forms of property would be detrimental to the economy of a city that enforced it. In a crucial chapter in his book, entitled "The Testimony of Reason," Ely made the claim that the polity may aspire to raise taxes on "intangible" forms of property, but a reasonable city government would avoid it on pragmatic grounds. In an age of boundless geographical horizons and itinerant capital, it would be imprudent for the city to tax property that could effortlessly flee. Ely reasoned that "there is a species of property which floats about from place to place with ease. We may say that property of this sort is endowed with a high degree of mobility." Since this form of property gains its remuneration independent of a particular locale, communities were powerless to impose limitations or taxes on it. Simply put, "If in our state it is oppressed, it will leave us for other regions, where it is more favorably treated." City governments must instead entice capital to their borders and remain cautious about driving it away.[5]

Liberal political economists since Adam Smith had portrayed the mobility of capital as a timeless principle. Ely's articulation of the principle of capital flight, in keeping with his training on the continent, cast it instead in a much more historicized perspective and grounded it in a particular place and time. This was neither a timeless principle nor the outcome of "modernity" as such, but rather a historically contingent situation. Ely did not deduce. Rather, he *observed*, noting that "interstate movement of floating capital was never so easy as it is to-day . . . capital of any high degree of mobility does, as a matter of fact, readily flow from state to state." As a result, it was, for example, as simple "to invest money in a mortgage a thousand miles from one's home as in a mortgage on land in one's own country." These new historical conditions called for a reorientation of tax policy. Rather than shaping policy from the perspective of the metropolitan economy, from the standpoint of "the individual city or the state," it had become necessary to examine a city or an industrial region as "a part of a larger whole"—the United States and even the world economy. The consequences of failing to make that adjustment could be disastrous. A city or region "may be well-nigh ruined by a failure to take into consideration interstate relations."[6]

Ely's advocacy that American states and cities should adapt to these conditions was a major concession to the emerging corporate order. Instead of taking the terms of national market integration as an open-ended question to be molded by a democratic political process as urban and western populists had done, he embraced what had been the position of financiers and their advocates, who argued that a fully integrated market in investments was already a fait accompli. "Like it or not," Ely explained, "as men of sense, we cannot wisely shut our eyes to the fact." The implications were far reaching. Instead of taxing mobile capital to actively spur metropolitan development, he argued that a wise tax policy ought to take "great care . . . to reduce interference with business and professional pursuits to a minimum." One of the main advantages of the income tax, as Ely envisioned it, was precisely its ability to generate government revenue, and do so in equitable fashion, while remaining decidedly noninterventionist in affecting market transactions. Unlike the property tax, a state income tax would not infringe on the separation between state and market. It would "allow business to proceed without obstruction in its natural channels." He assured readers that the rewards of his approach would filter down to the rest of the urban population—"make the flow of capital to [one's city] easier, and the benefits [would be] thus diffused throughout the community."[7] Those who supported such policies, he granted, were seeking not their own narrow goals but rather the good of their community as a whole. They "do not have in view the special interests of holders of such property [in financial assets], but the general welfare. . . . No practical man can fail to move carefully in this matter."[8]

Men "of sense" in American cities everywhere were indeed caught in a bind. Urban prosperity, to a significant degree, depended on capital investment. Investment, however, would not materialize if subjected to political "interference." The economic penalties a city suffered for political "meddling" were therefore severe. As a result, the formation of a continental financial network increasingly held in check the efforts to use political means to mold economic change. With the urban public sector thus stifled, the parameters of feasible policy were set not by ideology or urban politics but by the power of an increasingly national business leadership to disinvest and shift capital to friendlier pastures. Once one accepted these parameters, instead of pushing back against them, the viable spectrum of government action became greatly circumscribed. It certainly stacked the cards against publicly driven metropolitan development of the type envisioned by democratic constituencies in the postwar decades.

In this climate, with municipal finance under strain and progressive intellectuals steering away from taxing investment capital, urban elites, whose commitment to economic fairness fell short of that of Ely and his progressive intellectual cohort, became emboldened to launch an era of reform in city government. Earlier elite efforts to influence urban politics had fallen short. Their attempts to contain metropolitan expansion and rising municipal spending proved largely unsuccessful. Most emblematically, the opposition to the Tilden Commission of 1875—the notorious New York commission that proposed severe restrictions on the right to vote—demonstrated that direct attacks on universal suffrage held little prospect of success. Like their counterparts in New York, upper-class Bostonians learned that restricting the right to vote to property owners alone would not be a feasible strategy. Instead, they internalized the understanding that their influence in politics would have to come not from direct confrontation with the urban population but rather through methods that were more pragmatic.[9]

The leader of the reform movement in Boston, Mayor Nathan Matthews, was the leading visionary behind this crucial change in strategy. He acknowledged, as he himself put it, that change in urban politics would come not from "radical changes in the suffrage" or "the overthrow of representative institutions" but rather "along the more prosaic lines of a conservative experiment." Change had to come not through direct confrontation but rather "by slow degrees. . . . Success cannot be attained without the most thoughtful study and unceasing vigilance and effort." Granted, given the democratic foundations of government, the state could not be made to run as efficiently as a business, he reasoned. "A certain inefficiency, a certain waste, must be conceded as part of the price," he admitted, but this was a small sacrifice for the "blessings of free institutions." In other words, elites could achieve their goals in a democracy—secure their "freedoms"—by asserting themselves politically, building coalitions, and remaining ever watchful. Matthews framed this reinvigorated effort as a test of the elite's manliness. Unlike upper classes elsewhere, who had "lost the virility to resist," he called fellow men of privilege to assert themselves and prevent the city from becoming "a pauperized community of nationalists and socialists."[10]

Beyond his political deftness, Matthews had the social pedigree to lead the reform movement. He was a descendant of an old and distinguished New England family based in Yarmouth on Cape Cod. His father had left the Cape and come to Boston to begin a successful business career in commerce and then urban real estate, becoming at one point the largest taxpayer on real estate in Boston and a major developer in the luxurious Back Bay neighborhood. Born in 1854, the younger Matthews graduated from Harvard College, studied political economy and jurisprudence in Leipzig, and continued on to Harvard Law School. He joined the bar in 1880 and practiced law, focusing on urban real estate and trust administration. While at Harvard, Matthews joined the crew team, a sport that became a lifelong passion. He loved trees and laid out—allegedly with his own hands—a modern forest on the family's private property north of Boston, property that was later donated to Harvard as a scientific research lab (the family also underwrote the construction of Matthews Hall, a dormitory in Harvard Yard).[11] Matthews had an infatuation with bookkeeping and professed a love of figures. His college degree had a focus in mathematics. He was a member of the American Statistical Society and was fascinated with "tables of statistics."[12]

Matthews came from an old-line family of Democrats. He was not a "mugwump" like the many elite Bostonians who joined the party in 1884 to support the candidacy of Grover Cleveland. He nonetheless capitalized on the Brahmin frustration with politics in Massachusetts and looked for ways to make their voices heard. In 1888, he founded the Young Men's Democratic Club (YMDC), which became a vehicle for the gathering of campaign contributions from men of means in Boston and elsewhere in Massachusetts. He was aggressive and deliberate in his quest to secure the financial clout of his organization. "Will you not see what can be done in the way of getting funds from W. F. Weld, Charles Weld, and S. D. Warren?" he wrote in a typical letter to a supporter in the city's financial district. "We want to raise between ten and twenty thousand dollars, and to do it at once. We have several thousand dollars subscribed already, and think that the Welds and Warren might be induced to give at least $500 apiece, and we think that you are the best man to approach them."[13] In another letter to a supporter, he lamented the "considerable apathy among the Democrats in Boston" but was optimistic that the voters "can be aroused by the holding of rallies . . . particularly if we can obtain the necessary funds. . . . Will you not send me your check for such a sum as you feel that you can afford to give?"[14] Unlike previous such groups, the YMDC refused to move the proceeds to the official party institutions in the state. Rather, Matthews retained exclusive control over the funds and distributed them to a network of political affiliates. Access to the financial leadership of the state, including top figures such as John Murray Forbes, Charles Cabot Jackson, and Edward Atkinson, helped make the YMDC, in Matthews's words, "as influential as a political organization as any in the country with the exception of the great societies of New York City."[15]

The organizational effort of the YMDC helped Democrats capture the governorship of the state for three consecutive years after decades of almost uninterrupted Republican dominance. Matthews built on this success to take over the Democratic State Committee (DSC), the official leadership of the party in Massachusetts. He viewed the older leadership of the party as lackluster and inefficient. "Everybody knows that they get no money to do anything with . . . and that they don't do anything," he wrote in confidence to a friend. "This year and in '88 they did not put a single dollar into the campaign for registration or election day, and this year they did not raise or spend a cent for any purpose except headquarters and one rally." As the chairman of the DSC's executive committee, Matthews brought to the party an unprecedented organizational effort. He marked a decisive shift in Massachusetts politics in bringing administrative methods from the world of business to bear in the electoral sphere.

Long before Election Day, Matthews gathered systematic statistics on the population of the state, acquiring a complete set of all the publications of the state's Bureau of Statistics of Labor for the offices of both the party and the YMDC.[16] He worked to create a centralized database of relevant election information and to develop a statewide network for the dissemination of party literature. One circular sent out to correspondents throughout the state requested: "Will you kindly send me the names of all Grocers, Barbers and Druggists in your town who are Democrats, and can be relied on to keep Tariff Documents and other campaign literature in their shops, and assist in distributing it?"[17] Another questionnaire collected detailed information about each and every town, inquiring about the names of all prominent Democrats and their occupations, hotels and inns and the politics of their proprietors, all Democratic lawyers, all places suitable for public meetings, important newspapers and their proprietors' views, holders of liquor licenses, a copy of the town book, and the number of voters who would like their poll taxes paid for them. Matthews instructed operatives to make sure "those just coming of age" be put on the lists at the earliest possible date and offered financial assistance in mobilizing voters.[18]

No detail was too small. Matthews pushed for a reduction in the number of voting precincts to allow solicitation to be more effective. He worked on redesigning the ballot to make it simpler for illiterate voters to vote the party line. He fostered relationships with editorialists at sympathetic newspapers such as the Post and the Globe. He circulated election speeches to the press before they were delivered orally to allow prompt and comprehensive newspaper coverage of party gatherings. He corresponded directly with printers regarding flyers and political circulars: "Please have [the flyers] printed to the extent of 10,000 and send them to the Young Men's Club as fast as possible. Be sure to use as good card as the sample I have."[19]

Matthews built the party's identity around the catch phrase of "Jeffersonian Democracy," which he defined as the effort to "limit the functions of government and to oppose every unnecessary interference by the government with individual rights and action."[20] He gave guest speakers "talking points" to crystallize the party's message. When West Virginia representative William M. Wilson came to Boston, Matthews wrote that he had "taken pains to mark on the margin of these various documents in blue pencil the passages which have a Jeffersonian sound." To win supporters among workers, party publications took up the antitariff issue and explained the detrimental effects of protectionism on American consumers. One flyer, for example, listed basic staples and the direct effects of tariffs on their prices. The flyer explained that tariffs "oppress the consumer by increasing the cost of clothing, food, and shelter." They "stifle competition, limit production, and raise prices. . . . [Products] could and would be sold at far lower, though still profitable figures, were it not that the tariff, by restricting imports, enables the combination to run the price up to the tariff point."[21]

Matthews's access to superior financial resources and his organizational skills did not suffice to win electoral support. Crucial to his success was the alliance he forged with the state's immigrant political leadership. As one historian put it, this was a coalition of "Yankee money and Irish votes."[22] The Democratic State Committee that Matthews assembled reflected this partnership. Irish-born Patrick A. Collins and John H. Sullivan served as chairman and treasurer of the committee, respectively, while Matthews and fellow blue blood Josiah Quincy, became the chairman of the executive committee and the secretary, respectively. Those immigrant electoral power brokers proved willing participants in the movement Matthews and his cohort sought to advance. A remarkable man like Collins had risen from the inner wards of the city to serve as a state representative and senator. He temporarily suspended his political career to attend Harvard Law School and pursue a career as a lawyer and director on corporate boards. Far from the stereotypical image of a "party boss," he was a man who bridged the divide between Boston's immigrant neighborhoods and the highest echelons of the business community. He owed his success to both. This reform alliance inaugurated a new pluralist politics that sought to limit state intervention in civil affairs and to soften class antagonisms.

Matthews had full confidence in his partners and greatly helped defuse any animosity toward them among elite sponsors of the party. Endorsing John H. Sullivan for treasurer of the State Committee, Matthews emphasized to a suburban supporter that Sullivan was "not identified with any of the Boston factions any more than myself, [and] has the respect of all classes of the party and people." He stressed that Sullivan was "well off . . . and is a man who we can recommend to the people who furnish us with money as a safe depositary of funds."[23] The new partners shared the business elite's goal of fiscal retrenchment. In a note to the former mayor of Boston, Hugh O'Brien, who had been its first Irish-born mayor, Matthews thanked the man for pursuing a policy of municipal austerity against the spendthrift men in the City Council: "If . . . the extravagant schemes of the City Hall crowd come to naught, the result will be largely due to your efforts."[24] This relationship between the city's ethnic leadership and the upper class of Boston was more than a marriage of convenience. In the face of an ambitious statist agenda in state and city politics, the notion of pluralist politics appealed both to Matthews and to his immigrant supporters. Matthews actively worked to foster ethnic awakening within the polity and found willing participants in men like O'Brien and Collins.

Nowhere was the alignment between affluent Bostonians and immigrant leaders more explicitly articulated than in the debate over the authority of the commonwealth's school boards to supervise private schools. The parochial school movement, which had been inaugurated by the Catholic Church in the mid-1880s, had not yet gained traction at this point, and the majority of the immigrant population sent their children to the public school system, which was hailed as the best in the nation and was by far the most generously funded.[25] Although anti-immigrant sentiment inspired some support for stricter government supervision of Catholic schools, most residents of the state supported mandatory primary education in the public schools. The debate over the supervision of private schools, more than a debate about Catholic education, thus became a broader debate over the fundamental relationship between the state, society, and the individual citizen.

Matthews made the issue one of his pet peeves. At a hearing on the issue before the Joint Committee on Education of the Massachusetts legislature, he appeared on behalf of sixteen private schools, reminding the hearers that the private schools of the state are "both in numbers and number of students, mainly Protestant," not Catholic.[26] Of thirty or forty private schools in the city of Cambridge, only two or three were "parochial" schools. The issue went far beyond the status of a small number of religious schools, he argued. Rather, the effort to tighten government oversight was a blatant infringement on individual rights such as "the right of the parent to educate his children, as, and where, and to what extent he pleases, [which] ought never to be abridged by legislative interference." It attempted nothing less than the substitution of "the Christian family for the centralized paternalism of the 'State'" to create a state monopoly over the "means of education." Worse than antagonizing the "church of Rome," he warned, state supervision of private schools would introduce "into this Commonwealth . . . one of the worst forms of State Socialism." He explained that "the essential principle of Socialism is the regulation by the coercive power of government of the individual in all the departments and details of life, according to certain fixed and uniform standards." The supervision of private schools by local school boards would not only "subject the teacher of a private school to an inspection as inquisitional and arbitrary" but would compromise the basic liberties of the people, subjecting them to an experiment in social engineering. "The people," Matthews observed, "instead of being the creators of the government, are regarded as its creatures; and the government itself is magnified as the 'State,' into something superior to religion, to the family, to the rights of property, and to all the other institutions of civilized society."[27]

Matthews exaggerated but did not mischaracterize the views expressed by the commonwealth's board of education. The board indeed defined for the state a broad mandate in the field of primary education. They agreed with Matthews that at stake was far more than the prejudices of a minority: a contest over civil society itself. In typical fashion, their annual report insisted that, more than merely a service that government provided to its citizens, the state and its public schools had a "vital relation" and therefore enjoyed a special status. The board admitted that compulsory public education entailed an infringement on individual liberties. That, however, was a necessary sacrifice for the higher goal of a free, democratic society. "The idea of a system of free public schools originated in the same minds that established for us a free democratic state," they reasoned. "Neither can exist without the other." Public education therefore was a necessity of the first order for the preservation of democratic institutions. "A large association of ignorant men cannot, for any considerable period, oppose a successful resistance to tyranny and oppression from the educated few," they explained, since an uneducated polity will "inevitably sink into acquiescence to the will of intelligence, whether directed by the demagogue or by priestcraft." The violation of individual rights was justified in the case of education for a higher goal of fostering "moral relations which enable men to become a people," allowing them to develop a common identity, "and which enable a people to secure to themselves the unmolested enjoyment of their rights, and the full development of their social faculties."[28] The relationship between a free people and their government in a democratic society, far from being antagonistic, was in this view harmonious and mutually reinforcing.

The board was explicit about their support for a uniform educational foundation for all the children of the state. They argued that "there is some knowledge which all should know, and some mental cultivation which all should receive." If so, "a united effort should be made to bring all the children into the public schools, where they may receive such elementary training as will lay the foundation for those states of mind which will make of these persons one people in intelligence and virtue and love of country." In their vision, the state's public schools should provide a common foundation for all, allowing the diversity of civil society to thrive in other spheres, "leaving to the family, to the Sunday school and the church, the exercise of those influences which may direct the individual to particular forms of religious faith and worship."[29] Matthews rejected this emphasis on what he characterized as a form of coercive "uniformity," stating, "We object to the doctrine that all education in these or any branches of learning should be uniform, the same for all schools and for all scholars." "We deny this necessity, and repudiate the socialistic theories on which it is grounded," he argued. Against the board's definition of freedom as essentially social and collective, he proposed a definition of freedom that focused on individual choice. "Gentlemen, this country of ours was founded, not for protection, but for freedom."[30]

Matthews advocated a more pluralist education system, grounded in what he perceived to be a more natural order. Pegging the existing public system as a perverse imposition by the government, he explained that the "law of nature is diversity, not conformity," and this law applied "with equal force to human institutions, to industry, to education, and to government itself; individuality is the essential condition of all human happiness and progress." He denied his opponents' arguments that public schools were geared to give their students "certain 'social' advantages . . . tending to create class distinctions." Rather, private schools in his view enhanced the education system as a whole by pushing the public schools to excel. Private schools, he explained, offered to public education "that competition which is the indispensable prerequisite to progress in educational matters as in everything else." They allowed experimentation with new pedagogical methods that could not be undertaken within the public system. "The private school," Matthews argued, "is the 'experimental station of the public school.'" The private school in this manner could lead to improvements in public education.[31]

The school question was not without its own fiscal dimensions. As he started to eye a potential run for mayor of Boston on a platform of fiscal retrenchment, one cost-cutting opportunity Matthews focused on was the expenditure on school buildings. Matthews supported a moratorium on construction until the school controversy was resolved. In one of his speeches, he explained that he was "led to question, from a purely business standpoint, the propriety of building new schoolhouses. . . . I am opposed to the building of more public schools until the community know what attitude the public will assume in the future toward the school system and the present bigoted school committee."[32] In other words, Matthews aimed to (and then successfully went ahead and did) put the city's education system on a fiscal diet just as he moved to undercut its legitimacy, casting the school system as a form of socialist coercion. The board of education pushed in the opposite direction. To preserve the public system and the collective vision it carried, they explained that the state must continue to fund it generously. Only the continued fiscal resilience of the system could ensure its longevity in the face of the private challengers. "If it is not deemed politic to compel all the children of the State to attend the public schools, still it is plainly the duty of the State to make the public schools so good that all parents and guardians of children of school age will refuse, with an intelligent judgment and an unyielding will, to be deprived of their advantages."[33] Compromising the system's quality would be the first step toward jeopardizing its future and undermining its public goals.

Matthews entered office as mayor in 1891 and served four one-year terms. The approach that characterized his time in office was explained most explicitly in a detailed report that he published in 1895, at the tail end of his administration. More than an analysis of Boston's particular difficulties, the report was a treatise on the prospects and challenges of governing cities in a democracy. Not surprisingly, fiscal challenges stood at the center of the analysis. Corruption in city government, "about which we hear so much," Matthews explained, was "the least of [the city's] difficulties." The single biggest problem facing Boston, in his view, was "not Corruption, but

Expenditure." He attributed the situation to Bostonians' high expectations from their government—"the desire of the people of this city for more and better service from the municipality than is required in other cities . . . water supply, schools, streets, libraries, collection of garbage, public lighting, and similar municipal conveniences."[34] In addition to these urban amenities, the city subsidized ferry tolls and water rates (neglecting to adequately use them as sources of revenue) and paid high salaries to teachers, policemen, and firemen. Finally, over the previous three decades, the city had also undertaken costly improvements, spending $20 million on an extensive waterworks, $40 million on street widenings and grade changes, and $20 million on sewer and drainage problems. By all measures, these were enormous sums.

The problem of high government expenditure, as Matthews defined it, was hardly a local difficulty or a technocratic blunder. Despite views to the contrary, Matthews defined Boston's problem—and by implication that of all American cities—as a political one, rooted in the enfranchisement of male citizens. For this reason, in his view, it was useless for American cities to imitate well-run cities like Berlin or Paris. Matthews explained that those who look to emulate European models of city government will "omit to tell you that the basis of every political structure in this country . . . is universal local suffrage." Democratic politics made American cities fundamentally different from the cities of Europe, where local government was often administered by centralized national authorities or by property-based representation. "It is idle to point to the cities of modern Germany as illustrations of the fact that municipal corporation can be managed on strictly business principles," he explained, "for there the property-owners control the suffrage." The same applied to France, where "a large part of the local business is transacted by the national government," or to England, where "the suffrage is not yet equal, free, and universal, and the people have not yet learned their opportunities and power." Matthews explained that the conventional culprit of the "party system" was also a red herring. He observed that the divisions that animated city government were rarely partisan. Rather, almost all the issues before the City Council boiled down to questions of expenditure. The City Council was therefore split "in almost every case . . . between extravagance and economy, between expenditure and retrenchment, not between Democrats and Republicans."[35]

Runaway municipal spending represented the immense challenge of governing large cities in a democracy, potentially making them into a "training school for socialism," as Matthews put it. Despite surfacing in Boston in the most severe form for a variety of contingent reasons, the challenge far surpassed the case of one particular locality. It lay more broadly in democratic government, in the "chief danger of popular government: the demand for systematic distribution of wealth by taxes." The difficulty lay with "the demand of individuals, interests, classes, sections, and sometimes of the whole community, for extravagant expenditure." This difficulty keeps increasing as "the belief gains ground that the community in its corporate capacity owes a liberal living to its individual members." Indeed, Matthews observed, over the last generation, "a gradual change has come over the spirit of the people; and a large part of a population once the most independent and self-reliant in the world is now clamoring for support, as individuals or in classes, from the governments of this country." Consequently, he continued, there is "the difficulty of practicing economy in the face of the fact that a large portion of the people do not want economy; that another large portion insist upon expenditure as an indirect means of equalizing conditions; and of the fact that those who do not pay anything directly to the support of the government are in an immense and constantly increasing majority." He explained that "as long as the people at large, while in favor of economy as a general principle, yet desire appropriations for particular purposes on a scale that makes economy impossible, just so long will it be difficult to restrain the City Council, however constituted, from an improvident expenditure of the public funds."[36]

As mayor, Matthews made the reduction of municipal budgets his central goal. He enacted a long list of reforms to combat "extravagant" spending by city government. He introduced new business methods to the operation of departments, consolidated divisions where possible, and, with special ardor, systematized record keeping and department reports. He complained that "hopeless confusion" made it "entirely impossible for anyone to know how our city work is really carried on, or how much it is costing, so that anything like careful and intelligent scrutiny and criticism on the part of citizens is quite out of the question." Matthews conceded that Boston city departments had the most comprehensive reports of all American cities. The reports, however, were not designed in a uniform way to allow easy financial comparisons across departments or across years. This presented a challenge to anyone who examined these reports with a foremost goal of cutting costs. Despite volumes upon volumes of information and data, Matthews found it "impossible to find out in any satisfactory manner what work had been done or the cost of any work, excepting by taking the lump sum of money expended."[37]

Furthermore, the level of detail and the organizing principle of the reports did not allow direct supervision by a centralized executive. City departments described the services and goods they provided to the citizenry without itemizing every expense or evaluating the economic efficiency of their operations in any systematic way. Previously, in lean years, mayors who wanted to push for reduced spending had to rely on department heads to inform them how much they were able to cut from their operating expenses. They could not easily penetrate the dense operations of any particular department, which were often run by the same department heads for many years.[38] In large part, these layers of mediation within a decentralized system explained why government budgets were so difficult to cut, even in the absence of actual corruption. Matthews wanted to eliminate or weaken those "middlemen" and gain direct access to detailed information, which was necessary in order to change priorities. He therefore criticized the reports for lacking legibility, for being "confused and unintelligible, giving very little information that was of any importance, and no two were arranged on the same plan."[39] Matthews's complaints reflected the frustration of someone trying to infuse city government with a new logic of economy.

Looking to the future, Matthews proposed additional reforms, which included a reduction in the number of elective offices, the substitution of a single legislative branch for the bicameral system, longer terms in office, the enactment of civil service rules, the strict limitation of city indebtedness, the abolition of the district system of representation, and the concentration of further executive control in the mayor. All these measures were designed to restrict the function of city government as a representative and deliberative political body (or were "liable to degenerate into a debating society" in Matthews's terms) and redefine it as an apolitical administrative apparatus, to the extent possible.[40]

Nothing, however, received more attention from Matthews than fundamental reconstruction of the urban fiscal system. His analysis of municipal finance was telling. He had little to say about personal property in the form of shares and bonds escaping taxation, or wealthy taxpayers fleeing to the suburban towns around Boston. In line with Ely's diagnosis, he lamented the heavy tax charged on personal property—"the double taxation of many classes of personal estate is driving wealth and business away more rapidly than ever."[41] Instead, his complaints were directed at the residents of the city's "suburban wards," those neighborhoods that had been annexed to the city more than two decades earlier. In his view, these dense districts were at the core of the city's fiscal difficulties. They consumed large portions of the budget but paid back in taxes only about one-third or one-half of that sum.[42] This was true in terms of expenses on schools, library branches, and parks but was even more blatant in the case of residential development, which was heavily subsidized by public money. The "cost of street construction, like the cost of street widenings, sewers, and other similar improvements and conveniences," he argued, "falls upon the general taxpayer to an extent that would not be tolerated in any other progressive community." Whereas in other cities, New York and Chicago being the foremost examples, the cost of street construction, including sewers, street paving, and sidewalks, was taxed directly to the abutting land owners, in Boston, those costs were borne by the city's general tax fund. Matthews drew attention to this issue in Boston's fiscal structure more than any other, explaining that it was "of vital importance to a correct understanding of the problem of taxation in this city."[43]

According to Matthews, the peripheral wards not only consumed a disproportionate part of the budget but also dodged their fair share of the tax burden. He identified "systematic undervaluation" of real estate in "suburban and vacant lands, which results in . . . an inequitable distribution of the burdens of taxation." Whereas land downtown was assessed at between 60 percent and 90 percent of its market value, the assessed valuation of land in the peripheral districts ranged between 25 percent and 60 percent of market value. Additionally, suburban developers and homeowners—the beneficiaries of the extension of street, water, and sewer systems to outlying areas—successfully resisted efforts to assess them for the benefits they enjoyed. The law determined that three-fourths of the cost of sewers would be charged to the abutting landowners, but this measure was never enforced. Of about $23 million spent on street, water, and sewer improvements between 1867 and 1873, for example, only $3.5 million was assessed and only about $2 million was successfully collected.[44] Taxpayers in the business districts downtown paid the difference, in essence subsidizing development elsewhere in the city.[45]

Matthews argued that assessing "suburban" landowners in full would save the city half a million dollars annually. The public funds, he argued, "have always been regarded as held partly in trust for the development of real estate, and no administration has ever succeeded in getting rid of this radical vice in our financial system." Despite popular support for the use of public funds in the development of those districts, Matthews pegged them as the work of "selfish" men, who "but spend . . . [their] time in agitating for the expenditure of the public funds upon local and private improvements" and "under the pretence of advocating public improvements . . . actually succeed." Matthews spent his four years in office trying to reverse this development policy through action in the state legislature. He wrote that "every day's experience in the past four years has confirmed my belief in the wisdom and necessity of such a change."[46]

This was a direct attack on the metropolitan vision that had driven policy in the previous decades, policy that had led to annexation and to the resulting public spending on infrastructure in the peripheral districts. Those districts had the best amenities for working people, housing conditions that were much improved relative to the downtown area, viable prospects for property ownership by skilled workers, and the most favorable opportunities for proprietary businesses. Those neighborhoods were also crucial for the alleviation of housing density downtown. Matthews and his supporters advocated the marketization of real estate development to prevent what they saw as the redistribution of wealth through government spending on improvements. This would mean that private forces, not public policy, would instead guide development. Boston did not entirely escape these worse consequences of a privatized housing market, but public subsidies for residential development went a long way toward providing the population with quality housing on the periphery of the city. Matthews pressed hard against these subsidies.

Matthews focused his analysis on the undue resources consumed by the peripheral wards of the city. His views regarding the wealthy property owners of the city, whose property was held mostly in the form of personal property (stocks, bonds, debts, and other financial assets), were approximately articulated in the report of the Special Commission on Taxation, which he endorsed and presented to the City Council in 1891. The members of the commission were lawyer George G. Crocker, woolen-goods merchant and chairman of the Boston Executive Business Association Jonathan A. Lane, and lawyer and trustee William Minot Jr., Henry Davis Minot's older brother. The commission offered the thinly disguised perspective of the city's elite businessmen, which was nevertheless presented as the scientific expertise of that "class of persons who study the subject as a matter of pure reason."[47] The commission's report focused primarily on the heavy taxation borne in Boston by "personal property," which the report declared "unreasonable." Taxes on "personal property" werc more difficult to bear than those on "real estate," they explained, "because the burden of the tax is not so readily distributed."[48] Whereas taxes on real estate diffuse themselves among the population, through rents on working-class tenants, taxes on real estate fall directly on the owner of the property.

The commissioners elaborated why taxes on property were more difficult for the owner to shift to weaker segments of the population. To make their point, the commissioners gave their readers a short lesson in international finance, which Minot could describe from personal experience. They explained that whereas "the value of land, and the rent or profit is local," determined by conditions in the city itself, "the value of money and the interest or profit is universal." "Broadly speaking," the report explained, "all the money in the world forms one mass, which is constantly readjusting itself to a common level. The supply in London and Amsterdam affects the value of money here, so that the returns upon invested capital are about the same here as abroad." A local market, like the market in real estate, adjusted according to local conditions. Higher taxes would be translated into higher rents, allowing the investor to always recoup his investment. In the case of a financial asset, the return was determined in an international financial market and therefore could not be as easily adjusted to reflect the local tax. As a result, "the holder of a four percent bond of the C[hicago], B[urlington], & Q[uincy] R.R., if he is taxed, pays the tax out of his own pocket because his being taxed is an accident. It is not a payment under the universal law of trade, but a piece of ill-luck, like having his pocket picked of the same sum."[49] In a nationally integrated economy, the logic went, local politics presented themselves as arbitrary infringements on a self-regulating market system.

This analysis could be used to explain why taxes on personal property were in fact highly desirable from the perspective of the urban population at large. Unlike increased taxes on real estate, which percolated down to homeowners and tenants, taxes on financial instruments could not be easily diffused. To preclude this line of reasoning, the commission had to reiterate the risk of capital flight, which was then greater than ever. "In the present time," they explained, "rapid and cheap communication ha[s] brought the great rival competing cities . . . close together. It no longer takes days to travel, or ship goods, or communicate. Time and space are

annihilated. We are as much in close competition with New York and Philadelphia as if our boundaries touched." Under these circumstances, high
"double taxation" created a situation where "Boston and Massachusetts are
both avoided like a house guarded by a savage dog. It is true that one may
not be bitten; but it is pleasanter to go where the dog is not so fierce. Our
system is a scarecrow and a most efficient one." The damage of this policy
to the region's industrial economy was beyond measure. "Untold millions
of industrial capital has been warned away from Massachusetts, and driven
out of it by our oppressive and unreasonable laws, and many a millionaire
has feared to come here or left for the same reason." The commission elaborated how this affected the population as a whole. "The absence of great
industrial establishments in Boston is evident to everyone. . . . Supposing
an establishment employing $1,000,000 of capital and 500 men. Which is
worth most to the city of Boston, a tax on the million dollars, or the inci-
dental advantages?"[50]

Exemption of personal property, on the other hand, would deliver a wide
range of benefits: "labor would be better employed, and better paid; and
real estate, in spite of the greater burden laid upon it, would increase in
value more rapidly than in the past." Small businessmen in service sectors
would secure wealthy consumers: "Ask the driver of the corner cab, the
chore-man, the small grocer, the apothecary, all those who live on the expenditure of the wealthier classes, and they will tell you." The trickle-down
logic embraced by the commission articulated a view of prosperity that
emanated from the wealthiest residents of the city: "On one street on the
Back Bay there are some 400 houses. It has been estimated that the
householders expend on this street alone between $3,000,000 and
$4,000,000 yearly, or say $300,000 a month. Whether these people remain
in town one, or two, or three months longer, more or less, is a question
of expenditure of from $300,000 to $1,000,000 on this street alone, and
of money paid in to the general wealth of Boston instead of elsewhere, of
which cabmen, expressmen, carriers, choremen, mechanics, laborers, and
so on would get their share. The Commission guarantees that all of these
and more would be the advantages of relieving personal property from
double taxation."

This approach not only explained why taxing personal property was a misguided policy that put the city at a disadvantage vis-à-vis other cities. It also
provided a legitimizing rationale for tax evasion on a massive scale. Although
taxing out-of-state property was legally sanctioned, the commissioners

defined it as a form of illegitimate "double taxation." "When a resident of this State is taxed for the market value of his shares in a foreign corporation," they argued, "the property, real and personal, which makes up that market value is doubly taxed. It is taxed in the State where the person who owns an interest in that tangible property is; it is taxed in this State where the person who owns an interest in that tangible property lives." Their conclusion was far reaching: "It is not true that a vast amount of personal property wholly escapes taxation. The more correct statement is, that a vast amount of personal property escapes the double taxation which our laws attempt to impose on them."[51] This moral reasoning, which was totally at odds with the laws of the commonwealth, gave the wealthiest property owners in the city an ideological carte blanche to hide financial assets from tax assessors in the city.

Completing the capture of fiscal policy and ideology by elite reformers, a newly appointed tax commission in 1897 released its findings, renouncing the positions expressed in the report of 1875, which was authored by Thomas Hills. By 1895, the fiscal foundation of the large cities of the commonwealth had been gradually undermined. In part, this was the result of low valuations of personal property. Some witnesses before the committee estimated that only about a tenth of the $700 million in value of shares of foreign corporations held in Massachusetts was taxed. Aggravating the situation for cities like Boston was the flight of wealthy residents to suburban tax shelters. Despite systematically low valuations of personal property, the eighteen wealthiest towns in Massachusetts assessed personal property at about $55 million. Boston, the commercial and industrial center of the state, with about eight times the population of the eighteen towns around it, was assessed at $206 million.[52] The share of the property tax borne by real estate rose from about 55 percent in 1865 to almost 80 percent by 1898. This meant that taxes became more and more regressive, falling increasingly on the urban population at large (see Figure 6.1).

The commission of 1897, dominated by Thomas Jefferson Coolidge, the textile manufacturer turned financier, and F. W. Taussig, a Harvard economist, endorsed the abolition of the tax on "intangible" properties and supported a departure from the principle of equal taxation of all forms of property.[53] They sought to compensate for the loss of revenues with modest taxes on inheritances and on residential property, which, they claimed, would have the virtue of not "trench[ing] on the field which should fairly be left to other jurisdictions."[54] Renouncing any attempt to reinforce the

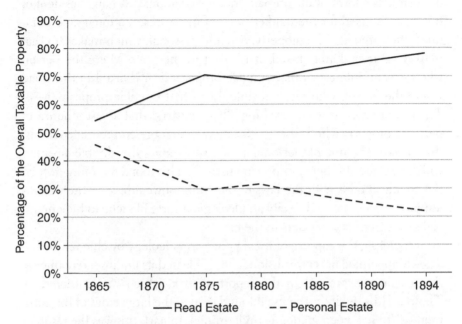

6.1. The divergence between taxes on "real" versus "personal" property. Compiled from Charles Phillips Huse, *The Financial History of Boston* (Cambridge: Harvard University Press, 1916).

administration of the property tax and more rigorously assess financial forms of property, they denounced it as an abject failure. "It is precisely this class" of property holders, they explained, that had the most open "opportunities for changes of investment or of residence." The effort to tax them most rigorously would be doomed to failure since those were precisely the citizens who "a system of rigidly taxing securities would be least likely to reach effectively."[55]

It was left to two dissenting voices on the commission to lament the direction of state policy. First, Alvan Barrus, of the rural county of Hampshire, decried the situation on behalf of the state's agrarian population. He decried the "untold millions" in state subsidies that had gone into railroad expansion but that had failed to benefit Massachusetts farmers. "While the farms of the State were being excessively taxed to forward these enterprises for the benefit of Boston," he argued, "Boston capital was seeking other worlds to conquer by aiding uncertain railroad enterprises, west and south, and by placing millions in western farm mortgages, many of which proved to be of the wild-cat order." Railroad traffic was overly focused on attracting commerce from other regions. "These railroads, fitted for first-class transportation and traffic from abroad, hardly pay that attention to local transportation in this State which the outlay by the State would seem to warrant." "Far from proving a benefit to [the farmer]," railroad policy "left his farm stranded on the hill-top, forced its abandonment . . . and, last but not least, brought new competitors to monopolize the markets which he formerly controlled."[56] Significantly, Barrus's support for government involvement in economic affairs was not shaken by his lifelong disappointment with the results of railroad policy. Although he held that the agrarian districts of the state paid more than their fair share, his support of taxation in support of government remained unshaken. "Some think it robbery to be compelled to pay a tax for the support of the government; but there is no place on this broad earth where men get so many good returns for their money expended as they do from a good government honestly administered." "The robbery," he insisted, "comes in not supporting it."[57]

More outspoken was George E. McNeill, one of the commonwealth's most renowned labor radicals.[58] His minority report registered a sense of outrage at the commission's resolutions, despite their presentation as scientific findings. "To exempt intangible properties" from taxation, he explained, amounted to an annuity of "more than 4 million a year of actual money to our wealthiest citizens." The sum was nothing less than an "extort[tion]" from the people of the state of a "perpetual tribute to a privileged class." McNeill did not support a reduction in taxes. He thought that the revenues of cities ought to be increased. He explained that "the city of Boston seriously needs the immense annual sum of which she would be robbed under the plan proposed by the majority." If a reduction were undertaken, however, it should be directed to other social groups, not to the most privileged citizens of the state. "Do these [the eighteen suburban towns], with State Street and the Back Bay, constitute the most desirable and needy region in which to pour out the largess of our exemption?" This approach meant the state would succumb to and reward "evasion, falsification, bribery and intimidation" of "the most wealthy of our citizens," setting a bad example that would "demoralize all classes of tax payers and the community at large."[59]

Again, the spirit of Thomas Hills hovered over the debate as McNeill referred to him as "an authority of national reputation, with the widest experience of any man living on the taxation of these properties." McNeill reminded readers that Hills, together with the other assessors of the state, was "inflexibly opposed to the exemption of intangible properties." This was because tax assessors could clearly recognize "the injustice and public injury of removing from our wealthiest class the body of their taxes, that they stand practically a unit—a peerless jury—in favor of the [existing] system." The assessors saw those who have to shoulder the tax payments that personal property holders successfully evade as those "laborers who bear tax through rent and lodging bills, farmers, merchants, manufacturers and the general community," who are "doubly taxed to make up the deficit caused by permitting the holders of such securities to escape."[60]

The state's fiscal challenge, McNeill explained, was connected with the process of national economic integration. Especially since the Civil War, the process had produced a growing amount of intangible property, "rendering the taxation of personalty [personal property] more difficult" and creating a class of capitalists whose investment strategies were entirely disembedded from their local environment, or, as McNeill put it, whose "love of home was in direct proportion to their exemption from bearing their share in the expenses of government." This mobility of capital presented difficult challenges for cities and states around the country. Against the reformers' argument that the taxation of out-of-state corporations amounted to double taxation, McNeill explained that the notion that capital was heavily taxed or doubly taxed was false. In fact, mobile capital managed to escape taxation almost everywhere. "The same motive that prompts a man to go to Vermont to escape taxation on his stock [in Massachusetts]," he argued, "would prompt him to escape taxation in Chicago." Across the country, the holders of intangible property had the upper hand. They had become "more numerous and influential than formerly." They were also "thoroughly organized," "maintain[ed] bureaus to present arguments favorable to their cause," "fill[ed] the press with planted matter, and employ[ed] able counsel to oppose propositions for more stringent laws who say, at the end of each success, 'You cannot tax personalty; therefore, it should be exempted.'" The other side in the debate, however, had "no organization and no money."[61]

In this interconnected environment, the competition among cities over investment led to a "race to the bottom," which translated into immense pressure to cut budgets and reduce taxes. McNeill, in line with the view of Thomas Hills two decades earlier, proposed an alternative way to understand the issue. He sought to reframe the problem. "The competition that threatens our Commonwealth," he responded to the reformers, "is not a competition between States as to which shall offer the best inducements for a tax-dodging constituency, nor a competition with a lower civilization." Rather, the competition ought to be over who provided the best public services. He insisted that "the only competition that [Massachusetts] has to fear is from such States as shall advance most on the lines in which she so long has led,—the State that affords to all her citizens the best economic and social environment, and furnishes the best schools, the best libraries, the largest opportunities of leisure and improvement." Social well-being and prosperity ought to be advanced "not by exemption of the wealthy but by those measures of relief and remedy that will inspire the humblest with hope, encourage enterprise and disseminate education and enlightenment." McNeill maintained a fundamental hope about the prospects of an industrial society. "As civilization advances," he argued, "the demand will be for more art, more skill and more value in the common necessities of a higher life, as well as the demand for more of those things which are now termed luxuries, but which ought to be and will be a part of the necessities of the life of the humblest."[62] To facilitate this vision, McNeill proposed a series of measures aimed at improving enforcement of the existing tax code, in addition to severe penalties for evading taxes. Despite these compelling words, neither McNeill and Barrus nor Coolidge and Taussig won the day. The political stalemate over the issue of public finance continued into the twentieth century, precluding the implementation of any significant reform. In the meantime, the fiscal condition of Boston and other cities continued to erode, further narrowing the boundaries of viable urban policy. Municipal debates in later decades took place within much tighter ideological confines.

Conclusion

At the turn of the twentieth century, a dramatic wave of mergers radically transformed the landscape of American capitalism. In what historians have called the "Great Merger Movement," more than 1,800 manufacturing companies in a variety of sectors, including food, oil, rubber, glass, chemicals, machinery, and metals, were soaked up in a surge of national consolidations. The total value of publicly listed industrial shares shot up from $33 million in 1890 to $1 billion by 1898, rapidly increasing to $7 billion by 1903.[1] The American industrial order was thus decisively restructured, taking on the corporate shape that characterized it for most of the twentieth century. A nation that only four decades earlier had been primarily an exporter of agricultural goods became home to some of the largest manufacturing concerns in the world—U.S. Steel, International Harvester, and General Electric, among others. This momentous shift— by some accounts, the most pivotal moment in the history of American capitalism—announced the United States' arrival as a global industrial power.

The avalanche of business mergers was rapid, but—as we have seen—the new corporate economy had been long in the making. Far from spontaneous or historically necessary, this shift was the culmination of many years of sustained elite mobilization in business, politics, and the public sphere writ large. Of the confluence of important factors that accounted for this transition, two in particular stood out. First, the emergence of large industrial corporations rested in critical ways on the growing strength of American finance. The United States continued to be a favored destination for European, and particularly British, capital. Foreign investment was nevertheless becoming less and less important compared with domestic savings, which were controlled by American financiers. This financial strength allowed the nation's leading investment bankers to engineer this wave of mergers and underwrite the formation of the new industrial giants with unprecedented amounts of capital.[2] The capaciousness of American moneymen, remarkably, was not itself a technocratic or managerial achievement. Investment banks remained unincorporated private partnerships, each organized around a tightly knit and carefully selected cohort of individuals. They hired few employees and maintained a slim bureaucratic apparatus. The partners at these firms were nevertheless able to forge dense and far-flung networks of affluent individuals, banking institutions, and reliable sources of information. These networks allowed them to pool together immense financial resources and mobilize these resources toward new business ventures—across economic sectors and across space.[3]

The business community of Boston was at the forefront of this marriage of finance and large-scale industry. A community that prided itself on its steadfast traditionalism and arch-conservative approach to business readily took charge of a massive revolutionary process. Two investment houses with old roots in the city—Lee, Higginson & Company and Kidder, Peabody & Company (the renamed investment house of Nathaniel Thayer)—dominated this activity. These two houses stood atop a robust financial sector in Boston that included dozens of commercial banks, trust companies, and brokerage firms, all in charge of investing the accumulated savings of the city's propertied elite.[4] With large pools of capital at their disposal, Kidder, Peabody underwrote cutting-edge industrial securities, overseeing, for example, the conversion of soap producer Proctor & Gamble and cigarette maker Pierre Lorillard from family-owned businesses to huge publicly owned corporations. They also floated large bond issues for the American Telephone and Telegraph Company (AT&T)—$15 million in total in 1899 and 1900 alone—facilitating the rapid expansion of the telecommunications giant.[5] Lee, Higginson was similarly active. It financed the formation of Westinghouse and, together with J. P. Morgan & Company, engineered the merger that created General Electric, a $50 million corporation.[6] Between 1907 and 1912, Kidder, Peabody and Lee, Higginson each purchased and distributed the securities of about one hundred national corporations, valued at more than $1 billion.[7]

Contrary to many accounts, the growing financial supremacy of Wall Street did not displace Bostonian investment houses. Instead, it opened up opportunities for profitable collaborations. Brahmin investors participated regularly in syndicates that were headed by New York houses, and vice versa. Between 1894 and 1934, Kidder, Peabody joined New York's House of Morgan on 164 different share issues for 71 different clients, floating securities that reached a total value of $753 million. Lee, Higginson participated in 149 deals with 64 different clients, floating a total of $353 million in securities, which were then distributed to institutional and individual investors in Boston. The two Bostonian houses were among Morgan's ten most important collaborators, and the only ones that were based outside of New York. These ongoing relationships sustained the vitality of the Bay State as a financial center into the twentieth century.[8] The business of these firms, of course, had by then little affinity to commerce or manufacturing activity in Boston and New England. Their portfolios reflected a broad geographical outlook and included properties far and wide throughout the continent, from Texas, Oregon, and California to Duluth, Detroit, Louisville, and Pittsburgh.[9] The assets of the old Hospital Life Insurance Company were emblematic of this new capitalist spatiality. By 1900, this vehicle of wealth management—founded in the early nineteenth century by Massachusetts merchants and controlled for decades by the cotton industrialists of New England—had not a single textile firm among the top ten largest collateral holdings. Its three heaviest holdings were in the Pere, Marquette Railroad, Chicago Junction Railways & Union Stockyards, and the Chicago, Burlington, and Quincy Railroad. Seven of the top ten assets of this firm were railroads and stockyard companies that carried out business in the West. Like the other ten trust companies in the city, which were all in control of very large pools of capital and frequent lenders to the city's bankers and brokers, the scope of its investments had become unquestionably national.[10]

A second and even more fundamental factor in this moment of industrial consolidation was the formation of a very large national market. As historian Alfred D. Chandler's canonical study of the process readily observed, the rise of national industrial corporations could not have occurred in the United States absent the extensive "geographical size" and the "very rapid growth of its domestic market," which far exceeded those of other industrializing nations.[11] There was, however, nothing preordained or technologically necessary about the continental scale of this domestic market. Nor was it a sudden creation that federal authorities could simply give birth to, as the myriad financial debacles surrounding the Congress-sponsored transcontinental railroads clearly demonstrated.[12] Rather, this large domestic market came into being gradually and grudgingly as the Great West became increasingly integrated into the economic orbit of the nation. It materialized as men of capital like Adams, Higginson, Agassiz, and Minot laboriously mobilized massive infusions of capital from east to west, financing the development of railroads and other large-scale industries. It took shape as they diverted the business orientation of eastern urban centers away from Atlantic commerce, regional industry, and metropolitan promotional projects toward western development, national ventures, and continental industrialization. It cohered consequently as the economy of western regions became more specialized and focused on the long-haul shipping of primary goods, suppressing countervailing efforts to advance relative regional autonomy. The ideological underpinnings of the national market were fortified as a new cultural orientation sanctioned the separation of production and consumption. Its legitimacy grew as universities, museums, and other civic institutions asserted private elite authority over science and taste, and enshrined the separation of intellectual and manual labor.[13]

And yet, for all its overwhelming force, the formation of an integrated domestic market and the corporate economy remained, at best, incomplete. Any notion of a totalized corporate "consolidation" of the American economy both greatly simplifies and overstates the case. Paradoxically, national unification accelerated in tandem with metropolitan and regional fragmentation. Federal authorities, and most notably the United States Supreme Court, indeed toiled in the 1880s and 1890s to forge a coherent regulatory framework on the national level. Aiming to remove domestic barriers to long-haul trade, the Court famously articulated the doctrines of "dual sovereignty" and "substantive due process." These doctrines upheld the exclusive authority of federal authorities over interstate commerce. They declared corporations to be legal persons and therefore free from state-level regulations that might impede "reasonable profits upon their invested capital."[14]

The Supreme Court thus affirmed the primacy of interregional commerce. The tenacious activism of the Supreme Court on behalf of the national market, however, was unthinkable without the robust efforts *to the contrary* on the part of state and city governments, who repeatedly and directly defied these new doctrines. In ways that the Supreme Court could not hope to fully contain, they advanced policies that prioritized regional and metropolitan interests over national ones. Driven by grassroots social forces, they invested public resources in city infrastructure in ways that bolstered urban manufacturing and trade, subsidized neighborhood development and housing, and validated a democratic industrial culture. They took pains to regulate railroad rates, tax out-of-state corporations, support labor mobilization, and broadly distribute and preserve natural resources. They passed hundreds if not thousands of statutes affecting every aspect of economic life, the large majority of which were legally upheld. As a result, as historians Gary Gerstle and William Novak have recently argued, the era of "laissez faire" was anything but. The period in fact inspired immense experimentation and expansion in the assertion of public control over the sphere of the market.[15] Instead of gradual growth of national authority at the federal level, the American political system in this era became locked in a contradiction between the competing pulls of national and subnational authorities. Far from a geographically homogeneous regulatory environment, it resembled a "jarring mix of institutional incoherence and strength," as political scientist Kimberley Johnson accurately observed.[16]

The regulatory policies of states and cities signaled in large measure attempts to divert resources away from national circuits of accumulation, and toward more balanced urban and regional development. These wrinkles in the blanket of centralized political power had a lasting economic impact. American railroads, for example, experienced prodigious expansion, from about 35,000 miles of track at the close of the Civil War to about 250,000 miles of track in 1915. They greatly improved their infrastructure, deployed increasingly powerful locomotives, and invented sophisticated management methods. As bridges spanned rivers and as the gauges of track became more standardized, shipping costs plummeted and the volume of interregional through traffic increased exponentially.[17] Nevertheless, as one government official put it, the United States still had "no such thing as a railway system." The rapid emergence of the network, not a priori by design but incrementally via the combination of local lines into regional carriers and regional carriers into interregional systems, did not result in a seamless whole. Despite their increased speed, regularity, and ubiquity, railroad traffic moved over a multiplicity of trunk lines, profusion of branches, indirect routes, and intricate rate schedules that only made sense when examined contextually from a regional perspective.[18] The massive presence of national industrial corporations notwithstanding, this uneven geography of the transportation system continued to serve not a monolithic corporate-dominated landscape but a diverse manufacturing economy that distributed goods in overlapping markets of varying scales—local, regional, national, and international. The outlying neighborhoods of Boston that suffered greatly from squeezed municipal budgets in the twentieth century but nevertheless continued to thrive as productive economic spaces were an important case in point.[19]

The same patterns characterized the financial system. For sure, the latter decades of the period witnessed the rise of an array of financial institutions—national commercial banks, private investment banks, trust companies, and insurance companies—all preoccupied with moving capital into emerging regions and industries. Investors in a northeastern city like Boston no longer confined themselves to regional ventures but instead expanded their business entanglements to the entire continent, financing industrial ventures of unprecedented magnitude. And yet, interregional and intraregional segmentation persisted and in some ways increased. The gap between the Northeast and other regions, in terms of access to capital, narrowed but did not disappear. The financing of the great majority of new business ventures was mediated through local business networks, not via formal financial institutions or securities markets.[20] Significant spreads remained between interest rates charged in New York or Boston and those charged by country banks in the western and southern regions. This was true both in the short-term bank loans and in the case of the market for long-term mortgage loans. Owing to "severe imbalances in regional supplies and demands" for mortgage finance and the inability of intermediaries to "move enough funds across space to equalize lending rates" (to use the economists' own parlance) the markets for home and farm mortgages developed unevenly and irregularly.[21] Mortgage lending therefore increased in overall size but nevertheless remained overwhelmingly anchored in local institutions—mutual savings banks and building and loan associations—whose geographical horizons were decidedly local. These institutions proliferated as small, single-neighborhood organizations, drawing on the saved resources of their adjoining communities.[22] Even as the infrastructure for channeling massive financial resources nationally dramatically improved, access to credit among farmers, small businessmen, and working-class homeowners remained as varied as ever. The contests that attended the process of market integration thus left a complex spatial legacy, producing not only national networks and institutions but also dynamic pockets of local political power and state-level autonomy. This legacy was not a residual remnant of an earlier age, destined to gradually fade, but a direct product of market integration itself and thus a fully integral aspect of the modern political economy. The efforts in the twentieth century to smooth out these wrinkles and promote regulatory homogeneity within the nation-state were never fully successful until a new wave of federalism at century's end removed the thin layer of national uniformity. It uncovered and once again accentuated disparities and inequalities.[23]

The politics of market formation—so central to American public life in the late nineteenth century—have come back of late into sharp relief. Long overshadowed by buoyant rhetoric about a technologically driven process of "globalization," the legal and political architecture of markets again captures headlines, be it via debates over transoceanic trade deals, continent-wide single markets, or massive cross-border labor migrations. What was once heralded as an apolitical form of human progress and accompanied by almost utopian pronouncements—the arrival of a borderless world, the triumph over distance, the growing intimacy of life in a global village—has been revealed as a quintessentially political project, with profound implications for social inequality, government policy, and public welfare. Markets, it has become quite clear, are far from level playing fields or platforms for competition between independent economic actors. They are, rather, politically made institutions that remain inescapably rigged to favor some over others. In setting the terms of economic engagement, these institutions forever and always shape the balance of power within and among societies, designating gains and setbacks, winners and losers.

The conversation about government policy has shifted accordingly. A discussion that for decades converged around a narrow set of taken-for-granted policy options, framed around making the world easily and lucratively navigable for investors, now confronts an explosion of alternatives on all levels of government. The spectrum of proposals on the agenda is wide and does not easily align with conventional ideological divides. It ranges from a resurgence of economic nationalism to radical reconfiguration of international arrangements, from greater fragmentation of political jurisdiction to accelerated centralization of authority, from re-democratization of economic policymaking to its uncompromising insulation from mobilized majorities. This conversation is most fundamentally a conversation about the relationship between states and markets on varying spatial scales—transnational, national, regional, metropolitan. Instead of anticipating the dawn of a "flat world," it grapples with a complex and layered geography of finance, trade, manufacturing, housing, and labor. There is no obvious or necessary blueprint for how the building blocks ought to be reassembled.

All of this would strike Gilded Age Americans as oddly familiar. They similarly stood in uncharted and highly malleable terrain, confronting the policy dilemmas posed by a massive economic transformation. They contended with footloose capital, tax policies, public investment, and labor strife. Their historical legacy cautions us against wistful longing for a simpler and more straightforward geography of governance. Rather, it urges clear-eyed engagement with the contradictory and asymmetrical aspects of political and economic life, which are still so little understood. This uneven landscape should not be rejected outright in favor of more easily comprehensible schemes. We should instead escape the either-or, in-or-out logic that underpins technocratic discourse and, in turn, fuels reactionary politics. For historians, the crucial step would be loosening the grip of conceptual frameworks that are informed, more or less blatantly, by overdetermined stage theories of change. We must instead recover what Americans in the late nineteenth century intuitively understood, namely, that the modern political economy would take shape not immanently according to expert projections but as a historically contingent outcome of political struggle.

Populism, it has been recently pointed out, is a label that political elites attach to policies that they disapprove of. But it is, of course, much more than that. Scholars have attended to the sentiments that drive populism, the symbolic universe of populist discourse, and the social movements that gave it its political weight. They, however, only very partially engaged with the content and substance of populist politics. They disregarded large spheres of public life where populist ideas informed and shaped policy. Mobilized voters in the late nineteenth century not only registered their discontent and anger or forged a unique rhetorical style, but also generated serious policy ideas that had real economic consequences. The contradictions of democracy and capitalism in our own day are much more than fixable design flaws in the machinery of our political economy. Rooted in a history of social conflict, they cannot be resolved through cloistered deliberations between investment bankers and policy experts. The reconstitution of our governing institutions, therefore, must inevitably draw on similar outpouring of creative energy from the grass roots. It cannot proceed without a much wider scope for democratic participation.

Notes

Introduction

1. "Sketch of the Rise, Progress, Cost, Earnings, etc., of the Railroads of the United States," in Henry Varnum Poor, *Manual of the Railroads of the United States* (New York: H. W. Poor, 1868), 9–32.
2. On Poor as the mouthpiece of Wall Street railroad promoters, see Alfred D. Chandler, *Henry Varnum Poor, Business Editor, Analyst, and Reformer* (Cambridge, MA: Harvard University Press, 1956).
3. On these midcentury intercity rivalries, see Arthur M. Schlesinger, "The City in American History," *The Mississippi Valley Historical Review* 27, no. 1 (June 1940): 43; D. W. Meinig, *The Shaping of America: A Geographical Perspective on 500 Years of History*, vol. 2: *Continental America, 1800–1867* (New Haven, CT: Yale University Press, 1995), 323–331; David M. Scobey, *Empire City: The Making and Meaning of the New York City Landscape* (Philadelphia: Temple University Press, 2002); Andrew Heath, "The Public Interest of the Private City: The Pennsylvania Railroad, Urban Space, and Philadelphia's Economic Elite, 1846–1877," *Pennsylvania History* 79, no. 2 (April 2012): 177–208.
4. Before the Civil War, of the overall freight on these interregional lines, through traffic averaged less than a fifth of the tonnage going east and less than a tenth going west. On the immense fragmentation within the railroad network of the United States, see the meticulous work by George Rogers Taylor and Irene D. Neu, *The American Railroad Network, 1861–1890* (Cambridge, MA: Harvard University Press, 1956). Mirroring the decentralized structure of the transportation system, the majority of midwestern industrial employment until at least 1880 was concentrated in sectors that served local and regional, not national, markets. See David R. Meyer, "Midwestern Industrialization and the American Manufacturing Belt in the Nineteenth Century," *The Journal of Economic History* 49, no. 4 (December 1989): 921–937.
5. Richard Franklin Bensel, *Yankee Leviathan: The Origins of Central State Authority in America, 1859–1877* (Cambridge: Cambridge University Press, 1990); Margaret G. Myers et al., *The New York Money Market* (New York: Columbia University Press, 1931). For data on the uneven geography of the

American financial system, see Richard Franklin Bensel, *The Political Economy of American Industrialization, 1877–1900* (Cambridge: Cambridge University Press, 2000), 56–75; Lance E. Davis, "The Investment Market, 1870–1914: The Evolution of a National Market," *The Journal of Economic History* 25, no. 3 (1965): 355–399; Richard Sylla, "Federal Policy, Banking Market Structure, and Capital Mobilization in the United States, 1863–1913," *The Journal of Economic History* 29, no. 4 (1969): 657–686; Kenneth A. Snowden, "Mortgage Rates and American Capital Market Development in the Late Nineteenth Century," *The Journal of Economic History* 47, no. 3 (September 1, 1987): 671–691.

6. United States Office of the Comptroller of the Currency, *Report of the Comptroller of the Currency* (Washington, DC: Government Printing Office, 1868).

7. For insightful emphasis on capital "immobility" and the pivotal role of eastern financiers in moving money across regions, see Lance E. Davis, "Capital Immobilities and Finance Capitalism: A Study of Economic Evolution in the United States, 1820–1920," *Explorations in Entrepreneurial History* 1 (1963): 88. Chandler proceeded from the assumption that in the case of the United States "the lack of a well-organized national capital market" was never a "constraint," thus relegating finance to an afterthought. See Alfred D. Chandler, *The Visible Hand: The Managerial Revolution in American Business* (Cambridge, MA: Belknap Press, 1977), 93. More recently, scholarly work has instead emphasized its "underdevelopment" in the late nineteenth century. See Mary O'Sullivan, "The Expansion of the U.S. Stock Market, 1885–1930: Historical Facts and Theoretical Fashions," *Enterprise and Society* 8, no. 3 (September 1, 2007): 489–542.

8. Richard White, *Railroaded: The Transcontinentals and the Making of Modern America* (New York: W. W. Norton, 2011), xxv–xxvi.

9. For a critique of "methodological nationalism" in the social sciences, see Neil Brenner, *New State Spaces: Urban Governance and the Rescaling of Statehood* (Oxford: Oxford University Press, 2006); Neil Brenner, "Beyond State-Centrism? Space, Territoriality, and Geographical Scale in Globalization Studies," *Theory and Society* 28, no. 1 (February 1, 1999): 39–78.

10. William J. Novak, *The People's Welfare: Law and Regulation in Nineteenth-Century America* (Chapel Hill: University of North Carolina Press, 1996); Richard R. John, "Ruling Passions: Political Economy in Nineteenth-Century America," *Journal of Policy History* 18, no. 1 (2006): 1–20. For government spending, taxing, and borrowing as an index of state capacity on the different levels, see John B. Legler, Richard Sylla, and John J. Wallis, "U.S. City Finances and the Growth of Government, 1850–1902," *The Journal of Economic History* 48, no. 2 (1988): 347–356; John Joseph Wallis, "American Government Finance in the Long Run: 1790 to 1990," *The Journal of Economic*

Perspectives 14, no. 1 (2000): 61–82. On the different theories of power separating the national government from state and local authorities, see Gary Gerstle, *Liberty and Coercion: The Paradox of American Government from the Founding to the Present* (Princeton, NJ: Princeton University Press, 2015).

11. Bensel, *Yankee Leviathan*; Bensel, *The Political Economy of American Industrialization, 1877–1900.*

12. Benjamin Madley, *An American Genocide: The United States and the California Indian Catastrophe, 1846–1873* (New Haven, CT: Yale University Press, 2016); Steven Hahn, "Slave Emancipation, Indian Peoples, and the Projects of a New American Nation-State," *The Journal of the Civil War Era* 3, no. 3 (2013): 307–330; Pekka Hämäläinen, *The Comanche Empire* (New Haven, CT: Yale University Press, 2008).

13. The federal structure of the American state should not be associated with a flat notion of government "weakness." See William J. Novak, "The Myth of the 'Weak' American State," *The American Historical Review* 113, no. 3 (June 1, 2008): 752–772; Brian Balogh, *A Government Out of Sight: The Mystery of National Authority in Nineteenth-Century America* (Cambridge: Cambridge University Press, 2009). On the Civil War as a fleeting moment of federal hegemony, see Kimberley S. Johnson, *Governing the American State: Congress and the New Federalism, 1877–1929* (Princeton: Princeton University Press, 2007), 4–5.

14. Gary Gerstle, "The Resilient Power of the States across the Long Nineteenth Century," in *The Unsustainable American State*, ed. Lawrence R. Jacobs and Desmond S. King (Oxford: Oxford University Press, 2009), 61–87; Thomas J. Sugrue, "All Politics Is Local: The Persistence of Localism in Twentieth-Century America," in *The Democratic Experiment: New Directions in American Political History*, ed. Meg Jacobs, William J. Novak, and Julian E. Zelizer (Princeton, NJ: Princeton University Press, 2003), 301–326; Amy Bridges, "Managing the Periphery in the Gilded Age: Writing Constitutions for the Western States," *Studies in American Political Development* 22, no. 1 (April 2008): 32–58.

15. Most paradigmatically, Robert H. Wiebe, *The Search for Order, 1877–1920* (New York: Hill and Wang, 1967). Important and inspirational exceptions to this tendency include Martin J. Sklar, *The Corporate Reconstruction of American Capitalism, 1890–1916: The Market, the Law, and Politics* (Cambridge: Cambridge University Press, 1988); James Livingston, *Origins of the Federal Reserve System: Money, Class, and Corporate Capitalism, 1890–1913* (Ithaca, NY: Cornell University Press, 1986); Gerald Berk, *Alternative Tracks: The Constitution of American Industrial Order, 1865–1917* (Baltimore: Johns Hopkins University Press, 1994); Elizabeth Sanders, *Roots of Reform: Farmers, Workers, and the American State, 1877–1917* (Chicago: University of Chicago

Press, 1999); Bensel, *The Political Economy of American Industrialization, 1877–1900*. See also Gerald Berk, "Corporate Liberalism Reconsidered: A Review Essay," *Journal of Policy History* 3, no. 1 (1991): 70–84.

16. On political "stability" as a key tenet of the notion of American exceptionalism, see Gregory P. Downs, "The Mexicanization of American Politics: The United States' Transnational Path from Civil War to Stabilization," *The American Historical Review* 117, no. 2 (2012): 387–409.

17. For a small sampling, see John M. Hart, *Empire and Revolution: The Americans in Mexico since the Civil War* (Berkeley: University of California Press, 2002); Jeremy Adelman, *Republic of Capital: Buenos Aires and the Legal Transformation of the Atlantic World* (Stanford, CA: Stanford University Press, 1999); Ekaterina A. Pravilova, *A Public Empire: Property and the Quest for the Common Good in Imperial Russia* (Princeton, NJ: Princeton University Press, 2014); Ritu Birla, *Stages of Capital: Law, Culture, and Market Governance in Late Colonial India* (Durham, NC: Duke University Press, 2009); Şevket Pamuk, *The Ottoman Empire and European Capitalism, 1820–1913: Trade, Investment, and Production* (Cambridge: Cambridge University Press, 1987).

18. Alfred Chandler famously emphasized the bureaucratic aspect of change, labeling it "a managerial revolution." See Chandler, *The Visible Hand*.

19. As Josephson argued in one typical teleological passage, financial manipulation "retarded" the formation of a consolidated national economy by "at least forty years after it had become a logical necessity." See Matthew Josephson, *The Robber Barons; the Great American Capitalists, 1861–1901* (New York: Harcourt, 1934), 191. See also Richard Hofstadter, *The American Political Tradition and the Men Who Made It* (New York: Knopf, 1948).

20. Chandler, *The Visible Hand*; Wiebe, *The Search for Order*.

21. Richard Hofstadter, *The Age of Reform; from Bryan to F. D. R.* (New York: Knopf, 1955); Lawrence Goodwyn, *Democratic Promise: The Populist Moment in America* (New York: Oxford University Press, 1976); Leon Fink, *Workingmen's Democracy: The Knights of Labor and American Politics* (Urbana: University of Illinois Press, 1983).

22. Practically alone in bridging the divide between economic and social history is James Livingston. See James Livingston, "The Social Analysis of Economic History and Theory: Conjectures on Late Nineteenth-Century American Development," *The American Historical Review* 92, no. 1 (1987): 69–95.

23. On the transition from the Atlantic economy of earlier decades to continental industrialization, see James Livingston, *Pragmatism and the Political Economy of Cultural Revolution, 1850–1940* (Chapel Hill: University of North Carolina Press, 1994), 31–49; Sven Beckert, *The Monied Metropolis: New York City and the Consolidation of the American Bourgeoisie, 1850–1896* (Cambridge: Cambridge University Press, 2001).

24. Edward Barbier, *Scarcity and Frontiers: How Economies Have Developed through Natural Resource Exploitation* (Cambridge: Cambridge University Press, 2011); Lance Edwin Davis and Robert E. Gallman, *Evolving Financial Markets and International Capital Flows: Britain, the Americas, and Australia, 1865–1914* (Cambridge: Cambridge University Press, 2001).
25. On how the history of globalization, rather than displacing local and regional histories, in fact reveals the full significance of all regions to world history as "actors and participants in the very processes being narrated," see Michael Geyer and Charles Bright, "World History in a Global Age," *The American Historical Review* 100, no. 4 (October 1995): 1044–1045.
26. Gerald Taylor White, *A History of the Massachusetts Hospital Life Insurance Company* (Cambridge, MA: Harvard University Press, 1955), xv.
27. Sven Beckert, *Empire of Cotton: A Global History* (New York: Knopf, 2014).
28. See, for example, Joyce Appleby, *Relentless Revolution: A History of Capitalism* (New York: W. W. Norton, 2010).
29. On the decline of old wealth, see most notably Hofstadter, *The Age of Reform*, 136–141. For a critical reassessment, see "The Moral and Intellectual Rehabilitation of the Ruling Class," in Christopher Lasch, *The World of Nations; Reflections on American History, Politics, and Culture* (New York: Knopf, 1973), 80–99. See also Jackson Lears, "The Managerial Revitalization of the Rich," in *Ruling America: A History of Wealth and Power in a Democracy*, ed. Steve Fraser and Gary Gerstle (Cambridge, MA: Harvard University Press, 2005), 181–214.
30. The relationship between business, politics, and ideology in the context of the American south has been most fruitfully problematized in Eugene D. Genovese, *The Political Economy of Slavery: Studies in the Economy & Society of the Slave South* (New York: Pantheon Books, 1965); Eugene D. Genovese, *Roll, Jordan, Roll: The World the Slaves Made* (New York: Pantheon Books, 1974). For inquiries in this vein in the northern context, see Michael Zakim, *Ready-Made Democracy: A History of Men's Dress in the American Republic, 1760–1860* (Chicago: University of Chicago Press, 2003); Michael Zakim and Gary J. Kornblith, eds., *Capitalism Takes Command: The Social Transformation of Nineteenth-Century America* (Chicago: University of Chicago Press, 2011); Beckert, *The Monied Metropolis*.
31. Leslie Butler, *Critical Americans: Victorian Intellectuals and Transatlantic Liberal Reform* (Chapel Hill: University of North Carolina Press, 2007); Louis Menand, *The Metaphysical Club* (New York: Farrar, Straus, and Giroux, 2001); T. J. Jackson Lears, *No Place of Grace: Antimodernism and the Transformation of American Culture, 1880–1920* (New York: Pantheon Books, 1981); John G. Sproat, *The Best Men; Liberal Reformers in the Gilded Age* (London: Oxford University Press, 1968); Geoffrey Blodgett, *The Gentle Reformers: Massachu-*

setts Democrats in the Cleveland Era (Cambridge, MA: Harvard University Press, 1966); Frederic Cople Jaher, *Doubters and Dissenters, Cataclysmic Thought in America, 1885–1918* (London: Free Press of Glencoe, 1964).

32. Thomas Piketty, *Capital in the Twenty-First Century*, trans. Arthur Goldhammer (Cambridge, MA: Harvard University Press, 2014).

33. See, for example, Jürgen Osterhammel, *The Transformation of the World: A Global History of the Nineteenth Century* (Princeton, NJ: Princeton University Press, 2014); Barbier, *Scarcity and Frontiers*; A. G. Hopkins and P. J. Cain, *British Imperialism, 1688–2000*, 2nd ed. (Harlow: Longman, 2002); Eric J. Hobsbawm, *The Age of Capital, 1848–1875* (New York: Vintage Books, 1996); Eric J. Hobsbawm, *The Age of Empire, 1875–1914* (New York: Vintage Books, 1989).

34. Giovanni Arrighi, *The Long Twentieth Century: Money, Power, and the Origins of Our Times*, 2nd ed. (New York: Verso, 2010); Fernand Braudel, *The Wheels of Commerce, Civilization and Capitalism, 15th–18th Century* (New York: Harper and Row, 1982).

35. The South was the third site, of course. See Downs, "The Mexicanization of American Politics"; Steven Hahn, "Slave Emancipation, Indian Peoples, and the Projects of a New American Nation-State"; Eric Foner, *Reconstruction: America's Unfinished Revolution, 1863–1877* (New York: Harper and Row, 1988).

36. On the historiography on American populism, see most notably John Donald Hicks, *The Populist Revolt: A History of the Farmers' Alliance and the People's Party* (Minneapolis: The University of Minnesota Press, 1931); Hofstadter, *The Age of Reform*; Goodwyn, *Democratic Promise*; Steven Hahn, *The Roots of Southern Populism: Yeomen Farmers and the Transformation of the Georgia Upcountry, 1850–1890* (New York: Oxford University Press, 1983); Charles Postel, *The Populist Vision* (Oxford: Oxford University Press, 2007); Robert D. Johnston, *The Radical Middle Class: Populist Democracy and the Question of Capitalism in Progressive Era Portland, Oregon* (Princeton, NJ: Princeton University Press, 2003).

1. Anatomy of a Crisis

1. The "Cottonham" experiment is described in Henry Lee Higginson and Bliss Barry, *Life and Letters of Henry Lee Higginson* (Boston: The Atlantic Monthly Press, 1921), 247–266; Charles F. Morse, *A Sketch of My Life Written for My Children* (Cambridge, MA: Privately printed at the Riverside Press, 1927), 26–32. The advice came from Higginson's wartime friend General Francis Channing Barlow. On the large-scale and much better known experiment of the Sea Islands of South Carolina, see Willie Lee Nichols Rose, *Rehearsal for Reconstruction: The Port Royal Experiment* (Indianapolis: Bobbs-Merrill, 1964); Steven Hahn, *A Nation under Our Feet: Black Political Struggles in the Rural*

South from Slavery to the Great Migration (Cambridge, MA: Harvard University Press, 2003); Eric Foner, *Reconstruction: America's Unfinished Revolution, 1863–1877* (New York: Harper and Row, 1988).

2. For Atkinson's advocacy on this issue, see Edward Atkinson, *Cheap Cotton by Free Labor* (Boston: A. Williams, 1861).

3. Higginson and Barry, *Life and Letters of Henry Lee Higginson*, 254–256.

4. Ibid., 253, 254.

5. Ibid., 254, 252.

6. Ibid., 264.

7. Ibid., 262, 257, 265. While the major orated to the former slaves in their church, Mrs. Higginson "preached in the kitchen" to the three house servants. Ibid., 259.

8. On the interregional links between the emergence of the Cotton Kingdom in the South and industrialization in the North, see Sven Beckert, *Empire of Cotton: A Global History* (New York: Knopf, 2014); Edward E. Baptist, *The Half Has Never Been Told: Slavery and the Making of American Capitalism* (New York: Basic Books, 2014); Walter Johnson, *River of Dark Dreams: Slavery and Empire in the Cotton Kingdom* (Cambridge, MA: Harvard University Press, 2013); Sven Beckert and Seth Rockman, eds., *Slavery's Capitalism: A New History of American Economic Development* (Philadelphia: University of Pennsylvania Press, 2016). The links between the destruction of slavery and post–Civil War industrialization have not received the same level of scrutiny.

9. On these interregional links, see Thomas H. O'Connor, *Lords of the Loom, the Cotton Whigs and the Coming of the Civil War* (New York: Scribner, 1968).

10. Quoted in Robert F. Dalzell, *Enterprising Elite: The Boston Associates and the World They Made* (Cambridge, MA: Harvard University Press, 1987), 49.

11. Robert Dalzell's account generally accepts this optimistic view, consistent with the founders' own view of themselves as articulated in Nathan Appleton, *Introduction of the Power Loom, and Origin of Lowell* (Lowell, MA: B. H. Penhallow, 1858). The most meticulous study of the beginnings of the industry remains Caroline F. Ware, *The Early New England Cotton Manufacture: A Study in Industrial Beginnings* (Boston: Houghton Mifflin, 1931). See also Spalding, "Promotion of the Textile Industry in New England"; Paul F. McGouldrick, *New England Textiles in the Nineteenth Century: Profits and Investment* (Cambridge, MA: Harvard University Press, 1968); Vera, *Economic History of a Factory Town; a Study of Chicopee, Massachusetts* (Northhampton, MA: Smith College, 1935).

12. Ware, *Early New England Cotton Manufacture*, 142. The interlocking boards in the cotton industry have been outlined in Shlakman, *Economic History of a Factory Town*, 39–42, 243–247. See also Spalding, "Promotion of the Textile Industry in New England," 87–88, 102, 107, 126, 127, 139.

13. About a third of the finished product went south. Ten percent was exported to places such as Brazil, Chile, and increasingly China. See Ware, *Early New England Cotton Manufacture*.

14. Dalzell, *Enterprising Elite*, 79, 233–238; Ronald Bailey, "The Slave(ry) Trade and the Development of Capitalism in the United States: The Textile Industry in New England," in *The Atlantic Slave Trade: Effects on Economies, Societies, and Peoples in Africa, the Americas, and Europe*, ed. Joseph E. Inikori and Stanley L. Engerman (Durham, NC: Duke University Press, 1992), 221; Robert Brooke Zevin, "The Growth of Cotton Textile Production after 1815," in *Reinterpretation of American Economic History*, ed. Robert Fogel and Stanley Engerman (New York: Harper and Row, 1971), 122–147.

15. Peter Dobkin Hall, *The Organization of American Culture, 1700–1900: Private Institutions, Elites, and the Origins of American Nationality* (New York: New York University Press, 1982); Ronald Story, *The Forging of an Aristocracy: Harvard & the Boston Upper Class, 1800–1870* (Middletown, CT: Wesleyan University Press, 1980); Frederic Cople Jaher, *The Urban Establishment: Upper Strata in Boston, New York, Charleston, Chicago, and Los Angeles* (Urbana: University of Illinois Press, 1982).

16. William Lawrence, *Life of Amos A. Lawrence, with Extracts from His Diary and Correspondence* (Boston: Houghton Mifflin, 1888).

17. Donald B. Cole, *Immigrant City: Lawrence, Massachusetts, 1845–1921* (Chapel Hill: University of North Carolina Press, 1963); Spalding, "Promotion of the Textile Industry in New England," 180–184, 199–209.

18. William Appleton, *Selections from the Diaries of William Appleton, 1786–1862*, ed. Susan Mason Lawrence Loring (Boston: Merrymount Press, 1922).

19. Among the investors were the topmost financial elite of Boston, including John Amory Lowell, William Sturgis, Nathan Appleton, George W. Lyman, Patrick Tracy Jackson Jr., James Lawrence, Thomas H. Perkins, and Samuel Lawrence. See Hamilton Andrews Hill, *Memoir of Abbott Lawrence* (Cambridge, MA: Privately printed at John Wilson and Son, 1883), 24–25. Investors at Holyoke included Edmund Dwight, James K. Mills, Samuel A. Eliot, Patrick Tracy Jackson Jr., Thomas H. Perkins, and George W. Lyman. See Spalding, "Promotion of the Textile Industry in New England," 199.

20. December 1, 1855, in Appleton, *Selections from the Diaries of William Appleton*, 180.

21. At one heated meeting of shareholders, Abbott Lawrence reportedly "talked for an hour (perhaps to keep others from talking) & smoothed over the irritations of some of the stockholders with great skill . . . keeping [them] from making trouble," quoted in Spalding, "Promotion of the Textile Industry in New England," 195, 197–198, 209–210.

22. Cole, *Immigrant City*; Green, *Holyoke, Massachusetts*.

23. On the panic of 1857 more broadly, see James L. Huston, *The Panic of 1857 and the Coming of the Civil War* (Baton Rouge: Louisiana State University Press, 1987).

24. "The price of the stock of the incorporated companies, fell lower than ever, and manufacturing property seemed to have no certain value," Boston Board of Trade, *Annual Report* (Boston: Press of George C. Rand and Avery, 1859), 163. On depreciation, see Spalding, "Promotion of the Textile Industry in New England," 210.

25. A. A. Lawrence, letterbook, October 19, 1857, Massachusetts Historical Society (MHS).

26. Entries on September 25 and October 1, 1857, in Appleton, *Selections from the Diaries of William Appleton.*

27. Although he suffered less than his neighbors, William Appleton estimated that his manufacturing stocks declined from about $600,000 to about $400,000. He noted that "The Honorable Abbott Lawrence" suffered a loss of about a million dollars. Amos A. Lawrence computed that his investment portfolio lost about a third of its value, shrinking from $453,400 to $294,004. See Amos A. Lawrence Papers, Box 11, September 1857, MHS.

28. Boston Board of Trade, *Annual Report* (Boston: Press of George C. Rand and Avery, 1859), 165. The price of middling cotton rose from 6.25 cents in 1843 to 16 cents in 1857. See Boston Board of Trade, *Annual Report* (Boston: Press of George C. Rand and Avery, 1858), 53.

29. Boston Board of Trade, *Annual Report*, 1859, 165.

30. Boston Board of Trade, *Annual Report*, 1858, 53–54.

31. See Ware, *Early New England Cotton Manufacture*, 113, 151, 153; Lance Edwin Davis, "Stock Ownership in the Early New England Textile Industry," *Business History Review* 32, no. 2 (June 1958): 209. Davis's examination of nine firms (Amoskeag, Dwight, Cabot, Perkins, Hamilton, Lancaster, Lawrence, Lyman, and Massachusetts) similarly indicated that profits as a percentage of total capital stock were on a downward trajectory, averaging 10.3 percent from 1830 to 1834; 9.4 percent from 1835 to 1839; 6.8 percent from 1840 to 1844; 12 percent from 1845 to 1849; 6.1 percent from 1850 to 1854; and 6.0 percent from 1855 to 1859. The decline of manufacturing stocks was generally known in Boston in the 1850s. The chronicler of the Boston Stock Market noted that the full extent of the crisis was obscured by large stock holdings that were not traded regularly: "We hear little said of the immense losses incurred by this class of stocks, although many now sell below 75 cents on a dollar and some would not bring 50 per cent. The small amount thrown upon the market, and the strength of parties holding them, prevent even further depression . . . considering that many of them pass not only one or two dividends, but sometimes half a dozen in succession." See Joseph G. Martin, *Twenty-One*

Years in the Boston Stock Market, Or, Fluctuations Therein: From January 1, 1835 to January 1, 1856 (Boston: Redding and Co., 1856), 42.

32. Boston Board of Trade, *Annual Report*, 1858, 54. This was an uncontroversial conclusion. On the "disinclin[ation] of capitalists to make further investments" and the "positive aversion to the whole business of manufacturing," see Erastus B. Bigelow, *Remarks on the Depressed Condition of Manufactures in Massachusetts: With Suggestions as to Its Cause and Its Remedy* (Boston: Little, Brown and Co., 1858), 23, 17. There was a lively conversation about the root causes of the crisis. Bigelow argued that the predicament proved the corporate form was simply ill suited for manufacturing ventures. James Ayer, another vocal critic, proposed that the industry suffered from nepotism and excessive concentration, leading to negligent management. See James C. Ayer, *Some of the Uses and Abuses in the Management of Our Manufacturing Corporations* (Lowell, MA: C. M. Langley & Co., 1863). There were also cases of outright fraud and malfeasance. See *Report of the Investigating Committee to the Stockholders of the Bay State Mills at Their Meeting, February 5, 1858* (Boston: J. H. Eastburn's Press, 1858). However, all agreed that the downturn was not temporary and that the system as constituted was in desperate need of reform. Nathan Appleton authored the apologia, pegging the downturn on excessive competition from smaller producers. See Appleton, *Introduction of the Power Loom, and Origin of Lowell*.

33. Whereas the shift to industry was pronounced and largely unidirectional, New Englanders' older involvements in long-distance commerce did not cease. Boston was the main American destination for East Indian, Baltic, and Mediterranean goods, remaining the second-largest port in the United States after New York, surpassing Philadelphia, Baltimore, and New Orleans. See Samuel Eliot Morison, *The Maritime History of Massachusetts, 1783–1860* (Boston: Houghton Mifflin, 1921), 214–215, 225. Several of the original incorporators at Waltham and Lowell—Israel Thorndike, James Lloyd, and Patrick Tracy Jackson—had their start in the East India trade. See James R. Fichter, *So Great a Proffit: How the East Indies Trade Transformed Anglo-American Capitalism* (Cambridge, MA: Harvard University Press, 2010), 265–267. Nathan Appleton's previous line of business before entering domestic manufacturing was trade in Canton silks and Bengal cottons. See Frances W. Gregory, *Nathan Appleton, Merchant and Entrepreneur, 1779–1861* (Charlottesville: University Press of Virginia, 1975), 60–61, 110–111, 113.

34. See Vera Shlakman, *Economic History of a Factory Town*, 30; Kenneth Wiggins Porter, *The Jacksons and the Lees; Two Generations of Massachusetts Merchants, 1765–1844* (Cambridge, MA: Harvard University Press, 1937), 123–124.

35. Gerald Taylor White, *A History of the Massachusetts Hospital Life Insurance Company* (Cambridge, MA: Harvard University Press, 1955), 71.
36. These investments tripled Cushing's fortune between his return from China in 1831 and his death in 1862, despite lavish spending of about $50,000 a year. The other big items were his large estate in Watertown, land in downtown Boston, shares in banks and insurance companies, railroads in upstate New York and Pennsylvania, government bonds, and notes and personal loans, including some to individuals and firms affiliated with the textile industry. "Schedule of Property," January 1, 1851, John Perkins Cushing Business Records, vol. 6, Baker Library Historical Collection, Harvard University. See also Henrietta Larsen, "A China Trader Turns Investor," *Harvard Business Review* 12, no. 3 (1934): 345–358.
37. Morison, *The Maritime History of Massachusetts*, 276.
38. Lance E. Davis, "The New England Textile Mills and the Capital Markets: A Study of Industrial Borrowing 1840–1860," *The Journal of Economic History* 20, no. 1 (March 1960): 1–30. Massive losses in the late 1850s did not appear in the official ledgers of the company, in what must have been very aggressive accounting. See the numbers in White, *History of Massachusetts Hospital Life Insurance Company*.
39. On the desperate efforts by the Massachusetts Hospital Life Insurance Company (MHLIC) to find outlets for its funds among Massachusetts farmers, see Tamara Plakins Thornton, "'A Great Machine' or a 'Beast of Prey': A Boston Corporation and Its Rural Debtors in an Age of Capitalist Transformation," *Journal of the Early Republic* 27, no. 4 (2007): 567–597. Not coincidentally, the leading figures of the textile industry assumed control of the company in those later years. Francis C. Lowell Jr., son of the original founder of the Boston Manufacturing Company, became the MHLIC's actuary. Amos Lawrence, Abbott Lawrence, and Nathan Appleton became members of the finance committee. Only very aggressive accounting sustained the reputation of the firm after the crisis of 1857. See "Appendix to Actuary Report," December 28, 1857, AA-1 Case 1, 1823–1956, in Massachusetts Hospital Life Insurance Co., Baker Library Historical Collections, Harvard University.
40. About 30,000 males and 51,500 females. See *Manufactures of the United States in 1860*, ix–x, lxxiii.
41. Gregory, *Nathan Appleton, Merchant and Entrepreneur*, 197–198, 271.
42. Amos A. Lawrence Papers, Box 11, September 1857, MHS.
43. In 1842, 390 different owners to be exact. The vast majority of shares, more than 90 percent, were owned by merchants, estate trustees, lawyers, manufacturers, physicians, literary institutions, females (typically widows and daughters of former shareholders), and "individuals retired from business." Farmers and

"clerks" owned less than 7 percent of the shares. See Ware, *Early New England Cotton Manufacture*. By 1859, about one-quarter of the shares in the industry were in the possession of heiresses and estate trustees. See Davis, "Stock Ownership in the Early New England Textile Industry," 216, 218.

44. This was at a time when the population of Boston reached almost 180,000. See Ware, *Early New England Cotton Manufacture*; Davis, "Stock Ownership in the Early New England Textile Industry"; Zevin, "The Growth of Cotton Textile Production after 1815," 294–295.

45. Ware, *Early New England Cotton Manufacture*, 149–150.

46. Ayer, *Uses and Abuses in the Management of Our Manufacturing*, 4.

47. Hall, *The Organization of American Culture*, 72, 110.

48. Dalzell, *Enterprising Elite*, 124–125; Ronald Story, "Class and Culture in Boston: The Athenaeum, 1807–1860," *American Quarterly* 27, no. 2 (May 1, 1975): 178–199. Its endowed assets included $152,000 in "productive property," excluding its real estate and magnificent collection of literature and fine art.

49. Story, *The Forging of an Aristocracy*.

50. Dalzell, *Enterprising Elite*, 159–160. See Seymour Edwin Harris, *Economics of Harvard*, Economics Handbook Series (New York: McGraw-Hill, 1970), 368.

51. My understanding of merchant capitalism as fundamentally distinct from industrial capitalism relies on the authoritative work of Pierre Gervais on this topic. See Pierre Gervais, "A Merchant or a French Atlantic?: Eighteenth-Century Account Books as Narratives of a Transnational Merchant Political Economy," *French History* 25, no. 1 (March 1, 2011): 28–47; Pierre Gervais, Yannick Lemarchand, and Dominique Margairaz, eds., *Merchants and Profit in the Age of Commerce, 1680–1830* (London: Pickering and Chatto, 2014).

52. The literature on bourgeois class consolidation in the United States concurs with this view. See Jaher, *The Urban Establishment*; Sven Beckert, *The Monied Metropolis: New York City and the Consolidation of the American Bourgeoisie, 1850–1896* (Cambridge: Cambridge University Press, 2001); Betty Farrell, *Elite Families: Class and Power in Nineteenth-Century Boston* (Albany: State University of New York Press, 1993).

53. The second-largest industry in Massachusetts, shoemaking, was made up of many hundreds of poorly capitalized establishments that, like other manufacturing in this period, were financed via personal borrowing by petty entrepreneurs. See Alan Dawley, *Class and Community: The Industrial Revolution in Lynn* (Cambridge, MA: Harvard University Press, 1976). On the disconnect between large financial institutions and investment in manufacturing more broadly, see Glenn Porter et al., *Merchants and Manufacturers; Studies in the Changing Structure of Nineteenth-Century Marketing* (Baltimore: Johns Hopkins Press, 1971). Davis also observes that, textiles and railroads aside, "private bonds were largely unknown." Government bonds were "unrewarding

and at times not even safe." See Davis, "Stock Ownership in the Early New England Textile Industry," 209.

54. Thomas Dublin, *Women at Work: The Transformation of Work and Community in Lowell, Massachusetts, 1826–1860* (New York: Columbia University Press, 1979), 137; Laurence F. Gross, *The Course of Industrial Decline: The Boott Cotton Mills of Lowell, Massachusetts, 1835–1955* (Baltimore: Johns Hopkins University Press, 1993), 63.

55. Ayer, *Uses and Abuses in the Management of Our Manufacturing.*

56. Between 1836 and 1860, the number of native-born females at the Hamilton Company in Lowell dropped sharply from 737 to 324. See Dublin, *Women at Work*, 138. See also Vera Shlakman, *Economic History of a Factory Town*, 138–150.

57. At the Hamilton Company, the percentage of workers in boarding houses declined from three-quarters in 1836 to one-third in 1860. See Ware, *Early New England Cotton Manufacture*, 4; Dublin, *Women at Work*, 138–139, 140–141; Gross, *The Course of Industrial Decline*, 24. The percentage of illiterate workers increased, growing from 11 percent in 1838 to 25 percent in 1876 at the Boott Company. See ibid., 63.

58. Sven Beckert and Katherine Stevens, *Harvard and Slavery: Seeking a Forgotten History* (Cambridge, MA: Privately printed, 2001); Craig Steven Wilder, *Ebony & Ivy: Race, Slavery, and the Troubled History of America's Universities* (New York: Bloomsbury Press, 2013); Samuel Eliot Morison, *Three Centuries of Harvard, 1636–1936* (Cambridge, MA: Harvard University Press, 1936), 287.

59. William F. Hartford, *Money, Morals, and Politics: Massachusetts in the Age of the Boston Associates* (Boston: Northeastern University Press, 2001).

60. "The Dangers That Threaten the Rights of Man in America" (July 2, 1854) and "The Chief Sins of the People" (April 10, 1851). See Theodore Parker, *The Collected Works of Theodore Parker*, ed. Frances Power Cobbe (London: Trübner, 1863), vol. 1, 257, vol. 6, 141. On the intersection of economic populism and antislavery in Parker's thought, see Dean Grodzins, "'Slave Law' versus 'Lynch Law' in Boston: Benjamin Robbins Curtis, Theodore Parker, and the Fugitive Slave Crisis, 1850–1855," *Massachusetts Historical Review* 12 (January 1, 2010): 1–33; Dean Grodzins, "Theodore Parker and the 28th Congregational Society: The Reform Church and the Spirituality of Reformers in Boston, 1845–1859," in *The Transient and Permanent: The Transcendentalist Movement and Its Contexts*, ed. Charles Capper, Conrad Edick Wright, and Austin Bearse (Boston: Massachusetts Historical Society, 1999), 73–117.

61. Grodzins, "'Slave Law' versus 'Lynch Law' in Boston."

62. Charles Sumner, *The Works of Charles Sumner* (Boston: Lee and Shepard, 1870), vol. 2, 81. Grassroots opposition movements had a longer history in Massachusetts, but they had been successfully contained earlier in the

century. See Andrew R. L. Cayton, "The Fragmentation of 'A Great Family': The Panic of 1819 and the Rise of the Middling Interest in Boston, 1818–1822," *Journal of the Early Republic* 2, no. 2 (1982): 143–167; Harlow W. Sheidley, *Sectional Nationalism: Massachusetts Conservative Leaders and the Transformation of America, 1815–1836* (Boston: Northeastern University Press, 1998).

63. Hartford, *Money, Morals, and Politics*; Steven Taylor, "Progressive Nativism: The Know-Nothing Party in Massachusetts," *Historical Journal of Massachusetts* 28 (2000), 167–184; John R. Mulkern, *The Know-Nothing Party in Massachusetts: The Rise and Fall of a People's Movement*, New England Studies (Boston: Northeastern University Press, 1990); Dale Baum, "Know-Nothingism and the Republican Majority in Massachusetts: The Political Realignment of the 1850s," *The Journal of American History* 64, no. 4 (1978): 959–986; William Gleason Bean, "Party Transformation in Massachusetts: With Special Reference to the Antecedents of Republicanism, 1848–1860" (Ph.D. diss., Harvard University, 1922).

64. Oliver Wendell Holmes, *The Autocrat of the Breakfast-Table* (Boston: Phillips, Sampson and Company, 1859), 304. See also Hall, *The Organization of American Culture*, 198–206.

65. Michael F. Holt, *The Political Crisis of the 1850s* (New York: Wiley, 1978), 201; John Ashworth, *Slavery, Capitalism, and Politics in the Antebellum Republic* (Cambridge: Cambridge University Press, 1995), 207–208, 442–445.

66. Barry A. Crouch, "In Search of Union: Amos A. Lawrence and the Coming of the Civil War" (Ph.D. diss., University of New Mexico, 1970), 64.

67. Ibid., 76–78; White, *History of Massachusetts Hospital Life Insurance Company*; Lawrence, *Life of Amos A. Lawrence*, 49–52.

68. Crouch, "In Search of Union," 53–57.

69. January 3, 1837 and January 10, 1837, Box 1, vol. 2A, Diaries of Amos A. Lawrence, MHS.

70. Amos A. Lawrence to Amos Lawrence, Amos Lawrence Papers, vol. 2, November 12 and December 22, 1836, MHS; O'Connor, *Lords of the Loom*, 47–48.

71. Crouch, "In Search of Union," 104.

72. Ibid., 169.

73. Ibid., 226, 237, 217.

74. Ibid., 218.

75. Ibid., 200–201.

76. Johnson, *River of Dark Dreams*.

77. Crouch, "In Search of Union," 228, 232.

78. Morison, *Three Centuries of Harvard, 1636–1936*, 290.

79. Charles Warren, *History of the Harvard Law School and of Early Legal Conditions in America* (New York: Lewis Publishing Company, 1908), vol. 2, 98;

Daniel R. Coquillette and Bruce A. Kimball, *On the Battlefield of Merit: Harvard Law School, the First Century* (Cambridge, MA: Harvard University Press, 2015), 223–235. For broad support for the enforcement of the fugitive slave act among Boston's "wealthy and most respectable," who cheered for the constitution as Georgia runaway Thomas Sims was remanded back to slavery in 1851, see Manisha Sinha, *The Slave's Cause: A History of Abolition* (New Haven, CT: Yale University Press, 2016), 509.

80. "The Slave Catcher's Commissioner Rebuked," *Commonwealth* (May 5, 1854); Coquillette and Kimball, *On the Battlefield of Merit*, 236–241, 265–266.

81. Louis Menand, *The Metaphysical Club* (New York: Farrar, Straus, and Giroux, 2001), 23–32.

82. Hall, *The Organization of American Culture*.

83. Ibid., 8.

84. Ibid., 90.

85. Ibid., 81.

86. Ibid., 134.

87. The involvement of Bostonian merchants in the transatlantic slave trade began in the seventeenth century and lasted in illicit ways into the early nineteenth century. See Hugh Thomas, *The Slave Trade: The Story of the Atlantic Slave Trade, 1440–1870* (New York: Simon and Schuster, 1997), 259–260, 534; James A. Rawley, *The Transatlantic Slave Trade: A History* (New York: W. W. Norton, 1981), 341–351.

88. Edward C. Kirkland, *Charles Francis Adams Jr., 1835–1915: The Patrician at Bay* (Cambridge, MA: Harvard University Press, 1965), 65. Will of C. F. Adams, Proved at Dedham in the County of Norfolk, on January 5th, 1887, Adams Real Estate Trust, 1871–1887, Adams Office Papers, MHS.

89. Kirkland, *The Patrician at Bay*.

90. Charles F. Adams, "The Reign of King Cotton," *The Atlantic Monthly*, April 1861. For the global transformation of the cotton economy in the wake of the Civil War, see Sven Beckert, "Emancipation and Empire: Reconstructing the Worldwide Web of Cotton Production in the Age of the American Civil War," *The American Historical Review* 109, no. 5 (December 2004): 1405–1438.

91. Charles Francis Adams, *Charles Francis Adams, 1835–1915: Autobiography* (Boston: Houghton Mifflin Co., 1916).

92. Thomas Jefferson Coolidge, *The Autobiography of T. Jefferson Coolidge, 1831–1920* (Boston: Houghton Mifflin, 1923), 1, 10, 13, 18; Ayer, *Uses and Abuses in the Management of Our Manufacturing*; Gross, *The Course of Industrial Decline*.

93. These new ventures certainly drew inspiration from several pioneering attempts to invest in western railroads in the 1850s, which were overshadowed in a city that was overwhelmingly beholden to the cotton economy. The financial viability of western ventures remained in question in the 1850s and in

the immediate aftermath of the war. See, for example, Higginson's brief experience as an employee of the undercapitalized and soon bankrupt Buckeye Oil Company in Ohio in Higginson and Barry, *Life and Letters of Henry Lee Higginson*, 240–247. For Boston's western investments prior to the Civil War, see John Lauritz Larson, *Bonds of Enterprise: John Murray Forbes and Western Development in America's Railway Age* (Cambridge, MA: Harvard University Press, 1984); Arthur M. Johnson and Barry E. Supple, *Boston Capitalists and Western Railroads: A Study in the Nineteenth-Century Railroad Investment Process* (Cambridge, MA: Harvard University Press, 1967); Thomas C. Cochran, *Railroad Leaders, 1845–1890* (Cambridge, MA: Harvard University Press, 1953).

94. See, for example, Lawrence's statement on the annexation of Texas. "What is more territory to us? Already our country reaches from the Atlantic to the Pacific and with its comparatively small population is almost ungovernable. . . . The territory is too large already. Rome fell from this cause—the more she grasped the less able was she to hold her possession." Quoted in Crouch, "In Search of Union," 62.

95. William Bryan Gates, *Michigan Copper and Boston Dollars: An Economic History of the Michigan Copper Mining Industry* (Cambridge, MA: Harvard University Press, 1951), 5, 8–9; *Annual Report of the Commissioner of Mineral Statistics of the State of Michigan* (Lansing, MI: W. S. George and Co., 1881), 11–12, 16.

96. Gates, *Michigan Copper and Boston Dollars*, 9–10.

97. *Annual Report of the Commissioner of Mineral Statistics of the State of Michigan*, 1881, 18; *Annual Report of the Commissioner of Mineral Statistics of the State of Michigan* (Marquette, MI: Mining Journal Steam Printing House, 1879), 151; Gates, *Michigan Copper and Boston Dollars*, 50. The most successful of the early mines, the "Cliff," had reached a depth of 1,200 feet when further exploration was discontinued. See ibid.

98. Gates, *Michigan Copper and Boston Dollars*, 10; *Annual Report of the Commissioner of Mineral Statistics of the State of Michigan*, 1879, 152–153, 12–13.

99. Agassiz took the reins of the enterprise from the man who first discovered the mine and came to Boston to raise funds for the enterprise, thus reducing himself to a historical footnote. See George Russell Agassiz, ed., *Letters and Recollections of Alexander Agassiz* (Houghton Mifflin, 1913), 54–56.

100. Gates, *Michigan Copper and Boston Dollars*, 61; *Annual Report of the Commissioner of Mineral Statistics of the State of Michigan*, 1879, 132.

101. Agassiz, *Letters and Recollections of Alexander Agassiz*, 75; Gates, *Michigan Copper and Boston Dollars*, 59; *Annual Report of the Commissioner of Mineral Statistics of the State of Michigan*, 1879, 156. It had been precisely forty-four years since September of 1823, when the water power wheel at Lowell started

"moving around its course majestically," as the founders reported. See
Spalding, "Promotion of the Textile Industry in New England," 42.

102. *Annual Report of the Commissioner of Mineral Statistics of the State of
Michigan,* 1879, 172–173; *Annual Report of the Commissioner of Mineral
Statistics of the State of Michigan,* 1881, 147–149. See also *Annual Report of the
Commissioner of Mineral Statistics of the State of Michigan* (Lansing, MI:
W. S. George and Co., 1884), 66–81.

103. Gates, *Michigan Copper and Boston Dollars,* 109–111.

104. Ibid., 113; Arthur W. Thurner, *Calumet Copper and People; History of a
Michigan Mining Community, 1864–1970* (Chicago: Book Concern, 1974), 41.

105. Quoted in Gates, *Michigan Copper and Boston Dollars,* 113–115.

106. Christopher J. Schmitz, "The World Copper Industry: Geology, Mining
Techniques and Corporate Growth, 1870–1939," *The Journal of European
Economic History* 29, no. 1 (2000): 77–105; C. Harry Benedict, *Red Metal, the
Calumet and Hecla Story* (Ann Arbor: University of Michigan Press, 1952), 80;
Gates, *Michigan Copper and Boston Dollars,* 197–198. Absolute production
continued to increase, but Michigan production declined in relative terms
after the mid-1880s with the development of new reserves in Montana and
Nevada.

107. Gates, *Michigan Copper and Boston Dollars,* 44. There were 800 shareholders,
almost all of them Bostonians, and almost half of the shares were held by the
intermarried Higginson, Shaw, Agassiz, and Russell families.

108. Christopher Schmitz, "The Rise of Big Business in the World Copper Industry
1870–1930," *The Economic History Review* 39, no. 3 (1986): 392–410.

109. Charles Nelson Glaab, *Kansas City and the Railroads: Community Policy in
the Growth of a Regional Metropolis* (Madison: State Historical Society of
Wisconsin, 1962).

110. Adams began visiting the area twice or three times a year (and traveled
throughout the West) between 1870 and 1890. See Charles Francis Adams II,
"Diary," vols. 4–20, MHS. See also Paul C. Nagel, "A West That Failed: The
Dream of Charles Francis Adams II," *The Western Historical Quarterly* 18, no.
4 (1987): 397–407.

111. Atkinson, "Kansas City's Livestock Trade and Packing Industry," 280–281.

112. Cuthbert Powell, *Twenty Years of Kansas City's Live Stock Trade and Traders*
(Kansas City, MO: Pearl Printing Company, 1893), 27–28. For ownership as
represented on boards of directors, see Henry Varnum Poor, *Manual of the
Railroads of the United States* (New York: H. W. Poor), 1872–1873, 356; 1873–
1874, 274; 1875–1876, 608.

113. Morse, *A Sketch of My Life,* 40. See also Charles F. Morse, Superintendent of
Atchison, Topeka, and Santa Fe, to "Engineers," April 4, 1878, 1876–1878,
Charles F. Morse collection, MHS.

114. Formed in 1883, 1884, and 1886, respectively. See Powell, *Kansas City's Live Stock Trade and Traders*, 101, 107, 140.
115. Cattle: 175,000 in 1875 to nearly 1.5 million by 1890; hogs: 150,000 in 1876 to 2.8 million by 1890; sheep 175,000 in 1875 to 1.5 million by 1890. See Atkinson, "Kansas City's Livestock Trade and Packing Industry," 328, 330.
116. Ibid., 341.
117. Ibid., 344–345, 303.
118. Ibid., 129–131. Kansas City's American National Bank was owned by easterners. "While a large amount of stock is held in Kansas City, the greater portion is divided among representatives of influential banking and other financial institutions of New York and New England (notably the latter), who command unlimited capital." See Theodore S. Case, *History of Kansas City, Missouri* (Syracuse, NY: D. Mason, 1888), 294–295.
119. Arthur M. Johnson and Barry E. Supple, *Boston Capitalists and Western Railroads: A Study in the Nineteenth-Century Railroad Investment Process* (Cambridge, MA: Harvard University Press, 1967), 294.
120. Ibid., 297.
121. Atkinson, "Kansas City's Livestock Trade and Packing Industry," 355, 357. Kansas City remained behind Chicago (3.6 million head of cattle, 7.6 million hogs) but well ahead of St. Louis (0.6 million head of cattle and 1.3 million hogs) and Omaha (0.6 million head of cattle and 1.4 million hogs).
122. Wilson J. Warren, *Tied to the Great Packing Machine: The Midwest and Meatpacking* (Iowa City: University of Iowa Press, 2006), 22, 207. See States United, *Census Reports, Twelfth Census of the United States Taken in the Year 1900, William R. Merriam, Director,* ed. William Rush Merriam et al. (Washington, DC: United States Census Office, 1901), ccviii.
123. Morse, *A Sketch of My Life,* 62, 60. For documentation of Morse's collaborations with Adams in various real estate investments, see "CFA2 & JQA Kansas City Investments 1878–1887," Adams Family Office Papers, MHS.
124. "CFA2 & JQA Kansas City Investments 1878–1887," Adams Family Office Papers, MHS.
125. Gross, *The Course of Industrial Decline.*
126. Ibid. Growth in the industry during the postwar decades was based on a radical change in the business model as mass production of coarse fabrics was replaced with shorter production runs of a great variety of higher-quality cloth. New England textile manufacturing continued to grow in absolute terms in the decades after the war, but its center moved south from the prewar centers, which had been financed and controlled from Boston, to Fall River and New Bedford, where mills were smaller, of lower capitalizations, and run and financed by local entrepreneurs who moved into the sector with a flexible production model. Between 1861 and 1875, twenty-two new mills were incorpo-

rated in Fall River. See "Fall River, Lowell, and Lawrence," in Massachusetts Bureau of Statistics of Labor, *Report on the Statistics of Labor* (Boston: Massachusetts Bureau of Statistics of Labor, 1881), vol. 13, 229, 241–242. See also Melvin Thomas Copeland, *The Cotton Manufacturing Industry of the United States* (Cambridge, MA: Harvard University Press, 1917). By 1882, the leading textile centers were Fall River (1,600,000 spindles), Lowell (800,000), New Bedford (440,000), Manchester, New Hampshire (315,000), and Lawrence (300,000). See Victor S. Clark, *History of Manufactures in the United States* (New York: P. Smith, 1929), vol. 2, 393. By the end of the century, Fall River and New Bedford were the established leaders in textile manufacturing. See Copeland, *Cotton Manufacturing Industry*, 28.

127. "Trial Balances," Coolidge Family Business Records, vols. 14–18, Baker Library Historical Collection, Harvard University. The transition from regional to western ventures is similarly documented in "Stock Ledger of J.E. Thayer" and "N. Thayer, 1858–1869," vol. 2, Kidder, Peabody and Co. Papers, Baker Library Historical Collections, Harvard University.

2. Cultivating the Laissez-Faire Metropolis

1. John T. Morse Jr., "Memoir of Henry Lee Higginson," in Massachusetts Historical Society, *Proceedings of the Massachusetts Historical Society, October, 1919–June, 1920* (Boston: Massachusetts Historical Society, 1920), vol. 3, 116.

2. I. Smith Homans Jr., ed., *Merchant's and Banker's Almanac* (New York: Bankers' Magazine and Statistical Register, 1868); Vincent P. Carosso, *More Than a Century of Investment Banking: The Kidder, Peabody & Co. Story* (New York: McGraw-Hill, 1979). For a more detailed overview of domestic capital movements as they related to American industrialization, with special emphasis on New England, see Richard Franklin Bensel, *The Political Economy of American Industrialization, 1877–1900* (Cambridge: Cambridge University Press, 2000), 56–75. See also Richard Franklin Bensel, *Yankee Leviathan: The Origins of Central State Authority in America, 1859–1877* (Cambridge: Cambridge University Press, 1990), 271–272, 284; Irwin Unger, *The Greenback Era; a Social and Political History of American Finance, 1865–1879* (Princeton, NJ: Princeton University Press, 1964), 145–146. Unger observed that "New England was better supplied with commercial banks, insurance and trust companies, and savings institutions than was any other part of the country. . . . The section exported capital in large amounts."

3. "These few examples make clear by illustration the westward development of railroads and mines and show how interest turned from New England mills and railroads to national undertakings." Marshall C. Stevens, *History of Lee, Higginson, and Co.* (Boston: Privately printed, 1927), 21–23.

4. Charles Francis Adams Jr., "The Canal and Railroad Enterprise of Boston," in *The Memorial History of Boston, Including Suffolk County, Massachusetts*, ed. Justin Winsor (Boston: J. R. Osgood and Company, 1881), vol. 4, 148.

5. James Livingston, *Pragmatism and the Political Economy of Cultural Revolution, 1850–1940* (Chapel Hill: University of North Carolina Press, 1994), 36.

6. Gerald Berk, *Alternative Tracks: The Constitution of American Industrial Order, 1865–1917* (Baltimore: Johns Hopkins University Press, 1994), 27; Sven Beckert, *The Monied Metropolis: New York City and the Consolidation of the American Bourgeoisie, 1850–1896* (Cambridge: Cambridge University Press, 2001), 150, 238.

7. Domenic Vitiello and George E. Thomas, *The Philadelphia Stock Exchange and the City It Made* (Philadelphia: University of Pennsylvania Press, 2010), 96, 98, 104–109, 120–127. On Stock Exchanges more generally as key facilitators of "interregional transfer of capital," see Bensel, *The Political Economy of American Industrialization*, 57.

8. More than in other peripheral regions around the world in this period, American development was driven predominantly (although far from exclusively) by financing from domestic sources. See Lance Edwin Davis and Robert E. Gallman, *Evolving Financial Markets and International Capital Flows: Britain, the Americas, and Australia, 1865–1914* (Cambridge: Cambridge University Press, 2001), 9, 27.

9. Charles F. Adams, "Boston," *North American Review* 106 (January 1868): 25, 3, 7.

10. For more on Adams as a reformer, see Nancy Cohen, *The Reconstruction of American Liberalism, 1865–1914* (Chapel Hill: University of North Carolina Press, 2002).

11. For a critique of the methodological localism in the social sciences, see Neil Brenner, "Is There a Politics of 'Urban' Development?: Reflections on the US Case," in *The City in American Political Development*, ed. Richardson Dilworth (New York: Routledge, 2009), 121–140. On cities as key sites for the process of market integration, see Saskia Sassen, "Spatialities and Temporalities of the Global: Elements for a Theorization," *Public Culture* 12, no. 1 (2000): 215–232; Saskia Sassen, *The Global City: New York, London, Tokyo* (Princeton, NJ: Princeton University Press, 1991).

12. On the fragmentation of political jurisdiction as a central feature of the modern American state, see Thomas J. Sugrue, "All Politics Is Local: The Persistence of Localism in Twentieth-Century America," in *The Democratic Experiment: New Directions in American Political History*, ed. Meg Jacobs, William J. Novak, and Julian E. Zelizer (Princeton, NJ: Princeton University Press, 2003), 301–326. Boston has long been the locus classicus for the study of American metropolitan development in the late nineteenth century under the rubric of "suburbanization." See Sam Bass Warner, *Streetcar Suburbs: The*

Process of Growth in Boston, 1870–1900, 2nd ed. (Cambridge, MA: Harvard University Press, 1978); Kenneth T. Jackson, *Crabgrass Frontier: The Suburbanization of the United States* (New York: Oxford University Press, 198/), 138–156; Michael Rawson, *Eden on the Charles: The Making of Boston* (Cambridge, MA: Harvard University Press, 2010), 129–178.

13. B. W. Harris, *The Annexation Question: Closing Argument of B. W. Harris, Esq., for the Remonstrants against the Annexation of Dorchester to Boston, before the Committee on Towns of the Massachusetts Legislature* (Boston: Rockwell and Rollins, printers, 1869).

14. For George's urban vision, see Lawrence M. Lipin, "Nature, the City, and the Family Circle: Domesticity and the Urban Home in Henry George's Thought," *The Journal of the Gilded Age and Progressive Era* 13, no. 3 (July 2014): 305–335. See also Jeffrey P. Sklansky, *The Soul's Economy: Market Society and Selfhood in American Thought, 1820–1920* (Chapel Hill: University of North Carolina Press, 2002), 105–136.

15. See Boston (Mass.), "City Document No. 105, Report by the Commission Appointed to Investigate the Subject of the Annexation of Certain Neighboring Cities and Towns to the City of Boston," Boston City Documents (Boston: Rockwell and Churchill, 1873), 15–16.

16. See "Annexation of Charlestown to Boston," *Boston Daily Atlas*, September 21, 1854; "Annexation of Charlestown to Boston," *Boston Daily Atlas*, September 12, 1854.

17. Alexander Gourevitch, *From Slavery to the Cooperative Commonwealth: Labor and Republican Liberty in the Nineteenth Century* (New York: Cambridge University Press, 2015); William E. Forbath, "The Ambiguities of Free Labor: Labor and Law in the Gilded Age," *Wisconsin Law Review* 4 (July–August 1985): 767–817; Eric Foner, *Free Soil, Free Labor, Free Men: The Ideology of the Republican Party Before the Civil War* (New York: Oxford University Press, 1970).

18. "In Board of Aldermen . . . Ordered," April 2, 1866, Board of Aldermen, Minutes, Boston City Archives. See also Boston (Mass.), "City Document No. 23, Report of the Commissioners on the Annexation of Roxbury," Boston City Documents (Boston: Rockwell and Churchill, 1867). These unions had to be consensual, but they still required a legislative act at the state level.

19. The report recommended immediate union with the first six, and with the others at a later date. See Boston (Mass.), "City Document No. 105," 38.

20. Boston (Mass.), "City Document No. 105," 8.

21. Boston (Mass.), "City Document No. 1, The Inaugural Address of Nathaniel B. Shurtleff" (Boston: Alfred Mudge and Son, 1869), 114.

22. Boston first developed a public water system in the 1840s, but it was limited to the inner city. See Michael Rawson, *Eden on the Charles: The Making of*

Boston (Cambridge, MA: Harvard University Press, 2010), 75–128; Carl S. Smith, *City Water, City Life: Water and the Infrastructure of Ideas in Urbanizing Philadelphia, Boston, and Chicago* (Chicago: University of Chicago Press, 2013).

23. Boston (Mass.), "City Document No. 80, Annual Report of the School Committee," Boston City Documents (Boston: Rockwell and Churchill, 1870).

24. The aldermen who passed the resolution consisted of what had become a typical mix of neighborhood businessmen—three grocers, two carpenters, a sail maker, a newspaper editor, an insurance agent, and four shopkeepers. The seven-member Joint Special Committee on the Annexation of Roxbury (aldermen and councilmen), which petitioned the legislature for annexation on behalf of Boston in March 1867, consisted of a printer, a carpenter-builder, a piano maker, a ship joiner, an iron roller, and two shopkeepers. Four of the seven were members of the Massachusetts Charitable Mechanic Association, including two future presidents of that organization.

25. Slack later became the chairman of Parker's Twenty-Eighth Congregational Society. See William Samuel Slack and Charles Wesley Slack, *The Slack Family* (Alexandria, LA: The Standard Printing Company, 1930); "Charles Wesley Slack," *New-England Historical and Genealogical Register*, October 1885; "Obituary: Charles Wesley Slack," *Boston Journal*, April 11, 1885.

26. This was the same Supreme Court that ruled in favor of the extradition of fugitive slaves. See *Triumph of Equal School Rights in Boston: Proceedings of the Presentation Meeting Held in Boston, Dec. 17, 1855: Including Addresses by John T. Hilton, Wm. C. Nell, Charles W. Slack, Wendell Phillips, Wm. Lloyd Garrison, Charles Lennox Remond* (Boston: R. F. Wallcut, 1856); Manisha Sinha, *The Slave's Cause: A History of Abolition* (New Haven, CT: Yale University Press, 2016), 329–330; Kyle G. Volk, *Moral Minorities and the Making of American Democracy* (Oxford: Oxford University Press, 2014), 125–130; Bruce Laurie, *Beyond Garrison: Antislavery and Social Reform* (Cambridge: Cambridge University Press, 2005), 280–282; Dean Grodzins, "Theodore Parker and the 28th Congregational Society: The Reform Church and the Spirituality of Reformers in Boston, 1845–1859," in *The Transient and Permanent: The Transcendentalist Movement and Its Contexts*, ed. Charles Capper, Conrad Edick Wright, and Austin Bearse (Boston: Massachusetts Historical Society, 1999), 73–117.

27. James M. McPherson, *The Struggle for Equality: Abolitionists and the Negro in the Civil War and Reconstruction* (Princeton, NJ: Princeton University Press, 1964), 120–121, 310–311.

28. "The Mechanics' Exhibition," *Commonwealth*, September 30, 1865.

29. *Commonwealth*, August 31, 1867; "Boston's Boundaries," *Commonwealth*, June 12, 1869.

30. Boston (Mass.), "City Document No. 28, Report of the Commissioners on the Annexation of Dorchester," Boston City Documents (Boston: Alfred Mudge and Son, March 1, 1869).

31. John Henry Clifford, *Argument on the Question of the Annexation of Roxbury to Boston, before the Legislative Committee, Thursday February 23, 1865* (Boston: Wright and Potter, 1867); Charles Russell Train, *Closing Argument in Behalf of the Petitioners for the Annexation of Dorchester to Boston, before the Committee on Towns* (Boston: Alfred Mudge and Son, 1869); Boston (Mass.), "City Document No. 28."

32. Edward Avery, *Annexation of Roxbury and Boston* (Boston: George C. Rand, 1865).

33. "Annexation of Roxbury," *Boston Daily Advertiser*, September 9, 1867. See also Nathaniel Wheeler Coffin, *A Few Reasons in Favor of the Annexation of a Part of the Town of Dorchester to the City of Boston* (Boston: Wright and Potter, State Printers, 1867); Clifford, *Argument on the Question of the Annexation of Roxbury to Boston.*

34. Harris, *The Annexation Question.*

35. Ibid.

36. Ibid.

37. George R. Minot & Others, Petitioners vs. City of Boston and Others, Brief for the Petitioners, Minot Business Papers, Carton 40, folder 1873, Massachusetts Historical Society. See also Theophilus P. Chandler v. Boston, 112 Mass. 200 (1873).

38. David Coolidge v. Brookline, 114 Mass. 592 (1874).

39. On this midcentury wave of partitions, see George Herbert McCaffrey, "The Political Disintegration and Reintegration of Metropolitan Boston" (Ph.D. diss., Harvard University, 1937), 176. For a detailed analysis of the West Roxbury case, see Alexander von Hoffman, *Local Attachments: The Making of an American Urban Neighborhood, 1850 to 1920* (Baltimore: Johns Hopkins University Press, 1994), 169–171.

40. On the flooding of the American art scene with bucolic images of New England landscapes, which were meant to be evocative "heritage" and "tradition," see Julia B. Rosenbaum, *Visions of Belonging: New England Art and the Making of American Identity* (Ithaca, NY: Cornell University Press, 2006).

41. Harris, *The Annexation Question.*

42. Arthur Williams Austin, *Address at Dedication of the Town-House at Jamaica Plain, West Roxbury* (Boston: Alfred Mudge and Son, 1868); Robert C. Winthrop, *Proceedings at the Dedication of the Town Hall, Brookline, February 22, 1873* (Brookline, MA: John Wilson and Son, 1873).

43. See William W. Wheildon, *Brief Review of Josiah Quincy's "Considerations Respectfully Submitted to the Citizens of Boston and Charlestown, on the Annexation of These Two Cities"* (Boston: Prentiss and Sawyer, 1854); McCaffrey, "Political Disintegration and Reintegration," 87. On the political uses of tradition, see Eric Hobsbawm and Terence Ranger, eds., *The Invention of Tradition* (Cambridge: Cambridge University Press, 1983).

44. "Sketch of the Rise, Progress, Cost, Earnings, etc., of the Railroads of the United States," in Henry Varnum Poor, *Manual of the Railroads of the United States* (New York: H. W. Poor, 1868).

45. "Our Waterworks," *Brookline Chronicle*, October 9, 1875.

46. William P. Marchione, "Uncommon Suburbs: Suburbanization at the Western Edge of Boston, 1820–1873" (Ph.D. diss., Boston College, 1994), 456–457. On Atkinson as a liberal reformer, see Harold Francis Williamson, *Edward Atkinson; the Biography of an American Liberal, 1827–1905* (Boston: Old Corner Book Store, 1934).

47. My emphasis. Alfred D. Chandler, *Annexation of Brookline to Boston: Opening Argument for the Town of Brookline before the Committee on Towns of the Massachusetts Legislature, Thursday, March 11, 1880* (Brookline, MA: T. R. Marvin, 1880); Alfred D. Chandler and T. P. Chandler, *Chandler vs. the City of Boston and the Town of Brookline, in Equity: Argument for the Complainants, June, 1873* (Boston: Alfred Mudge and Son, 1873).

48. Like Chandler, Charles F. Adams was a staunch supporter of the town form of government and mourned the transformation of his home town of Quincy, where he served on the board of selectmen for fifteen years, into a city in 1887. The transition, he noted, was promoted by "Americans of Irish descent [who] took pride in calling themselves Knights of Labor" and promoted labor-friendly policies such as a minimum wage in public works and a nine-hour day, "regardless of logic, expense or legality, and without listening to reason." See Charles Francis Adams, *Three Episodes of Massachusetts History: The Settlement of Boston Bay; the Antinomian Controversy; a Study of Church and Town Government* (Cambridge, MA: The Riverside Press, 1892), 990, 1007.

49. Harris, *The Annexation Question*.

50. Alexander Von Hoffman, "Weaving the Urban Fabric: Nineteenth-Century Patterns of Residential Real Estate Development in Outer Boston," *Journal of Urban History* 22, no. 2 (1996): 191–230. One property owner voiced a pervasive grumble among elites when he complained that high city taxes after annexation consumed almost 60 percent of the annual income he was able to extract from his rural property in West Roxbury, forcing him to sell it to housing developers. See Von Hoffman, "Weaving the Urban Fabric," 200.

51. See Nathan Matthews, *The City Government of Boston* (Boston: Rockwell and Churchill City Printers, 1895), 192. Charlestown's population increase also surpassed that of the inner city but by a less impressive margin, given that it was territorially small and more urbanized at the time of its annexation.

52. See, for example, enumeration district 781 in Dorchester (Ward 23) or 768 in West Roxbury (Ward 24) in *U. S. Federal Population Census, 1880* (NARA microfilm publication Series T9). Records of the Bureau of the Census, Record Group 29, National Archives, Washington, DC, which have been digitized by Ancestry.com. For a detailed analysis of the heterogeneous demographics of the new districts, see Von Hoffman, *Local Attachments*, 23–43; Warner, *Streetcar Suburbs*, 67–117; Noam Maggor, "Politics of Property: Urban Democracy in the Age of Global Capital, Boston 1865–1900" (Ph.D. diss., Harvard University, 2010), 129–148, which examines occupational data for heads of households throughout the entire city as enumerated in the Federal Census of 1880. The two groups whose relative numbers plunged, to take the Jamaica Plain area in West Roxbury as an example, were "farmers," "professionals," and "major proprietors," whose portions of the population declined from 10.1, 6.7, and 21.1 percent of the population to 0, 3.9, and 5.7, respectively, between 1850 and 1880. "Skilled workers," "semiskilled workers," "clerks and salesmen," and "petty proprietors" made up the difference. See Von Hoffman, "Weaving the Urban Fabric," 36.

53. The percentages represent the ratio in each ward of the number of property-owning voters to the number of poll-tax payers (all males over the age of twenty) in 1893. See Nathan Matthews, *The City Government of Boston* (Boston: Rockwell and Churchill City Printers, 1895), 193. See also Von Hoffman, "Weaving the Urban Fabric," 196–197. For patterns in the inner city, see David Ward, "The Industrial Revolution and the Emergence of Boston's Central Business District," *Economic Geography* 42, no. 2 (1966): 152–171; Walter Irving Firey, *Land Use in Central Boston* (Cambridge, MA: Harvard University Press, 1947). For Manhattan, see Elizabeth Blackmar, *Manhattan for Rent, 1785–1850* (Ithaca, NY: Cornell University Press, 1989).

54. On the physical proximity of landlords to their property, see Warner, *Streetcar Suburbs*, 185; Von Hoffman, "Weaving the Urban Fabric," 193.

55. Von Hoffman, *Local Attachments*, 54–62.

56. Warner, *Streetcar Suburbs*, 67. Warner's canonical interpretation viewed this varied outcome as ironic in light of the "rural ideal" that allegedly drove development on the periphery. As this chapter shows, however, this was fully intentional.

57. Sam Bass Warner made this very point, observing that "the development of residential land . . . might have remained in the hands of big syndicates had

not the City of Boston undertaken its large-scale street and sanitation program." See Warner, *Streetcar Suburbs*, 124.

58. Warner counted over 9,000 different applicants for housing permits in
Roxbury, West Roxbury, and Dorchester between 1870 and 1900. These
builders constructed roughly 22,500 units: 12,000 single-family homes, 6,000
two-family homes, 4,000 three-family, and 500 larger buildings. He detected
no housing moguls building on a mass scale. See Warner, *Streetcar Suburbs*,
35–37, 125–131, 184.

59. Von Hoffman, "Weaving the Urban Fabric," 192–195. Large-scale financing
was shut out of an inhospitable urban mortgage market. This market was
dominated by private loans and by neighborhood institutions like mutual
savings banks and building societies that enjoyed access to better information and lent in their immediate vicinity. Between 1865 and 1875, savings
banks in Massachusetts, whose investments in corporate securities were
legally constrained, increased their mortgage lending more than tenfold,
from $16 million to $120 million. See John T. Croteau, "The Development
of the Mutual Savings Banks in Massachusetts" (Ph.D. diss., Clark University, 1935), 83–85; Warner, *Streetcar Suburbs*, 118–120; Kenneth A. Snowden,
"Mortgage Rates and American Capital Market Development in the Late
Nineteenth Century," *The Journal of Economic History* 47, no. 3 (September
1, 1987): 671–691; D. M. Frederiksen, "Mortgage Banking in America,"
Journal of Political Economy 2, no. 2 (1894): 203–234. All these characteristics
were typical of the American construction industry prior to the New Deal,
which created national standards and allowed national financial institutions
to enter the home mortgage business. See, for example, Michael J. Doucet
and John C. Weaver, "Material Culture and the North American House:
The Era of the Common Man, 1870–1920," *Journal of American History* 72
(1985): 560.

60. Ronald D. Karr, "The Evolution of an Elite Suburb: Community Structure
and Control in Brookline, Massachusetts, 1770–1900" (Ph.D. diss., Boston
University, 1981), 212, 215–216, 267.

61. Quoted in Karr, "The Evolution of an Elite Suburb," 265.

62. In 1870, more than 90 percent of the residents of the Marsh were of Irish
descent. Brookline had a large working-class population, but it largely consisted of service providers for elite families, including maids, cooks, nursery
girls, laundresses, coachmen, gardeners, masons, carpenters, and farm
laborers. These dependent employees were in no position to challenge elite
families on the annexation question. Nevertheless, elites mobilized aggres-
sively whenever a vote on the question was in the offing. Among the methods
used to mobilize voters were torchlight processions, rockets displays, thousands
of handbills, and banners with slogans such as "Brookline the Paradise of

Working Men" and "Great Cities, Great Sores." See Marchione, "Uncommon Suburbs," 406, 475–480.

63. On the American fiscal state, with an emphasis on the local and state levels, see Clifton K. Yearley, *Money Machines: The Breakdown and Reform of Governmental and Party Finance in the North, 1860–1920* (Albany: State University of New York Press, 1970); Robin L. Einhorn, *American Taxation, American Slavery* (Chicago: University of Chicago Press, 2008); Robin L. Einhorn, *Property Rules: Political Economy in Chicago, 1833–1872* (Chicago: University of Chicago Press, 2001); Ajay K. Mehrotra, *Making the Modern American Fiscal State: Law, Politics, and the Rise of Progressive Taxation, 1877–1929* (New York: Cambridge University Press, 2013); Isaac William Martin, Ajay K. Mehrotra, and Monica Prasad, eds., *The New Fiscal Sociology: Taxation in Comparative and Historical Perspective* (Cambridge: Cambridge University Press, 2009). For a quantitative analysis, see John B. Legler, Richard Sylla, and John J. Wallis, "U.S. City Finances and the Growth of Government, 1850–1902," *The Journal of Economic History* 48, no. 2 (1988): 347–356; John Joseph Wallis, "American Government Finance in the Long Run: 1790 to 1990," *The Journal of Economic Perspectives* 14, no. 1 (2000): 61–82.

64. Yearley, *Money Machines*, 4.

65. Charles Phillips Huse, *The Financial History of Boston from May 1, 1822, to January 31, 1909* (Cambridge, MA: Harvard University Press, 1916), 371. The figures have been adjusted using the "GDP Deflator"; see EH.Net, http://eh.net/hmit/. On the rapid rise in municipal spending in New York, see Sven Beckert, *The Monied Metropolis*, 174–175.

66. See "The Crisis of the Tax States," in Joseph Alois Schumpeter, *The Economics and Sociology of Capitalism* (Princeton, NJ: Princeton University Press, 1991), 99–140; Charles Tilly, foreword to Isaac William Martin, Ajay K. Mehrotra, and Monica Prasad, eds., *The New Fiscal Sociology*. Schumpeter insightfully identifies "the public finances" as "one of the best starting points for an investigation of society." Tilly sees analysis of the tax regime as "a sort of CT scan for a regime's entire operation."

67. Exempt were furniture under $1,000, wearing apparel, and tools under $300 necessary for carrying on a trade. U.S. bonds were exempt under federal law, a provision greatly begrudged by local officials. Massachusetts corporations were taxed by the state for property exceeding their property in real estate, which was assessed locally. See entry for April 11, 1866, Assessors Department Ledger, Boston Municipal Archives, West Roxbury, Boston. See also David A. Wells, Dodge Edwin, and George W. Cuyler, *Report of the Commissioners to Revise Laws for Assessment and Collection of Taxes in the State of New York* (New York: Harper and Brothers, 1871); Boston (Mass.), *Ordinances and Rules and*

Orders of the City of Boston, Together with the General and Special Statutes of the Massachusetts Legislature Relating to the City (Boston: Alfred Mudge and Son, 1869), 691. The state limited the poll tax to $2, which meant it gradually made a diminishing contribution to public revenue.

68. For a long history of the tax before 1860, see Bullock, "The Taxation of Property and Income in Massachusetts"; Einhorn, *American Taxation, American Slavery,* 53–78. See also Robin L. Einhorn, "Institutional Reality in the Age of Slavery: Taxation and Democracy in the States," *Journal of Policy History* 18, no. 1 (2006): 21–43.

69. *Ordinances and Rules and Orders of the City of Boston, together with the General and Special Statutes of the Massachusetts Legislature Relating to the City* (Boston: Alfred Mudge and Son, 1869), 691; Commonwealth of Massachusetts, "House Document No. 15, Report of the Commissioners Appointed to Inquire into the Expediency of Revising and Amending the Laws Relating to Taxation and Exemption Therefrom," *House Documents* (Boston: Wright and Potter, 1875), 53–54; "Record of the Joint Special Committee on Retrenchment of Municipal Expenditure, 1877," Boston Municipal Archives, West Roxbury, Boston, 45.

70. See Charles J. Bullock, "The Taxation of Property and Income in Massachusetts," *The Quarterly Journal of Economics* 31, no. 1 (1916): 1.

71. Commonwealth of Massachusetts, "House Document No. 15," 53.

72. Bullock, "The Taxation of Property and Income in Massachusetts," 14; Charles Phillips Huse, *The Financial History of Boston from May 1, 1822, to January 31, 1909* (Cambridge, MA: Harvard University Press, 1916), 376–377.

73. Sporadic references to Hills and his defense of the property tax depict him as "diligent" but misguided, "ruggedly honest" yet imprudent. See Huse, *The Financial History of Boston,* 147; Bullock, "The Taxation of Property and Income in Massachusetts," 15–16; Yearley, *Money Machines,* 48.

74. Thomas Hills, Membership Questionnaire, November 15, 1897, Special Collections Department, New England Historic Genealogical Society. See also city directories digitized by the Tufts University Boston Streets Project, http://bcd.lib.tufts.edu/.

75. Fred Bunyan Joyner, *David Ames Wells, Champion of Free Trade* (Cedar Rapids, IA: The Torch Press, 1939), 28. For information about the Loyal Publication Society, see Sven Beckert, *The Monied Metropolis: New York City and the Consolidation of the American Bourgeoisie, 1850–1896* (Cambridge: Cambridge University Press, 2001), 129–131.

76. Stephen Meardon, "Postbellum Protection and Commissioner Wells's Conversion to Free Trade," *History of Political Economy* 39, no. 4 (2007): 571.

77. On the connection between New Englanders' political outlook and their business orientation, see, for example, Richard Franklin Bensel, *Yankee*

Leviathan: The Origins of Central State Authority in America, 1859–1877 (Cambridge: Cambridge University Press, 1990), 284.

78. Herbert Ronald Ferleger, "David A. Wells and the American Revenue System, 1865–1870" (Ph.D. diss., Columbia University, 1942), 185–186; Joyner, *David Ames Wells,*

79. Charles F. Adams, "Boston II," *North American Review* 106 (April 1868): 36.

80. Wells, Edwin, and Cuyler, *Report of the Commissioners*, 9, 6.

81. Ibid., 106.

82. Ibid., 105.

83. Ibid., 113; emphasis in original.

84. Ibid., 104, 113.

85. Ibid., 94–95.

86. Ibid., 105.

87. Ibid., 116–118.

88. The same basic questions were debated earlier in the century, in the context of a very different social configuration, when the state was under the solid control of Boston's mercantile elite. See Oscar Handlin, *Commonwealth; a Study of the Role of Government in the American Economy: Massachusetts, 1774–1861* (New York: New York University Press, 1947); Morton J. Horwitz, *The Transformation of American Law, 1780–1860* (Cambridge, MA: Harvard University Press, 1977).

89. Boston (Mass.), *Ordinances and Rules and Orders of the City of Boston, Together with the General and Special Statutes of the Massachusetts Legislature Relating to the City* (Boston: Alfred Mudge and Son, 1869), 691.

90. Wells, Edwin, and Cuyler, *Report of the Commissioners*, 11.

91. *Boston Daily Advertiser*, February 21, 1871; *Boston Daily Advertiser*, December 16, 1871.

92. Boston (Mass.), "City Document No. 26, Report of the Hearing before the Special Committee of the Common Council on the Subject of Abolishing the Tolls on the East Boston Ferries," Boston City Documents (Boston: Alfred Mudge and Son, 1871), 21, 31–32.

93. City of Boston, *Auditor of Accounts' Annual Report of the Receipts and Expenditures of the City of Boston* (Boston: Alfred Mudge and Son, 1871), 253.

94. Ibid., 286.

95. Ibid., 264, 261–262.

96. Ibid., 265, 274–275, 277; emphasis in the original.

97. Ibid., 279, 283.

98. It is worth noting that Hills represented not only the prevailing view in Massachusetts, which was conceded even by his fiercest critics, but a much broader public sentiment. A commission appointed in Maryland a few years

later reached similar conclusions to those of the one in Massachusetts. The commissioners in Maryland argued that "it would hardly be the part of prudence to strike from our taxable basis the large amount represented by the above mentioned classes of personal property," primarily the "stock and bonds of non-resident or foreign corporations. . . . It can hardly be proper for the State to abandon the taxation of personal property, because some of its citizens threaten to commit perjury rather than assume a portion of the public burdens which their fellows are bearing." See Tax Commission of Maryland State, *Report of the Maryland Tax Commission to the General Assembly, January, 1888* (Baltimore: King Brothers, 1888), 12–13.

99. "Critical Notices: Reports of the Tax Commissioners of Massachusetts," *The North American Review* 120 (April 1875): 477–485.

100. David Ames Wells, "The Reform of Local Taxation," *The North American Review* 122 (April 1876): 357–403; Commonwealth of Massachusetts, "House Document No. 15," 205.

101. Wells, Edwin, and Cuyler, *Report of the Commissioners*, 94–95.

102. Ibid., 4, 10.

103. Cooley, the most prominent legal authority on the issue and an advocate for strict judicial supervision of local taxation, explained that taxation was rooted "in the reciprocal duties of protection and support between the state and the citizens. . . . The citizen and the property owner owes to the government the duty to pay taxes, that the government may be enabled to perform its functions, and he is supposed to receive his proper and full compensation in the protection which the government affords to his life, liberty and property, and in the increase to the value of his possessions by the use to which the money contributed is applied." See Thomas McIntyre Cooley, *A Treatise on the Law of Taxation: Including the Law of Local Assessments* (Chicago: Callaghan, 1876), 2.

104. Commonwealth of Massachusetts, "House Document No. 15," 9–10.

105. Ibid., 10.

106. Ibid., 9–10.

107. William Minot, *Taxation in Massachusetts* (Boston: Alfred Mudge and Son, 1877); Wells, "The Reform of Local Taxation."

108. Commonwealth of Massachusetts, "House Document No. 15," 532, 512, 516; Ronald Story, *The Forging of an Aristocracy: Harvard & the Boston Upper Class, 1800–1870* (Middletown, CT: Wesleyan University Press, 1980); Peter Dobkin Hall, *The Organization of American Culture, 1700–1900: Private Institutions, Elites, and the Origins of American Nationality* (New York: New York University Press, 1982).

109. Commonwealth of Massachusetts, "House Document No. 15," 182.

110. Ibid., 183.

111. Ibid., 184.

112. Ibid., 188.
113. One of the Boston papers then wrote that "Harvard College belongs to the people of Massachusetts and by the grace of God, the people . . . will yet have it and hold it." Quoted in Samuel Eliot Morison, *Three Centuries of Harvard, 1636–1936* (Cambridge, MA: Harvard University Press, 1936), 288.
114. Commonwealth of Massachusetts, "House Document No. 15," 192–193.
115. Ibid., 193. Hills directed his critique to elite Protestant churches of Boston, not to working-class Catholic churches. Catholic churches, although larger on average, owned only about 25 percent of the exempted property. See ibid., 511–512.
116. Ibid., 194.
117. Ibid., 371.
118. Ibid., 392.
119. William Minot Jr., *Taxation* (Boston: Alfred Mudge and Son, 1881).
120. Ibid.

3. Brahminism Goes West

1. "The Car Telescoped," *Rocky Mountain News*, November 15, 1890.
2. "Telescoped a Sleeper Saturday," *The Daily Inter Ocean*, November 15, 1890.
3. "A Useful Life Ended," *Daily Leader*, November 15, 1890. See also Henry Davis Minot Papers, "Tributes and Obituaries" folder, Box 2, Massachusetts Historical Society (MHS); "Fast Trains Collide," *Daily Picayune*, November 15, 1890.
4. "Juggernaut of Death," *Morning Oregonian*, November 15, 1890.
5. "Henry D. Minot, the Life of One of the Victims of the Collision," *New York Times*, November 15, 1890.
6. "Superior's Sad Loss," *Daily Leader*, November 15, 1890; Henry Davis Minot Papers, "Tributes and Obituaries" folder, Box 2, MHS.
7. "An Untimely Death," *Daily Pioneer*, November 15, 1890.
8. "The Chamber of Commerce Takes Action to Show Its Respect for Superior's Friend," *Daily Leader*, November 15, 1890; Henry Davis Minot Papers, "Tributes and Obituaries" folder, Box 2, MHS.
9. For this declension narrative, see, most emblematically, Richard Hofstadter, *The Age of Reform: From Bryan to F. D. R.* (New York: Knopf, 1955), 136–141. See also Frederic Cople Jaher, *The Urban Establishment: Upper Strata in Boston, New York, Charleston, Chicago, and Los Angeles* (Urbana: University of Illinois Press, 1982). For a critique, see "The Moral and Intellectual Rehabilitation of the Ruling Class," in *The World of Nations; Reflections on American History, Politics, and Culture,* ed. Christopher Lasch (New York: Knopf, 1973), 80–99; Jackson Lears, "The Managerial Revitalization of the Rich," in *Ruling America: A History of Wealth and Power in a Democracy,* ed. Steve Fraser and Gary Gerstle (Cambridge, MA: Harvard University Press, 2005), 181–214.

10. For gentlemanly bankers in the British context, see P. J. Cain and A. G. Hopkins, *British Imperialism: Innovation and Expansion, 1688–1914* (London: Longman, 1993).

11. William T. Davis, *Professional and Industrial History of Suffolk County, Massachusetts* (Boston: Boston History Co., 1894), vol. 1, 639; Henry Wilder Foote, *Annals of King's Chapel from the Puritan Age of New England to the Present Day* (Boston: Little, Brown, 1882), vol. 2, 365.

12. See Elizabeth Blackmar, "Inheriting Property and Debt: From Family Security to Corporate Accumulation," in *Capitalism Takes Command: The Social Transformation of Nineteenth-Century America*, ed. Michael Zakim and Gary J. Kornblith (Chicago: University of Chicago Press, 2011), 93–117, and Peter Dobkin Hall, "What the Merchants Did with Their Money: Charitable and Testamentary Trusts in Massachusetts, 1780–1880," in *Entrepreneurs: The Boston Business Community, 1700–1850*, ed. Conrad Edick Wright and Katheryn P. Viens (Boston: Massachusetts Historical Society, 1997), 365–421. See also David Grayson Allen, *Investment Management in Boston: A History* (Boston: University of Massachusetts Press, 2015), 61–80. For the impact of New England jurisprudence on trusts beyond the region, primarily in New York, and the resulting "Bostonization of American Wealth" at the end of the nineteenth century, see Peter D. Hall and George E. Marcus, "Why Should Men Leave Great Fortunes to Their Children?" in *Inheritance and Wealth in America*, ed. Robert K. Miller and Stephen J. McNamee (New York: Plenum Press, 1998), 158–160.

13. As Tocqueville argued, "What is most important for democracy is not that there are no great fortunes; it is that great fortunes do not rest in the same hands. . . . Wealth circulates there with incredible rapidity, and experience teaches that it is rare to see two generations reap the rewards of wealth." See Alexis de Tocqueville, *Democracy in America*, trans. Eduardo Nolla and James T. Schleifer (Indianapolis: Liberty Fund, 2012), 79–80, 85.

14. Joseph Story, "Chancery Jurisdiction," in *The Miscellaneous Writings of Joseph Story*, ed. William W. Story (Boston: C. C. Little and J. Brown, 1852).

15. William J. Curran, "The Struggle for Equity Jurisdiction in Massachusetts," *Boston University Law Review* 31 (1951): 269–296; Edwin Woodruff, "Chancery in Massachusetts," *Law Quarterly Review* 5 (1889): 370–386.

16. Joseph Story, "Chancery Jurisdiction."

17. Harvard College and Massachusetts General Hospital v. Amory (1830).

18. Harvard College and Massachusetts General Hospital v. Amory.

19. Davis, "History of the Bench and Bar," 581; William Minot, *Private Letters* (Boston: Rockwell and Churchill, 1895), 10.

20. William Minot, *Private Letters* (Boston: Rockwell and Churchill, 1895), 11.

21. Jonathan Edwards and Catharine Maria Sedgwick, Katharine's aunt, are two of many notable members of the Sedgwick family. See Hubert M. Sedgwick, *A Sedgwick Genealogy: Descendants of Deacon Benjamin Sedgwick* (New Haven, CT: New Haven Colony Historical Society, 1961).

22. Minot, *Private Letters*, 5–6.

23. For a history of country estates and their cultural significance in nineteenth-century Boston, see Tamara Plakins Thornton, *Cultivating Gentlemen: The Meaning of Country Life among the Boston Elite, 1785–1860* (New Haven, CT: Yale University Press, 1989).

24. Minot, *Private Letters*, 6–7.

25. Henry Davis Minot, *The Land-Birds and Game-Birds of New England; with Descriptions of the Birds, Their Nests and Eggs, Their Habits and Notes* (Salem, MA: Naturalist's Agency; Estes and Lauriat, 1877).

26. Theodore Roosevelt and Henry Davis Minot, *The Summer Birds of the Adirondacks in Franklin County, N.Y.* (Salem, MA: Samuel E. Cassino, 1877).

27. Henry Davis Minot to Dr. Folsom, April 18, 1878, Henry Davis Minot Papers, "January–September 1878" folder, Box 1, MHS.

28. Henry Davis Minot to William Minot, September 14, 1878, Henry Davis Minot Papers, "January–September 1878" folder, Box 1, MHS.

29. John T. Morse Jr., "Memoir of Henry Lee Higginson," *Proceedings of the Massachusetts Historical Society* (October 1919–June 1920), 116.

30. Henry Davis Minot to William Minot, July 14, 1882, Henry Davis Minot Papers, "Personal correspondence, January 1866–June 1886" folder, Box 1, MHS; Henry Davis Minot to William Minot Jr., July 25, 1882, Henry Davis Minot Papers, "1882" folder, Box 1, MHS; Henry Davis Minot to Unknown, August 25, 1882, Henry Davis Minot Papers, "Railroad 1882–1886" folder, Box 5, MHS.

31. Henry Davis Minot to William Minot Jr., July 8, 1882, Henry Davis Minot Papers, "1882" folder, Box 1, MHS; Henry Davis Minot to William Minot Jr., July 25, 1882, Henry Davis Minot Papers, "1882" folder, Box 1, MHS.

32. William Minot Jr. to Henry Davis Minot, July 16, 1882, in Minot, *Private Letters*, 60, supplement.

33. Henry Davis Minot to Unknown, August 25, 1882, Henry Davis Minot Papers, "Railroad 1882–1886" folder, Box 5, MHS.

34. Ibid.

35. Henry Davis Minot to William Minot Jr., July 25, 1882, Henry Davis Minot Papers, "1882" folder, Box 1, MHS.

36. The details of some of these trips can be reconstructed based on Henry's notebooks, where he recorded all the trip's expenses, his letters to his family and employers in Boston, and reports on his findings, which he composed at

the end of the journey. See Henry Davis Minot Papers, "Railroad journal, 1883," vol. 25, Box 9, and Henry Davis Minot Papers, "Reports 1883," folders 7–10, Box 5, MHS.

37. A. K. Sandoval-Strausz, *Hotel: An American History* (New Haven, CT: Yale University Press, 2007), 101.

38. Among expenses for hotels, Henry recorded expenses for train tickets, telegrams, a horse and saddle, and new shoes to replace a worn-out pair. See Henry Davis Minot Papers, "Railroad journal, 1883," vol. 25, Box 9, MHS.

39. For more on this hierarchy, see Thomas C. Cochran, *Railroad Leaders, 1845–1890* (Cambridge, MA: Harvard University Press, 1953).

40. Henry Davis Minot to William Minot Jr., April 18, 1883, Henry Davis Minot Papers, "January–May 1883" folder, Box 1, MHS.

41. Henry Davis Minot to William Minot Jr., May 28, 1883, Henry Davis Minot Papers, "January–May 1883" folder, Box 1, MHS.

42. Henry Davis Minot to William Minot Jr., June 11, 1883, Henry Davis Minot Papers, "June–December 1883" folder, Box 1, MHS.

43. Henry Davis Minot to William Minot Jr., June 21, 1883, Henry Davis Minot Papers, "June–December 1883" folder, Box 1, MHS.

44. Henry Davis Minot to William Minot Jr., August 21, 1883, "June–December 1883" Folder, Box 1, HDM Papers, MHS.

45. Henry Davis Minot to Alice Minot, September 22, 1883, "June–December 1883" Folder, Box 1, HDM Papers, MHS.

46. Henry Davis Minot, "Special Report on the Flint, Pere Marquette R.R.," 4, 6, 13, 14, September 29, 1883, "Reports 1883," Folder, Box 5, HDM Papers, MHS.

47. This moment also marked Henry's reconnection with Theodore Roosevelt. Henry wrote, "It is a delightful prospect to me that of returning my intercourse with him. . . . His manners show no change, and our old cordiality seems young again." See Henry Davis Minot to William Minot Jr., August 21, 1883, Henry Davis Minot Papers, "June–December 1883" folder, Box 1, MHS.

48. Massachusetts was the only state to grant such license at that point. Two other corporations were chartered under the provision, one for another railroad in Mexico, the other for a railroad in the area of the Ottoman Empire known as Palestine. See Commonwealth of Massachusetts, "An Act in Addition to the 'General Railroad Act' of the Year Eighteen Hundred and Seventy Four, to Authorize the Formation of Corporations to Construct Railroads in Foreign Countries," chapter 274, 1879, approved April 28, 1879. For information about the railroad's board and offices, see Henry Varnum Poor, *Manual of the Railroads of the United States* (New York: H. W. Poor, 1884), 974–976. By 1885, with the support of forty-nine such concessions, American financiers had constructed a railway system of nearly 6,000 miles in Mexico. See John M. Hart,

Empire and Revolution: The Americans in Mexico since the Civil War (Berkeley: University of California Press, 2002), 121.

49. Sandra Kuntz Ficker, "Economic Backwardness and Firm Strategy: An American Railroad Corporation in Nineteenth-Century Mexico," *Hispanic American Historical Review* 80, no. 2 (2000): 267–298; Sandra Kuntz Ficker, *Empresa Extranjera Y Mercado Interno: El Ferrocarril Central Mexicano, 1880–1907* (México, D. F.: Colegio de México, 1995).

50. Kuntz Ficker, "Economic Backwardness and Firm Strategy," 284. On concessions more generally, see Cyrus Veeser, "A Forgotten Instrument of Global Capitalism? International Concessions, 1870–1930," *The International History Review* 35, no. 5 (October 1, 2013): 1136–1155; Cyrus Veeser, "Concessions as a Modernizing Strategy in the Dominican Republic," *Business History Review* 83, no. 04 (December 2009): 731–758.

51. "New Conquest of Mexico," *Boston Daily Advertiser*, March 10, 1884. The title and content of the article drew a sharp contrast between this conquest and the original one, described in William H. Prescott's classic history *Conquest of Mexico*, which was published in 1843.

52. Henry Davis Minot to William Minot Jr., April 8, 1884, Henry Davis Minot Papers, "Letterbook 1884–1888," vol. 1, MHS.

53. Henry Davis Minot Papers, "Expense Book for Mexico Trip, 1884," vol. 26, Box 9, MHS.

54. Henry Davis Minot to William Minot Jr., May 22, 1884, Henry Davis Minot Papers, "Letterbook 1884–1888," vol. 1, MHS.

55. Henry Davis Minot to William Minot Jr., June 17, 1884, Henry Davis Minot Papers, "Letterbook 1884–1888," vol. 1, MHS.

56. Kuntz Ficker, "Economic Backwardness and Firm Strategy," 282, 286. As late as 1907, branch lines added up to less than ten percent of overall mileage of the road. See ibid., 286.

57. Henry Davis Minot, "Report on the Mexican Central Railway," December 31, 1884, 2, "August–December 1884" folder, Box 5, MHS.

58. And yet again, he concluded, any rise in wages would be counterproductive as "the present low price of labor is to-day one of the best elements in Mexico's progress." Ibid., 23.

59. Kuntz Ficker, "Economic Backwardness and Firm Strategy," 287–288. See also Lorena Parlee, "Porfirio Diaz, Railroads, and Development in Northern Mexico: A Study of Government Policy toward the Central and National Railroads, 1876–1910" (Ph.D. diss., University of California, San Diego, 1981), 72–77.

60. To compound the problem, as public resources concentrated on railroad development, investment in road construction nearly stopped, further diminishing prospects for more robust regional traffic. The Mexican highway system barely

grew from 2,000 to 2,500 miles between 1876 and 1911. See Kuntz Ficker, "Economic Backwardness and Firm Strategy," 278.

61. See Hart, *Empire and Revolution*, 127. See also John H. Coatsworth, *Growth against Development: The Economic Impact of Railroads in Porfirian Mexico* (DeKalb, IL: Northern Illinois University Press, 1981).

62. Henry Davis Minot, "Report on the Mexican Central Railway," December 31, 1884, 2, Henry Davis Minot Papers, "August–December 1884" folder, Box 5, MHS.

63. Saul Engelbourg and Leonard Bushkoff, *The Man Who Found the Money: John Stewart Kennedy and the Financing of the Western Railroads* (East Lansing: Michigan State University Press, 1996); Albro Martin, *James J. Hill and the Opening of the Northwest* (New York: Oxford University Press, 1976).

64. Engelbourg and Bushkoff, *The Man Who Found the Money*, 117; Ralph W. Hidy et al., *The Great Northern Railway: A History* (Boston: Harvard Business School Press, 1988), 46–49.

65. Engelbourg and Bushkoff, *The Man Who Found the Money*, 117; Martin, *James J. Hill*; Hidy et al., *The Great Northern Railway*, 37.

66. As in his previous report, Henry covered issues ranging from demographics (settlement density), agriculture (prospects for the region's wheat and for the endurance of soil), technical matters (condition of the rails, equipment, and facilities), fiscal matters (the purging of the old debt, annual revenues, cost of operations, value of land owned by the corporation), and political issues (taxation, legal disputes, freedom to set rates). See Henry Davis Minot, *The Saint Paul, Minneapolis, and Manitoba Railway Company as Investment Property* (Boston: Privately printed for Lee, Higginson, & Co., 1885).

67. For the correspondence, see Henry Davis Minot to Charles E. Perkins, June 3, 1885, Minot Family Business and Financial Papers, Box 60, MHS; Henry Davis Minot to Charles E. Perkins, June 5, 1885, Minot Family Business and Financial Papers, Box 60, MHS; Henry D. Minot to John Murray Forbes, July 7, 1885, Henry Lee Higginson Business Papers, Box XII-2A, Baker Library; Henry D. Minot to Lee, Higginson, and Co., August 1, 1885, Henry Lee Higginson Business Papers, Box XII-2A, Baker Library.

68. Donald Meinig provides a useful typology of the different patterns of development within the national railroad network. See D. W. Meinig, *The Shaping of America: A Geographical Perspective on 500 Years of History*, vol. 3, *Transcontinental America, 1850–1915* (New Haven, CT: Yale University Press, 2000), 253–265.

69. Quoted in Hidy et al., *The Great Northern Railway*, 40.

70. Ibid., 39–44.

71. Henry Davis Minot to William Minot Jr., January 20, 1886, Henry Davis Minot Papers, "Letterbook 1884–1888," vol. 1, MHS.

72. Hidy et al., *The Great Northern Railway*, 55.

73. Minot articulated his view of the harmony between financial and executive operation during his visit to Mexico. Capturing his assessment of his own merits, he wrote to Henry Lee Higginson that the Mexican Central needs "above all else a railroad man of first rate ability, who shall stand between the financial and operating departments of the road; who shall supervise the plans and estimates and construction of the company's coast lines; who shall study the character of the Mexican people, the resources of the country, the competitive forces at work there, and every possible development of the Mexican Central's traffic; and who shall have the power, subject to the Government's approval, of fixing rates." Henry Davis Minot, "Report on the Mexican Central Railway," December 31, 1884, "August–December 1884" folder, Box 5, HDM Papers, MHS.

74. Henry Davis Minot to William Minot Jr., May 16, 1886, Henry Davis Minot Papers, "Letterbook 1884–1888," vol. 1, MHS; Henry Davis Minot to William Minot Jr., October 11, 1886, Henry Davis Minot Papers, "Letterbook 1884–1888," vol. 1, MHS; Henry Davis Minot to William Minot Jr., November 2 and November 12, 1886, Henry Davis Minot Papers, "Letterbook 1884–1888," vol. 1, MHS.

75. Henry Davis Minot to William Minot Jr., September 11, 1886, Henry Davis Minot Papers, "July–December 1886" folder, Box 2, MHS.

76. Henry Davis Minot to William Minot Jr., June 6, 1888, Minot Family Business and Financial Papers, Box 71, MHS; "List of Stockholders St. Paul, Minneapolis, and Manitoba Railway, closing of books April 17th 1888," April 17, 1888, Minot Family Business and Financial Papers, Box 71, MHS.

77. Henry Davis Minot to William Minot Jr., September 11, 1886, Henry Davis Minot Papers, "July–December 1886" folder, Box 2, MHS.

78. The Helena Board of Trade, *Helena Illustrated, Capital of the State of Montana; a History of the Early Settlement and the Helena of to-Day, Showing the Resources of the City, Its Commercial Advantages, Manufactures and Wonderful Growth with Illustrations of Public Buildings, Prominent Business Blocks, Beautiful Homes, Portraits and Biographical Sketches of Leading Citizens* (Minneapolis, MN: F. L. Thresher, 1890).

79. Henry Davis Minot to William Minot Jr., October 21, 1885, Henry Davis Minot Papers, "Letterbook 1884–1888," vol. 1, MHS.

80. New Englanders in earlier eras were, of course, much more ambivalent about the virtues of material accumulation. See Bernard Bailyn, *The New England Merchants in the Seventeenth Century* (Cambridge, MA: Harvard University Press, 1955).

81. George Edward Ellis, *Memoir of Nathaniel Thayer, Reprinted from the Proceedings of the Massachusetts Historical Society* (Cambridge: J. Wilson and Son, 1885), 12.

82. Ibid., 13.
83. Ibid., 14.
84. Ibid., 17.
85. Ibid., 15–16.

4. The Contest over the Common

1. In 1860, Boston's Suffolk County had roughly $14.5 million invested in manufacturing, far less than, for example, Middlesex County ($26.9 million), where Waltham and Lowell were situated, and Bristol County ($24.1 million), where Taunton, Fall River, and New Bedford were situated. Suffolk County also had far fewer men and women employed in manufacturing (19,093), compared with Essex County (46,377), where Lynn was situated, Middlesex (36,822), and Worcester (31,393). See *Manufactures of the United States in 1860: Compiled from the Original Returns of the Eighth Census* (New York: Norman Ross Publishing, 1990), 251.

2. In 1880, the total manufacturing product of Boston's Suffolk County was estimated at $134.5 million, more than Middlesex ($128 million) and Essex ($103 million). The county employed 60,985, more than Essex (59,869), which had been the leader prior to 1860, and a little less than Middlesex (61,135). See Francis Amasa Walker and Chas W. Seaton, eds., *Tenth Census of the United States, 1880* (New York: Norman Ross Publishing, 1991), 130.

3. In Lowell, the textile sector included "cotton goods," "dyeing and finishing," "woolen goods," and "worsted goods." In Lawrence, the textile sector included "cotton goods," "dyeing and finishing," "mixed textiles," "woolen goods," and "worsted goods." See *Tenth Census of the United States, 1880*, 402, 408–410.

4. In Lynn, the shoe and boot industry included "boots and shoes," "boots and shoes cut stock," "boot and shoe finding," "leather curried," and "leather tanned." See *Tenth Census of the United States, 1880*, 410.

5. *Tenth Census of the United States, 1880*, 385–386.

6. Compared with $72,315 and 70.8 at Lowell, $81,654 and 73.0 at Lawrence, and $17,185 and 36.2 at Lynn. *Tenth Census of the United States, 1880*, 402, 408–410. Ninety percent of all industrial establishments in the city were capitalized at less than $20,000. They employed more than half the industrial workforce in the city and paid more than half of the total wages. See Noam Maggor, "Politics of Property: Urban Democracy in the Age of Global Capital, Boston 1865–1900" (Ph.D. diss., Harvard University, 2010), 145–148. On alternatives to mass production in this period, but with scant attention to politics and ideology, see Charles Sabel and Jonathan Zeitlin, "Historical Alternatives to Mass Production: Politics, Markets and Technology in Nineteenth-Century Industrialization," *Past and Present*, no. 108 (1985): 133–176; Charles F. Sabel and Jonathan Zeitlin, eds., *World of Possibilities: Flexibility and Mass Produc-*

tion in Western Industrialization (New York: Cambridge University Press, 1997); Philip Scranton, *Proprietary Capitalism: The Textile Manufacture at Philadelphia, 1800–1885* (Cambridge: Cambridge University Press, 1983); Philip Scranton, *Endless Novelty: Specialty Production and American Industrialization, 1865–1925* (Princeton, NJ: Princeton University Press, 1997); Philip Scranton and Patrick Fridenson, *Reimagining Business History* (Baltimore: Johns Hopkins University Press, 2013).

7. Mona Domosh, *Invented Cities: The Creation of Landscape in Nineteenth-Century New York & Boston* (New Haven, CT: Yale University Press, 1996), 99–109. See also Bainbridge Bunting, *Houses of Boston's Back Bay: An Architectural History, 1840–1917* (Cambridge, MA: Belknap Press of Harvard University Press, 1967).

8. Domosh, *Invented Cities*, 110–122.

9. The concentration of elite families in this neighborhood was remarkable. One study found Back Bay to be the home of 1,166 upper-class families by 1905, compared with 242 on Beacon Hill and out of a total number of 1,635 upper-class families in the city. See Walter Irving Firey, *Land Use in Central Boston* (Cambridge, MA: Harvard University Press, 1947), 115. Residents of Back Bay held vast amounts of property in out-of-state corporations (both shares and bonds) and in western mortgages. No other ward in the city came close. For partial but very telling numbers for the year 1889, see William Minot, Jonathan Abbot Lane, and George G. Crocker, *Message of the Mayor Transmitting Report of the Special Commission on Taxation* (Boston: Rockwell and Churchill, 1891).

10. *Boston Daily Advertiser*, February 5, 1877.

11. The first petition of the remonstrants had forty-three signers. Thirty-four of forty-three recognized names among them belonged to a small set of occupations: five financiers, four industrialists, thirteen lawyers, nine merchants, an architect, a physician, and a real estate broker. A second petition against the exhibition included about 250 names (signed by initials only, making them difficult to trace). The mechanics association had about 800 members, representing a variety of trades. All of them had served apprenticeships in their youth and rose either as small proprietary businessmen (a highly volatile status) or as overseers in larger manufacturing establishments. Three petitions from nonmembers of the association in support of the mechanics included ninety-eight names, eighty-nine of which were recognized in city directories. The major urban industries were heavily represented—leather (seven), boots and shoes (eight), clothing (four), piano manufacturing (nine), and publishing (seven)—alongside traders/dealers (eight), grocers, retailers, carpenters, jewelers, real estate agents, clerks, and salesmen. Five bankers also supported the mechanics. Occupations are taken from city directories digitized by the Tufts University Boston Streets Project. See http://bcd.lib.tufts.edu/.

12. Boston (Mass.), "City Document No. 26, Evidence Taken at the Hearing before the Joint Standing Committee on Common and Public Grounds on the Petition of the Massachusetts Charitable Mechanic Association for Leave to Erect a Building on Boston Common," Boston City Documents (Boston: Rockwell and Churchill, 1877).

13. Massachusetts Charitable Mechanic Association, *Annals of the Massachusetts Charitable Mechanic Association, 1795–1892* (Boston: Press of Rockwell and Churchill, 1892), 521–522; Boston (Mass.), *A Catalogue of the City Councils of Boston, 1822–1908, Roxbury, 1846–1867, Charlestown, 1847–1873 and of the Selectmen of Boston, 1634–1822, Also of Various Other Town and Municipal Officers* (Boston: City of Boston Printing Department, 1909). Both men had also served terms in the state legislature.

14. Boston (Mass.), City Document No. 26, 3.

15. Ibid., 13.

16. A Committee of Citizens, *The Public Rights in Boston Common* (Boston: Rockwell and Churchill, 1877), 33.

17. Ibid., 33, 35.

18. Ibid., 5; "The Charitable Mechanic Association and the Common," *Boston Daily Advertiser*, February 22, 1877.

19. *The Public Rights in Boston Common*, 5.

20. Ibid., 5.

21. Ibid., 35. On this very point, see the exchange between Charles F. Adams Jr. and his brother Henry, who argued in a typical vein that "[New England's] wealth and life are drawn irresistibly towards more promising markets." Henry Adams to Charles Francis Adams Jr., July 30, 1867, in Henry Adams, *The Letters of Henry Adams* (Cambridge, MA: Harvard University Press, 1982), vol. 1, 541–546.

22. Boston (Mass.), City Document No. 26, 11, 8; *The Public Rights in Boston Common*, 4.

23. "The Last Hearing," *Boston Daily Advertiser*, February 17, 1877.

24. *The Public Rights in Boston Common*, 8.

25. Ibid., 31, 34.

26. Boston (Mass.), City Document No. 26, 21, 20.

27. *The Public Rights in Boston Common*, 11.

28. Ibid., 10.

29. Ibid., 24.

30. Ibid. Olney himself lived on a large estate in rural West Roxbury, which had recently been annexed to Boston against the will of its most affluent residents.

31. Ibid., 15.

32. Ibid., 40.

33. Ibid., 54. Quincy himself lived on Park Street, adjacent to the Common. Quincy's eulogist noted the man's reputation for putting his foot in his mouth: "He had the ambition but not the arts of the politician, and a candor of thought and speech which is often incompatible with political popularity." See Samuel Arthur Bent, *Eulogy on Samuel Miller Quincy* (Boston: T. R. Marvin and Son, 1887), 17.

34. *The Public Rights in Boston Common*, 9.

35. Boston (Mass.), City Document No. 26, 3; *The Public Rights in Boston Common*, 35.

36. *The Public Rights in Boston Common*, 33.

37. On this contest as fundamental to the politics of industrialization in this period, see James Livingston, *Pragmatism and the Political Economy of Cultural Revolution, 1850–1940* (Chapel Hill: University of North Carolina Press, 1994), 43–49; Alexander Gourevitch, *From Slavery to the Cooperative Commonwealth: Labor and Republican Liberty in the Nineteenth Century* (Cambridge: Cambridge University Press, 2015). See also Kristin Ross, *Communal Luxury: The Political Imaginary of the Paris Commune* (London: Verso, 2015), 39–65, and Jacques Rancière, *The Nights of Labor: The Workers' Dream in Nineteenth-Century France* (Philadelphia: Temple University Press, 1989). For a critique of the ideological divide between theoretical and applied knowledge, see Lissa Roberts, Simon Schaffer, and Peter Dear, eds., *The Mindful Hand: Inquiry and Invention from the Late Renaissance to Early Industrialisation* (Amsterdam: Koninkliijke Nederlandse Akademie van Wetenschappen, 2007), and Richard Sennett, *The Craftsman* (New Haven, CT: Yale University Press, 2008).

38. Ibid., 21, 5; Boston (Mass.), City Document No. 26, 11.

39. Boston (Mass.), City Document No. 26, 11.

40. Ibid., 11.

41. *The Public Rights in Boston Common*, 21.

42. Ibid., 24.

43. Ibid., 34; Boston (Mass.), City Document No. 26, 12.

44. Quoted in Michael Rawson, *Eden on the Charles: The Making of Boston* (Cambridge, MA: Harvard University Press, 2010), 52. For the long history of the Common, see Domosh, *Invented Cities*, 127–133; Rawson, *Eden on the Charles*, 22–74.

45. Domosh, *Invented Cities*, 129–130; Rawson, *Eden on the Charles*, 32–35.

46. Rawson, *Eden on the Charles*, 35–40, 43–67.

47. "An Old Lady of Boston," *Boston Daily Advertiser*, March 19, 1869, quoted in P. S. Gilmore, *History of the National Peace Jubilee and Great Musical Festival* (Boston: Lee, Shepard, and Dillingham, 1871).

48. Quoted in ibid., 219.

49. *The Public Rights in Boston Common*, 38.

50. For the elite's embrace of the "vanishing" medieval artisan, see T. J. Jackson Lears, *No Place of Grace: Antimodernism and the Transformation of American Culture, 1880–1920* (New York: Pantheon Books, 1981).

51. Massachusetts Charitable Mechanic Association, *The Tenth Exhibition of the Massachusetts Charitable Mechanic Association at Faneuil and Quincy Halls in the City of Boston* (Boston: Wright and Potter, 1865), vi; Massachusetts Charitable Mechanic Association, *The Fourteenth Exhibition of the Charitable Mechanic Association* (Boston: Alfred Mudge and Son, 1881), vii.

52. Massachusetts Charitable Mechanic Association, *The Fourteenth Exhibition*, xxiv.

53. Ibid., xxvi; Massachusetts Charitable Mechanic Association, *The Tenth Exhibition*, vi.

54. Ibid., 31.

55. Alexander Hamilton Bullock, *The Mechanic Arts Favorable to Liberty and Social Progress* (Boston: Wright and Potter, 1865), 10, 8.

56. Ibid., 13, 10.

57. Massachusetts Charitable Mechanic Association, *The Fourteenth Exhibition*, xxiv.

58. Massachusetts Charitable Mechanic Association, *The Twelfth Exhibition of the Massachusetts Charitable Mechanic Association* (Boston: Alfred Mudge and Son, 1874), 206.

59. Alexander Gourevitch, *From Slavery to the Cooperative Commonwealth: Labor and Republican Liberty in the Nineteenth Century* (New York: Cambridge University Press, 2015); Kristin Ross, *Communal Luxury: The Political Imaginary of the Paris Commune* (London: Verso, 2015); Bruce Robertson, "The South Kensington Museum in Context: An Alternative History," *Museum and Society* 2, no. 1 (March 2004): 1–14.

60. Bullock, *The Mechanic Arts*, 21.

61. Massachusetts Charitable Mechanic Association, *The Twenty-first Triennial Festival at Music Hall, November 18, 1869, Address by Charles W. Slack Esq.* (Boston: Alfred Mudge and Son, 1869).

62. Bullock, *The Mechanic Arts*, 21–22.

63. Ibid., 17–18.

64. Massachusetts Charitable Mechanic Association, *The Fourteenth Exhibition*, xxiv.

65. Massachusetts Charitable Mechanic Association, *The Twenty-first Triennial Festival, Address by Charles W. Slack Esq.*, 32–36. For the full sermon, see Theodore Parker, *The Collected Works of Theodore Parker: Lessons from the World of Matter and the World of Man*, 3rd ed. (London: Trübner and Co., 1872), 377–385.

66. See Neil Harris, "The Gilded Age Revisited: Boston and the Museum Movement," *American Quarterly* 14, no. 4 (1962): 545–566; Paul DiMaggio, "Cultural Entrepreneurship in Nineteenth-Century Boston: The Creation of an Organizational Base for High Culture in America," *Media, Culture and Society* 4, no. 1 (1982): 33–50; Paul DiMaggio, "Cultural Entrepreneurship in Nineteenth-Century Boston, Part II: The Classification and Framing of American Art," *Media, Culture and Society* 4, no. 4 (1982): 303–322; Lawrence Levine, *Highbrow/Lowbrow: The Emergence of Cultural Hierarchy in America* (Cambridge, MA: Harvard University Press, 1990).

67. Quoted in Walter Muir Whitehill, *Museum of Fine Arts, Boston: A Centennial History* (Cambridge, MA: Belknap Press, 1970).

68. Quoted in ibid., 42.

69. Quoted in ibid., 58.

70. Whitehill, *Museum of Fine Arts, Boston*, 51–52.

71. Quoted in DiMaggio, "Cultural Entrepreneurship in Nineteenth-Century Boston, Part II," 306–307.

72. Massachusetts Charitable Mechanic Association, *The Fourteenth Exhibition*, 229.

73. Boston (Mass.), *Reports of Proceedings of the City Council of Boston for the Year 1877* (Boston: City of Boston, n.d.), 113, 115.

74. Boston (Mass.), "City Document No. 27, Report on Petition of Mass. Charitable Mechanic Association for Use of a Portion of Boston Common on which to Erect Their Exhibition Building," Boston City Documents (Boston: Rockwell and Churchill, 1878).

5. Eastern Money and Western Populism

1. See Howard Roberts Lamar, *Dakota Territory, 1861–1889: A Study of Frontier Politics* (New Haven, CT: Yale University Press, 1956).

2. The federal government, of course, was not absent from the region, flexing its long muscles to assert U.S. sovereignty, remove the indigenous population, map the territory, and survey natural resources. See most notably Richard White, *"It's Your Misfortune and None of My Own": A History of the American West* (Norman: University of Oklahoma Press, 1991). All these issues remained under federal jurisdiction and control, and therefore they were not discussed by delegates at state-level constitutional conventions.

3. Eager settlers formed self-proclaimed territorial governments, with rudimentary regulatory authority, in anticipation of federal legislation. The Denver area, for example, had no less than three different bodies claiming government jurisdiction before the official establishment of the Colorado Territory in February 1861. See Dale A. Oesterle and Richard B. Collins, *The Colorado State Constitution: A Reference Guide* (Westport, CT: Greenwood Press, 2002), 3–4.

4. *Second Annual Report of the Denver Chamber of Commerce and Board of Trade, Denver, Colorado* (Denver: New Printing Company, April 15, 1885).

5. The classic study on this topic remains John Donald Hicks, *The Constitutions of the Northwest States* (Lincoln: University of Nebraska, 1923). I am deeply indebted to Hicks as well as to Amy Bridges's more recent and comprehensive effort to grapple with this overshadowed dimension of American state formation. See Amy Bridges, "Managing the Periphery in the Gilded Age: Writing Constitutions for the Western States," *Studies in American Political Development* 22, no. 1 (April 2008): 32–58. State-level constitutionalism has gained increasing attention from legal scholars under the rubric of "federalism." See, for example, Christian G. Fritz, "The American Constitutional Tradition Revisited: Preliminary Observations on State Constitution-Making in the Nineteenth-Century West," *Rutgers Law Journal* 25 (1994): 945–998; Marsha L. Baum and Christian G. Fritz, "American Constitution-Making: The Neglected State Constitutional Sources," *Hastings Constitutional Law Quarterly* 27 (2000): 199–242; Gordon Morris Bakken, *Rocky Mountain Constitution Making, 1850–1912* (New York: Greenwood Press, 1987); David Alan Johnson, *Founding the Far West: California, Oregon, and Nevada, 1840–1890* (Berkeley: University of California Press, 1992); G. Alan Tarr, *Understanding State Constitutions* (Princeton, NJ: Princeton University Press, 1998); John J. Dinan, *The American State Constitutional Tradition* (Lawrence: University Press of Kansas, 2006); Emily J. Zackin, *Looking for Rights in All the Wrong Places: Why State Constitutions Contain America's Positive Rights* (Princeton, NJ: Princeton University Press, 2013). These constitutional debates reveal the complex ideological and doctrinal backdrop against which Supreme Court laissez-faire jurisprudence developed. Bensel's exploration of the federal "judicial construction of the national market" recognizes that "left to their own devices, the legislatures of the individual states would have erected significant barriers to the consolidation of the national market in the late nineteenth century" but does not take the efforts of these legislatures, and their notable successes, seriously enough. See Richard Franklin Bensel, *The Political Economy of American Industrialization, 1877–1900* (Cambridge: Cambridge University Press, 2000), 321. For a more thoughtful consideration of the possibilities, but again with overwhelming emphasis on federal institutions, see Gerald Berk, *Alternative Tracks: The Constitution of American Industrial Order, 1865–1917* (Baltimore: Johns Hopkins University Press, 1994).

6. The analysis here affirms Charles Postel's profound insight that "modernity" itself was not in question for the populists, but it pushes to better elaborate what precisely set the populist agenda apart from the reigning liberal orthodoxy of this and later periods.

7. The following territories gained statehood status in the years after the Civil War: Colorado (1875), Montana (1888), North Dakota (1889), South Dakota (1889), Washington (1889), Idaho (1890), and Wyoming (1890).

8. *Proceedings and Debates of the Constitutional Convention: Held in the City of Helena, Montana, July 4th, 1889, to August 17th, 1889* (Helena, MT: State Publishing Company, 1921), 806.

9. *Journal of the Constitutional Convention for North Dakota Held at Bismarck, Thursday, July 4 to Aug. 17, 1889, Together with the Enabling Act of Congress and the Proceedings of the Joint Commission Appointed for the Equitable Division of Territorial Property* (Bismarck, ND: Tribune, 1889), 67.

10. "No subject" in their deliberations, they explained, caused "more anxiety and concern than the troublesome and vexed question pertaining to corporations." See *Proceedings of the Constitutional Convention Held in Denver, December 20, 1875: To Frame a Constitution for the State of Colorado, Together with the Enabling Act Passed by the Congress of the United States and Approved March 3, 1875, the Address to the People Issued by the Convention, the Constitution as Adopted and the President's Proclamation* (Denver: Smith-Brooks Press, state printers, 1907).

11. *Journal and Debates of the Constitutional Convention of the State of Wyoming: Begun at the City of Cheyenne on September 2, 1889, and Concluded September 30, 1889* (Cheyenne, WY: Daily Sun Book and Job Printing, 1893), 668; Ichabod S. Bartlett, *History of Wyoming* (Chicago: The S. J. Clarke Publishing Company, 1918), vol. 3, 102–105.

12. *Journal and Debates of the Constitutional Convention of the State of Wyoming*, 498; Marie H. Erwin, *Wyoming Historical Blue Book; a Legal and Political History of Wyoming, 1868–1943* (Denver: Bradford-Robinson Printing Company, 1946), 642.

13. *Journal and Debates of the Constitutional Convention of the State of Wyoming*, 295.

14. *Proceedings and Debates of the Constitutional Convention: Held in the City of Helena in Montana*, 61; A. W. Bowen, *Progressive Men of the State of Montana* (Chicago: A. W. Bowen & Company, 1900), 57–58.

15. *Proceedings and Debates of the Constitutional Convention: Held in the City of Helena in Montana*, 137; *The Journal of the Washington State Constitutional Convention, 1889* (Seattle: Book Publishing Company, 1962), 203.

16. *Proceedings and Debates of the Constitutional Convention of Idaho, 1889* (Caldwell, ID: Caxton Printers, 1912), 1162. "There may be in ordinary years enough water to supply all of the people that settle along a ditch or canal," Claggett explained regarding the principle of "sufficiency," "but when there comes a dry season, is one-half of the farms to be absolutely destroyed because

the other man has an absolute priority, or is there to be an equitable distribution under such rules and regulations as may be provided by law?" See ibid., 1181.

17. *Proceedings and Debates of the Constitutional Convention: Held in the City of Helena in Montana*, 896; Bowen, *Progressive Men of the State of Montana*, 440–442, 281–283. Luce had come to Montana on behalf of the federal government to negotiate with the Crow Indians for the Northern Pacific Railroad's right of way.

18. *Proceedings and Debates of the Constitutional Convention: Held in the City of Helena in Montana*, 498.

19. *Proceedings and Debates of the Constitutional Convention of Idaho*, 1373–1374.

20. *The Journal of the Washington State Constitutional Convention*, 297–301; *Proceedings and Debates of the Constitutional Convention of Idaho*, 1372–1395; *Proceedings and Debates of the Constitutional Convention: Held in the City of Helena in Montana*, 196–217; *Journal of the Constitutional Convention for North Dakota*, 366–371.

21. *Proceedings and Debates of the Constitutional Convention: Held in the City of Helena in Montana*, 130; Bowen, *Progressive Men of the State of Montana*, 62.

22. *Proceedings and Debates of the Constitutional Convention: Held in the City of Helena in Montana*, 129.

23. Ibid., 143.

24. *Journal and Debates of the Constitutional Convention of the State of Wyoming*, 402; Erwin, *Wyoming Historical Blue Book*, 172.

25. *Proceedings and Debates of the Constitutional Convention: Held in the City of Helena in Montana*, 142. The Wyoming convention collectively heralded this "prohibition on the importation of foreign police to usurp local authority" as one of its most important achievements. See *Journal and Debates of the Constitutional Convention of the State of Wyoming*, 119.

26. *Journal of the Constitutional Convention for North Dakota*, 380.

27. *Proceedings and Debates of the Constitutional Convention of Idaho*, 1708–1709.

28. *The Journal of the Washington State Constitutional Convention*, 680, 474.

29. *Proceedings and Debates of the Constitutional Convention: Held in the City of Helena in Montana*, 553.

30. *Proceedings and Debates of the Constitutional Convention of Idaho*, 1716; Dennis C. Colson, *Idaho's Constitution: The Tie That Binds* (Moscow, ID: University of Idaho Press, 1991), 10.

31. *Journal and Debates of the Constitutional Convention of the State of Wyoming*, 684. Comparisons to other states at times supported the opposite conclusion, emboldening delegates to take a harder stance vis-à-vis corporate power. As Mayhew argued in Idaho, in anything relating to corporations, "it is best for us to follow some of the examples of other states . . . or territories now forming" and adopt "such provisions in constitutions of this character, in order to protect

the people against these institutions." See *Proceedings and Debates of the Constitutional Convention of Idaho*, 1068–1069.

32. *Proceedings and Debates of the Constitutional Convention: Held in the City of Helena in Montana*, 569; Bowen, *Progressive Men of the State of Montana*, 1176–1178.

33. *Proceedings and Debates of the Constitutional Convention of Idaho*, 889; Colson and Idaho, *Idaho's Constitution*, 9.

34. *Journal and Debates of the Constitutional Convention of the State of Wyoming*, 453, 691; A. W. Bowen, *Progressive Men of the State of Wyoming* (Chicago: A. W. Bowen & Company, 1903), 840–841.

35. *The Journal of the Washington State Constitutional Convention*, 188–189, 475.

36. *Journal and Debates of the Constitutional Convention of the State of Wyoming*, 672.

37. *Proceedings and Debates of the Constitutional Convention: Held in the City of Helena in Montana*, 127; Bowen, *Progressive Men of the State of Montana*, 137–139.

38. *Journal and Debates of the Constitutional Convention of the State of Wyoming*, 672.

39. *The Journal of the Washington State Constitutional Convention*, 188–189.

40. *Proceedings and Debates of the Constitutional Convention of Idaho*, 1743.

41. *Journal and Debates of the Constitutional Convention of the State of Wyoming*, 443; Erwin, *Wyoming Historical Blue Book*, 632.

42. *Proceedings and Debates of the Constitutional Convention of Idaho*, 888.

43. *Proceedings and Debates of the Constitutional Convention: Held in the City of Helena in Montana*, 675.

44. *Proceedings and Debates of the Constitutional Convention of Idaho*, 885–886.

45. *Proceedings and Debates of the Constitutional Convention: Held in the City of Helena in Montana*, 704.

46. Newspaper coverage readily observed this dynamic. Commenting on the convention in Washington, the *Seattle Times* noted that "there was great hue and cry raised about the necessity of giving encouragement to capital seeking investment in this state, and the specious plea was made and made often that any restraint upon corporations would be an injury to capital. It was under this cloak that the corporation tools in the convention did their work, and endeavored, by exhibiting a tender interest in the welfare of capital, to defeat those clauses particularly obnoxious to their masters. They succeeded in pulling wool over the eyes of some of the delegates—perhaps because they did not particularly object to being deluded." See *Seattle Times*, August 7, 1889. When delegates themselves failed to meet corporate expectations, outside lobbying occasionally came into play. After the delegates in Washington voted to create a powerful railroad commission, the territory's business groups sprang into

action. In the days after the decision, they overwhelmed the convention with a barrage of petitions. The boards of trade of Yakima and Ellensburg moved first to cast the railroad commission as "inimical to the best interests of our state," particularly to the "speedy development of our resources by . . . foreign capital." The boards of trade of Spokane Falls, Aberdeen, Montesano, and Vancouver then joined the chorus with their own petitions to protect "the liberty of contract," calling for the new article to be "in letter, and spirit . . . entirely expunged," alongside any other article that would "tend to alarm and drive away the capital so greatly needed at this time." When the question was again brought before the convention several days later, a dozen of the delegates had changed their votes, and the commission initiative was struck down. See *Tacoma Morning Globe*, July 29, August 2–3, 1889. After winning 39 votes in favor on August 3, 1889, the commission was brought up for another vote on August 6, losing by a vote of 47 to 23. See *Tacoma Morning Globe*, August 4, 7, 1889.

47. Bensel, *The Political Economy of American Industrialization*, 1–18.

48. *Proceedings and Debates of the Constitutional Convention: Held in the City of Helena in Montana*, 899. In Idaho, Mayhew similarly appealed to "reason," arguing that, "Corporations should be in some measure checked, that is to say, to hold them within the bounds of reason." See *Proceedings and Debates of the Constitutional Convention of Idaho*, 817. Ironically, it is precisely this embrace of "reason" that earned westerners a rebuke from Adams for being "deaf to reason."

49. On the concept of "legibility," see James C. Scott, *Seeing Like a State: How Certain Schemes to Improve the Human Condition Have Failed* (New Haven, CT: Yale University Press, 1998). David Montgomery's notion of "workers' control" of the production floor finds its macro-level political analog. See David Montgomery, *Workers' Control in America: Studies in the History of Work, Technology, and Labor Struggles* (Cambridge: Cambridge University Press, 1979); David Montgomery, *The Fall of the House of Labor: The Workplace, the State, and American Labor Activism, 1865–1925* (Cambridge: Cambridge University Press, 1987).

50. *Proceedings and Debates of the Constitutional Convention: Held in the City of Helena in Montana*, 899.

51. Ibid., 504. The issue of taxation, if administered by local assessors, introduced a similar element of "uncertainty." As Beatty pointed out in Idaho: "If you . . . give the eastern capitalist to understand that the surface ground of their mines is exactly in the power of the assessors of the state. How many eastern men are coming out here to invest their money in property that will be so uncertain as that?" Claggett likewise warned about the consequences of an absence of "a fixed and certain fiscal policy with regard to . . . taxation. . . . If you simply leave the whole matter to be the football of the legislative session, there is never anybody who will ever know two years in advance as to what the laws

with regard to mining property are going to be. . . . [This] will be a terrible discouragement to the investment of capital." See *Proceedings and Debates of the Constitutional Convention of Idaho*, 1750–1751, 1762 1763. Elizabeth Sanders has emphasized the significance of social movements' trust in legislative power as opposed to administrative state power controlled by experts. See Elizabeth Sanders, *Roots of Reform: Farmers, Workers, and the American State, 1877–1917* (Chicago: University of Chicago Press, 1999), 387–389.

52. David Schorr, *The Colorado Doctrine: Water Rights, Corporations, and Distributive Justice on the American Frontier* (New Haven, CT: Yale University Press, 2012), 104–138. As Schorr discusses, the effort to create a clear registry of water rights in later years was in fact invalidated by the state supreme court. Beatty commented on this very feature of "beneficial use" in Idaho, saying that the main objection was that it made "all interests uncertain." See *Proceedings and Debates of the Constitutional Convention of Idaho*, 1181.

53. This disparity registered in lending companies' reluctance, and even outright refusal, to accept water rights as collateral for credit. See Schorr, *The Colorado Doctrine*, 127–128.

54. Richard White, *Railroaded: The Transcontinentals and the Making of Modern America* (New York: W. W. Norton, 2011), chapter 4.

55. *Proceedings and Debates of the Constitutional Convention: Held in the City of Helena in Montana*, 709–710.

56. Both George Miller's classic study and Berk's more recent one engage this point. See George Hall Miller, *Railroads and the Granger Laws* (Madison: University of Wisconsin Press, 1971); Berk, *Alternative Tracks*.

57. *Proceedings and Debates of the Constitutional Convention: Held in the City of Helena in Montana*, 499.

58. Ibid., 127. My emphasis.

59. *Journal and Debates of the Constitutional Convention of the State of Wyoming*, 672.

60. See the following articles from state constitutions: Idaho Article XI, 10, 14; Montana Article XV, 11, 15; Wyoming Article X, "railroads," 8, Washington Article XII, 7; Colorado Article XV, 10; North Dakota Article VII, 136, 140.

61. The predominant interpretation of low long-haul freight rates as an expression of strict economic and thus apolitical terms, driven by the railroad's high fixed costs, dates back to Arthur Twining Hadley, *Railroad Transportation, Its History and Its Laws* (New York: G. P. Putnam's Sons, 1885). It has been most lucidly explained in William Cronon, *Nature's Metropolis: Chicago and the Great West* (New York: W. W. Norton, 1991). Richard White has more recently questioned this view, noting that in fact "the ratio of variable to fixed costs was almost the reverse of what Hadley posited." The railroads, White concluded, "did not base their rates on the cost of service, which they were incapable of

determining," but rather "set rates experimentally" according to "what the traffic would bear." In other words, the inexorable tendency of the economy of railroads to prioritize long over short and medium haul has been vastly overstated. See White, *Railroaded*, 331, 160. White bases his observations on Gerald Berk, *Louis D. Brandeis and the Making of Regulated Competition, 1900–1932* (Cambridge: Cambridge University Press, 2009), 74–78; Gregory L. Thompson, "Misused Product Costing in the American Railroad Industry: Southern Pacific Passenger Service between the Wars," *The Business History Review* 63, no. 3 (October 1, 1989): 510–554.

62. Idaho Articles XIV, 6, XIII, 3, VIII, 1, XIII, 2.
63. Idaho Articles XI, 5, 6, 10, 14, VII, 2, 4, 8.
64. Idaho Article XV, 1, 3, 4, 2.
65. Idaho Article XIII, 2; Montana Article XVIII, 2; Wyoming Article XIX, 1.
66. Colorado Article XVI, 2, 3; Wyoming Article IX, 2; Washington Article II, 35.
67. Montana Article XVIII, 3; Idaho Article XIII, 4; Wyoming Article IX, 3; Colorado Article XVI, 2; North Dakota Article XVII, 209. Wyoming's constitution prohibited all females from working in the mines. It did not, however, include a prohibition on blacklisting of labor organizers, use of convict labor, or the formation of a labor bureau.
68. Montana Article XV, 5; Idaho Article XI, 5; Washington Article XII, 18; North Dakota Article VII, 142. The struggle in Washington aborted the formation of a permanent regulatory body, stipulating merely that "a railroad and transportation commission *may* be established." See Washington Article XII, 18.
69. Montana Article XV, 5, 7; Idaho Article XI, 5, 6; Wyoming Articles X, 7, XII, 15; Washington Article XII, 13; Colorado Article XV, 4; North Dakota Article VII, 142.
70. Colorado Article X, 3; Wyoming Article XV, 3; Montana Article XII, 3.
71. Montana Article III, 15; Washington Article XXI, 1; North Dakota Article XVII, 210; Idaho Article XV, 1–6; Colorado Article XVI, 5–8; Wyoming Article VIII, 1–5.
72. Bensel, *The Political Economy of American Industrialization*, 321.

6. The Age of Reform

1. On Ely and his cohort of progressive tax reformers, see Ajay K. Mehrotra, *Making the Modern American Fiscal State: Law, Politics, and the Rise of Progressive Taxation, 1877–1929* (Cambridge: Cambridge University Press, 2013). More broadly about the new wave of economic thought, see Mary O. Furner, *Advocacy & Objectivity: A Crisis in the Professionalization of American Social Science, 1865–1905* (Lexington: University of Kentucky Press, 1975); Daniel T. Rodgers, *Atlantic Crossings: Social Politics in a Progressive Age* (Cambridge, MA: Harvard University Press, 1998); Nancy Cohen, *The*

Reconstruction of American Liberalism, 1865–1914 (Chapel Hill: University of North Carolina Press, 2002).

2. "Only an anarchist can take any other view," Ely wrote. See Richard Theodore Ely, *Taxation in American States and Cities* (New York: T. Y. Crowell, 1888), 13–14. For this departure from the classical liberal view, see Mehrotra, *Making the Modern American Fiscal State*, 110–117.

3. Ibid., 14.

4. Ibid., 287–288, 300, 297. On support for "expert" tax administration on the state level, see Mehrotra, *Making the Modern American Fiscal State*, 204–208.

5. Ely, *Taxation in American States and Cities*, 218.

6. Ibid., 217, 219.

7. Ibid., 218, 242, 220.

8. Ibid., 231, 230, 218.

9. For elite responses to democratic politics in this era throughout the United States and the West, see Alexander Keyssar, *The Right to Vote: The Contested History of Democracy in the United States* (New York: Basic Books, 2001); Sven Beckert, "Democracy and Its Discontents: Contesting Suffrage Rights in Gilded Age New York," *Past and Present* 174, no. 1 (2002): 116; Eric J. Hobsbawm, *The Age of Empire, 1875–1914* (New York: Vintage Books, 1989), 110–111.

10. Nathan Matthews, *The City Government of Boston* (Boston: Rockwell and Churchill, 1895), 181–182. See also, Matthews's speech at Phillips Academy at Exeter, quoted in ibid., 182.

11. On the links between modern forestry and the origins of scientific management, see James C. Scott, *Seeing Like a State: How Certain Schemes to Improve the Human Condition Have Failed* (New Haven, CT: Yale University Press, 1998).

12. George R. Nutter, *Nathan Matthews* (Cambridge, MA: N.p., 1928); Robert A. Silverman, "Nathan Matthews: Politics of Reform in Boston, 1890–1910," *The New England Quarterly* 50, no. 4 (1977): 626–643.

13. "Letter to John T. Wheelwright, 39 Court St., October 10, 1889," Nathan Matthews Political Papers, vol. 1889, Widener Library, Harvard University (WLHU).

14. "Letter to S. N. Aldrich, Post Office Building, October 10, 1889," Nathan Matthews Political Papers, vol. 1889, WLHU.

15. "Letter to James M. Beck, April 4, 1890," Nathan Matthews Political Papers, vol. 1890, WLHU.

16. "Letter to H. C. Wadlin Esq., Chief of the Bureau of Statistics of Labor, 20 Beacon Street, January 20, 1890," Nathan Matthews Political Papers, vol. 1890, WLHU.

17. See Nathan Matthews Political Papers, vol. 1890, WLHU, 747.

18. "Democratic State Committee: Instructions," Nathan Matthews Political Papers, vol. 1890, WLHU, 851.

19. "Letter to M. J. Kiley, Esq., 7 Spring Lane, March 31, 1890," Nathan Matthews Political Papers, vol. 1890, WLHU.

20. "Letter to the Springfield Republican, November 27, 1889," Nathan Matthews Political Papers, vol. 1889, WLHU.

21. "Letter to William M. Wilson, House of Representatives, April 1, 1890," Nathan Matthews Political Papers, vol. 1890, WLHU; "Some Reasons for Reducing these Tariff Taxes," Nathan Matthews Political Papers, vol. 1890, WLHU, 795–796.

22. Silverman, "Nathan Matthews," 628. On the harmony between the immigrant leadership and the Boston business elite at this juncture, see Geoffrey Blodgett, *The Gentle Reformers: Massachusetts Democrats in the Cleveland Era* (Cambridge, MA: Harvard University Press, 1966); Geoffrey Blodgett, "Yankee Leadership in a Divided City: Boston, 1860–1910," *Journal of Urban History* 8, no. 4 (1982): 371; Oscar Handlin, *Boston's Immigrants 1790–1880: A Study in Acculturation* (Cambridge, MA: Harvard University Press, 1959); Silverman, "Nathan Matthews"; Thomas H. O'Connor, *The Boston Irish: A Political History* (Boston: Northeastern University Press, 1995). O'Connor writes of the Hugh O'Brien mayoralty, for example, that "he was cordial to the Brahmins individually, and deferential to the traditions of the city they personified . . . [he was] a 'good' Irishman, an 'acceptable' Irishman, the kind of Irishman Yankees would seek out and encourage to become the leaders of the Irish and eventually the leaders of the city." As mayor, O'Brien embraced the goal of limiting government spending. See O'Connor, *The Boston Irish*, 132.

23. "Letter to David Hill Esq., Easthampton, Mass., January 4, 1890," Nathan Matthews Political Papers, vol. 1890, WLHU.

24. "Letter to Hon. Hugh O'Brien, February 25, 1890," Nathan Matthews Political Papers, vol. 1890, WLHU.

25. O'Connor, *The Boston Irish*, 150.

26. Nathan Matthews, *The Citizen and the State* (Boston: G. H. Ellis, printer, 1889), 5.

27. Ibid., 7, 8.

28. Commonwealth of Massachusetts, *Annual Report of the Board of Education* (Boston: Wright and Potter, 1889), 76.

29. Ibid., 75, 80.

30. Matthews, *The Citizen and the State*, 19.

31. Ibid., 6.

32. "How Boston Is Governed," *Boston Herald*, February 8, 1890, also included in Nathan Matthews Political Papers, vol. 1890, WLHU, 701.

33. Commonwealth of Massachusetts, *Annual Report of the Board of Education*, 81.
34. Matthews, *The City Government of Boston*, 174, 29.
35. Ibid., 190, 183, 180, 178.
36. Ibid., 175, 181, 14.
37. Ibid., 25–26.
38. "Record of the Joint Special Committee on Retrenchment of Municipal Expenditure, 1877," Boston Municipal Archives, West Roxbury, Boston. The department heads were assertive in their resistance to any cuts. The superintendent of the public library explained: "I see no way of cutting down the expenses of the library without imperiling the service. On the contrary, I see every reason for their being increased." The head of the assessment department explained, "I do not think that you can reduce the force without hurting the city. One man could do the work, with plenty of clerical help, but, in my opinion, each reduction would be always at the expense of the city and the convenience of the citizens," 20, 45.
39. Matthews, *The City Government of Boston*, 25.
40. Ibid., 13.
41. Ibid., 39–40.
42. This is by Matthews's own calculation, which given his attention to bookkeeping is most probably correct. Matthews complained that the municipality "cannot provide every suburban village within the municipality with schoolhouses, fire-engine houses, and police-stations; it cannot build streets and sewers for the benefit of speculative land-owners . . . without an inordinate annual expenditure and a correspondingly heavy tax rate." See ibid., 175.
43. Ibid., 89. The distributive effects of special assessments differed widely depending on context, which accounts for why elites elsewhere mobilized against special assessments. On the instrument of special assessments in other American cities, see Elizabeth Blackmar, *Manhattan for Rent, 1785–1850* (Ithaca, NY: Cornell University Press, 1989); Robin L. Einhorn, *Property Rules: Political Economy in Chicago, 1833–1872* (Chicago: University of Chicago Press, 2001); Stephen Diamond, "The Death and Transfiguration of Benefit Taxation: Special Assessments in Nineteenth-Century America," *The Journal of Legal Studies* 12, no. 2 (1983): 201–240.
44. Charles Phillips Huse, *The Financial History of Boston from May 1, 1822, to January 31, 1909* (Cambridge, MA: Harvard University Press, 1916), 154–155.
45. Matthews, *The City Government of Boston*, 37.
46. Ibid., 60, 92, 90.
47. William Minot, Jonathan Abbot Lane, and George G. Crocker, *Message of the Mayor Transmitting Report of the Special Commission on Taxation* (Boston: Rockwell and Churchill, 1891), 7. William's father explained that "to give [his son] leisure to examine these subjects [and work on this tax report] he needs a

week of seclusion . . . so we think of going to Lenox the latter part of the week and making ourselves comfortable at the hotel. The chambers have steam heat and open fires, and the table is good; and Will, with his stenographer, could work without interference." See William Minot, *Private Letters* (Boston: Rockwell and Churchill, 1895), 153.

48. Minot, Lane, and Crocker, *Message of the Mayor*, 8–9.
49. Ibid.
50. Ibid., 24–25.
51. Ibid., 15, 23.
52. Huse, *The Financial History of Boston*, 377; Commonwealth of Massachusetts, *Report of the Commission Appointed to Inquire into the Expediency of Revising and Amending the Laws of the Commonwealth Relating to Taxation* (Boston: Wright and Potter, 1897), 50. The eighteen towns selected were Arlington, Belmont, Brookline, Cohasset, Easton, Falmouth, Groton, Hopedale, Lancaster, Lincoln, Manchester, Mattapoisett, Milton, Nahant, Stockbridge, Swampscott, Wellesley, and Weston.
53. This embrace of a "classified" property tax, which promised to reduce or entirely eliminate taxes on "intangible" forms of wealth, became the standard position among business elites and experts. See Charles J. Bullock, "The Taxation of Property and Income in Massachusetts," *The Quarterly Journal of Economics* 31, no. 1 (1916): 1–61, and Mehrotra, *Making the Modern American Fiscal State*, 208–213.
54. Commonwealth of Massachusetts, *Report of the Commission*, 111.
55. Ibid., 83–84.
56. Ibid., 125–126.
57. Ibid., 133.
58. On McNeill, see Alexander Gourevitch, *From Slavery to the Cooperative Commonwealth: Labor and Republican Liberty in the Nineteenth Century* (New York: Cambridge University Press, 2015); David Montgomery, *Beyond Equality: Labor and the Radical Republicans, 1862–1872* (New York: Knopf, 1967).
59. Commonwealth of Massachusetts, *Report of the Commission*, 162, 148, 166.
60. Ibid., 159, 157.
61. Ibid., 172, 138.
62. Ibid., 141.

Conclusion

1. Naomi R. Lamoreaux, *The Great Merger Movement in American Business, 1895–1904* (Cambridge: Cambridge University Press, 1985); William G. Roy, *Socializing Capital: The Rise of the Large Industrial Corporation in America*

(Princeton, NJ: Princeton University Press, 1997), 4–5; Richard Franklin Bensel, *The Political Economy of American Industrialization, 1877–1900* (Cambridge: Cambridge University Press, 2000), 319; Thomas R. Navin and Marian V. Sears, "The Rise of a Market for Industrial Securities, 1887–1902," *The Business History Review* 29, no. 2 (1955): 105–138.

2. Roy, *Socializing Capital*, 250–251. For data on foreign investment as a declining portion of overall investment, see Lance Edwin Davis and Robert E. Gallman, *Evolving Financial Markets and International Capital Flows: Britain, the Americas, and Australia, 1865–1914* (Cambridge: Cambridge University Press, 2001), 9, 27.

3. Vincent P. Carosso, *Investment Banking in America, a History*, Harvard Studies in Business History 25 (Cambridge, MA: Harvard University Press, 1970), 85–87; Susie Pak, *Gentlemen Bankers: The World of J. P. Morgan* (Cambridge, MA: Harvard University Press, 2013); Julia C. Ott, *When Wall Street Met Main Street: The Quest for an Investors' Democracy* (Cambridge, MA: Harvard University Press, 2011).

4. On the interlocking directorates of these financial institutions and the federal investigation of the "money trust," see United States, *Money Trust Investigation. Investigation of Financial and Monetary Conditions in the United States under House Resolutions nos. 429 and 504, before a Subcommittee of the Committee on Banking and Currency*, eds. Arsène Paulin Pujo et al. (Washington, DC: Government Printing Office, 1913), 2003–2020.

5. Vincent P. Carosso, *More than a Century of Investment Banking: The Kidder, Peabody & Co. Story* (New York: McGraw-Hill, 1979), 30.

6. Thomas R. Navin and Marian V. Sears, "The Rise of a Market for Industrial Securities, 1887–1902," *The Business History Review* 29, no. 2 (1955): 124–125; Carosso, *Investment Banking in America*, 43–44.

7. Carosso, *More than a Century of Investment Banking*, 40–41. This was not so for the securities houses of Chicago, which as of 1900 remained distinctly regional, participating neither in the reorganization of railroads nor in underwriting major industrial consolidations. See Carosso, *Investment Banking in America*, 106–107.

8. Pak, *Gentlemen Bankers*, 25. J. P. Morgan also took on hefty portions of issues headed by Lee, Higginson ($120 million between 1894 and 1914) and Kidder, Peabody ($90 million in the same period of time). See ibid., 100. As late as 1930, the Boston Stock Exchange listed 265 different corporations in railroads, mining, manufacturing, and many other sectors, representing 365 different issues with a face value of over $3 billion. See David Grayson Allen, *Investment Management in Boston: A History* (Amherst: University of Massachusetts Press, 2015), 53.

9. For details about the portfolios and dealings of the two leading firms, and their partners, see United States, *Money Trust Investigation*, 1898–1951.

10. Gerald Taylor White, *A History of the Massachusetts Hospital Life Insurance Company* (Cambridge, MA: Harvard University Press, 1955), 125–126; William Thomas David, *Professional and Industrial History of Suffolk County, Massachusetts* (Cambridge, MA: Riverside Press, 1894), 432–442. For the geographically diverse portfolios of insurance companies, see *Thirty-Sixth Annual Report of the Insurance Commissioner of the Commonwealth of Massachusetts* (Boston: Wright and Potter, 1891), 22–31.

11. It was the monumental size of the market, in Chandler's analysis, that allowed American manufacturers to better "exploit the economies of scale and scope than anywhere else in the world." See Alfred D. Chandler, *Scale and Scope: The Dynamics of Industrial Capitalism* (Cambridge, MA: Belknap Press, 1994), 52–53.

12. Richard White, *Railroaded: The Transcontinentals and the Making of Modern America* (New York: W. W. Norton & Company, 2011). Richard Bensel notes the light traffic on the transcontinentals relative to other interregional railroads. See Bensel, *The Political Economy of American Industrialization*, 300.

13. See, for example, William Leach, *Land of Desire: Merchants, Power, and the Rise of a New American Culture* (New York: Pantheon Books, 1993). The hegemony of these ideas, of course, remained feeble. See Stefan Link, "Transnational Fordism: Ford Motor Company, Nazi Germany, and the Soviet Union in the Interwar Years" (Ph.D. diss., Harvard University, 2013); Ott, *When Wall Street Met Main Street*; Donald Finlay Davis, *Conspicuous Production: Automobiles and Elites in Detroit, 1899–1933* (Philadelphia: Temple University Press, 1988); James Livingston, *Pragmatism and the Political Economy of Cultural Revolution, 1850–1940* (Chapel Hill: University of North Carolina Press, 1994), 48–49.

14. See the majority decision in Chicago, Milwaukee, and St. Paul Railway Company v. Minnesota. For a meticulous explanation of the "judicial construction of the national market," see Bensel, *The Political Economy of American Industrialization*, 321–349.

15. William J. Novak, "Law and the Social Control of American Capitalism" *Emory Law Journal* 60, no. 2 (2010): 377–405; Gary Gerstle, "The Resilient Power of the States across the Long Nineteenth Century," in *The Unsustainable American State*, ed. Lawrence R. Jacobs and Desmond S. King (Oxford: Oxford University Press, 2009), 61–87.

16. Kimberley S. Johnson, *Governing the American State: Congress and the New Federalism, 1877–1929* (Princeton: Princeton University Press, 2007). See also Harry N. Scheiber, "Federalism and the American Economic Order, 1789–1910," *Law & Society Review* 10, no. 1 (1975): 57–118; William R. Childs, "State

Regulators and Pragmatic Federalism in the United States, 1889–1945,"
Business History Review 75, no. 4 (2001): 701–738.

17. Alfred D. Chandler, *The Visible Hand: The Managerial Revolution in American Business* (Cambridge, MA: Belknap Press, 1977); Bensel, *The Political Economy of American Industrialization*, 296.

18. Interstate Commerce Commission, *Second Annual Report* (1888), 245, quoted in D. W. Meinig, *The Shaping of America: A Geographical Perspective on 500 Years of History*, vol. 3: *Transcontinental America, 1850–1915* (New Haven, CT: Yale University Press, 2000), 247, 345–365.

19. Philip Scranton, *Endless Novelty: Specialty Production and American Industrialization, 1865–1925* (Princeton, NJ: Princeton University Press, 1997); Walter Licht, *Industrializing America: The Nineteenth Century* (Baltimore: John Hopkins University Press, 1995); Robert D. Lewis, *Chicago Made: Factory Networks in the Industrial Metropolis* (Chicago: University of Chicago Press, 2008); Robert Lewis, "The Changing Fortunes of American Central-City Manufacturing, 1870–1950," *Journal of Urban History* 28, no. 5 (2002): 573. For Boston, see Albert J. Kennedy and Robert A. Woods, eds., *The Zone of Emergence: Observations of the Lower Middle and Upper Working Class Communities of Boston, 1905–1914*, 2nd ed. (Cambridge, MA: MIT Press, 1969).

20. See, for example, Naomi R. Lamoreaux, Margaret Levenstein, and Kenneth L. Sokoloff, "Financing Invention during the Second Industrial Revolution: Cleveland, Ohio, 1870–1920," in *Financing Innovation in the United States, 1870 to the Present*, ed. Naomi R. Lamoreaux et al. (Cambridge, MA: MIT Press, 2007), 39–84.

21. Lance E. Davis, "The Investment Market, 1870–1914: The Evolution of a National Market," *The Journal of Economic History* 25, no. 3 (1965): 368; Richard Sylla, "Federal Policy, Banking Market Structure, and Capital Mobilization in the United States, 1863–1913," *The Journal of Economic History* 29, no. 4 (1969): 672; Kenneth A. Snowden, "Mortgage Rates and American Capital Market Development in the Late Nineteenth Century," *The Journal of Economic History* 47, no. 3 (September 1, 1987): 671–691; Kenneth A. Snowden, "The Evolution of Interregional Mortgage Lending Channels, 1870–1940: The Life Insurance–Mortgage Company Connection," in *Coordination and Information: Historical Perspectives on the Organization of Enterprise*, ed. Naomi R. Lamoreaux and Daniel M. G. Raff (Chicago: University of Chicago Press, 1995), 242.

22. Snowden, "The Evolution of Interregional Mortgage Lending Channels," 216–219. This remained the case until the middle of the twentieth century, when the federal government stepped in to create national standards and indeed create a national mortgage market. See Louis Hyman, *Debtor Nation: The History of America in Red Ink* (Princeton, NJ: Princeton University Press, 2011).

23. See, for example, Thomas Sugrue, "All Politics Is Local," in *The Democratic Experiment: New Directions in American Political History*, ed. Meg Jacobs, William J. Novak, and Julian E. Zelizer (Princeton, NJ: Princeton University Press, 2003), 301–326; Tami J. Friedman, "Exploiting the North–South Differential: Corporate Power, Southern Politics, and the Decline of Organized Labor after World War II," *The Journal of American History* 95, no. 2 (2008): 323–348; Elizabeth Tandy Shermer, *Sunbelt Capitalism: Phoenix and the Transformation of American Politics* (Philadelphia: University of Pennsylvania Press, 2013); Johnson, *Governing the American State.* See also Neil Brenner, *New State Spaces: Urban Governance and the Rescaling of Statehood* (Oxford: Oxford University Press, 2006).

Acknowledgments

When I embarked upon the journey that led me to write this book several years prior to the economic crisis of 2008, it still seemed plausible for observers to proclaim, or seriously debate, the "end of history." Scholars and journalists at the time contemplated the imminent triumph of global capitalism under the auspices of liberal democracy as the end point of humanity's political evolution. A great deal has changed in the decade or so since. Excitement over the boundless possibilities of globalization, as well as anxieties about market volatility, gave way to much more somber concerns about deepening economic inequality. The sense of unbridled optimism regarding economic interconnectedness drastically eroded in Europe, the United States, and elsewhere. The formation of integrated markets, which was at one point the rarefied domain of experts and technocrats, became a hot button electoral issue across the political spectrum. History has clearly resumed, and the question of capitalism remains as relevant as ever.

In grappling with this enduring question in my own inquiry, I had the privilege to learn from truly inspirational teachers, friends, and colleagues. The completion of this book affords me the opportunity to thank them and express my profound gratitude. This book began at Harvard University, where I benefited from a committee of dedicated and engaged advisers. Sven Beckert nurtured the project from the outset with his unending enthusiasm and keen eye for grand historical drama. His travels to all corners of the globe as he was researching his own book emboldened me to examine the particularities of American history from a very broad perspective. Liz Cohen was an immensely generous mentor as she introduced me to the fundamentals of the historical craft. She provided the forum where the early pieces of this manuscript were first presented and thoroughly workshopped. Alex Keyssar played a crucial role as a useful and smart skeptic. He was also a gateway into a rich tradition of historical scholarship on capitalism in America.

Several senior scholars have been equally supportive and important. Elizabeth Blackmar first set me on this path, explained that property is not "things," and taught me to think about history in space. My debt to her will never be repaid, especially since I continue to draw on the account. Gary Gerstle embraced me as his protégé, affirmed my interest in how elites govern, and shared his insights about the American state. Jeff Sklansky offered much-needed encouragement at crucial moments and remains a model of scholarly integrity. Paul Kramer's critical perspective, and our spatial history reading group, helped me crystallize my core arguments. Dan Sharfstein gave this manuscript its title, thereby imparting coherence to the entire endeavor. The draft of my early work that Michael Zakim painstakingly annotated from start to finish became the starting point for its revision into a book.

Many others along the way have also offered invaluable comments or feedback on the manuscript or parts of it. I want to thank all of them, and particularly Robert Johnston, Christine Desan, Pierre Gervais, Paul Groth, Sarah Igo, Roy Kreitner, Pam Laird, Richard John, Ben Johnson, Colleen Dunlavy, Rosanne Currarino, Walter Johnson, Jon Levy, and Robin Einhorn. My main interlocutors in developing this project, however, were more junior scholars, with whom I spent many hours elbow-to-elbow in libraries, archives, and seminar rooms, not to mention over coffee, at lunch tables, and on bar stools. I am especially grateful to Ann Marie Wilson, George Blaustein, Erin Royston Battat, Betsy More, Benjamin Waterhouse, Andrew Kinney, Clinton Williams, Angus Burgin, Eduardo Canedo, Rachel Gordan, Bill Rankin, Katherine Stevens, Jamie Jones, Sarah Carter, Caitlin Rosenthal, Ariel Ron, David Singerman, Hannah Farber, Rachel Tamar Van, Eli Cook, Manuel Covo, Vanessa Ogle, Ellie Shermer, Louis Hyman, Nicolas Barreyre, Martin Giraudeau, Joane Chaker, Yael Sternhell, Michael Kimmage, and, of course, Mark Hanna. No one understood and shared the underlying goals of this project from its incipient stages more than Stefan Link. He has been my co-conspirator, vital draft reader, indispensable critic, and dear friend during this Sisyphean climb.

The book required financial and institutional backing, which I have been fortunate to receive from a variety of sources, most notably the Department of History at Vanderbilt University, the School of Historical Studies at Tel Aviv University, and the Charles Warren Center at Harvard. Additional funding came from the Graduate School of Arts and Sciences at Harvard, Whiting Foundation, New England Regional Consortium, Massachusetts Historical Society, New York Public Library, Harvard Business School, the Taubman Center for State and Local Government, and Cornell University.

At Harvard University Press, Joyce Seltzer adopted the project early on and helped it come together as a book. Brian Distelberg and Kathleen Drummy patiently guided me through the process. The outside reviewers for the press offered reassuring and essential feedback that enabled me to enhance the final draft. Some of the ideas in Chapters 1 and 4 were explored previously in "To 'Coddle and Caress These Great Capitalists': Eastern Money and the Politics of Market Integration in the Great American West," *American Historical Review* 122, no. 1 (February 2017).

Finally, my greatest debt is to my close family and friends: my father Eli, whose love and support have been unwavering, my brother Erez, who read every chapter and was not deterred from pursuing his own forays into political economy, and my sister Shira, who sustained the home base during my long absence. Niza and Eric Knoll welcomed me into their lives a long time ago and have since put up with my many eccentricities. Linda Burnley, Lorna Moritz, Talaya Delaney, Yael Feldman-Maggor, Smadar Eyal, Ori Aronson, Hila Shamir, Ido Kalir, Oren Askarov, and Doron Kilshtein bestowed encouragement and companionship over many years. Raya Maggor has brought immeasurable joy and wisdom to my life. One of Lev Maggor's first complete sentences was: "Aba, are you at work?" He will be relieved to hear me respond in the negative more often, at least in the near future. Above all, Rebekah Maggor has been an inspiration and animating force behind this project for a very long time, contributing to its development in countless ways. She spared no sacrifice to make sure it came to its fruition. Throughout what was a long process of discovery, I learned the most from her.

Index